JUDGES AND RUTH

This commentary brings to life the world portrayed in the stories in Judges and Ruth to demonstrate why they are an important part of the Bible. The intention is to prepare the reader to understand social norms and customs, such as hospitality codes, marriage customs, inheritance laws, and agricultural practices, when they appear in the stories. By setting the cultural stage, the commentary functions as an effective guide to the "insider" perspective on the narratives. Having established a cultural and literary context for Judges and Ruth, the commentary then treats each episode separately and as a whole. It is written to be accessible for a wide audience – including clergy, scholars, teachers, seminarians, and interested laypeople. A "Suggested Reading" list – a feature of all volumes in the New Cambridge Bible Commentary – serves as a point of entry for the new serious students of Judges and Ruth, and the entire NRSV translation is provided throughout the text as a convenience to the reader.

Victor H. Matthews has authored or coauthored eleven books, including, most recently, *A Brief History of Ancient Israel* (2002) and *Old Testament Themes* (2000). Since 1984, he has been a member of the religious studies department at Southwest Missouri State University, where he currently is Professor of Religious Studies and Associate Dean of the College of Humanities and Public Affairs.

NEW CAMBRIDGE BIBLE COMMENTARY

GENERAL EDITOR: Ben Witherington III

HEBREW BIBLE/OLD TESTAMENT EDITOR: Bill T. Arnold

The New Cambridge Bible Commentary (NCBC) aims to elucidate the Hebrew and Christian Scriptures for a wide range of intellectually curious individuals. While building on the work and reputation of the Cambridge Bible Commentary popular in the 1960s and 1970s, the NCBC takes advantage of many of the rewards provided by scholarly research over the last four decades. Volumes utilize recent gains in rhetorical criticism, social scientific study of the Scriptures, narrative criticism, and other developing disciplines to exploit the growing edges in biblical studies. Accessible, jargon-free commentary, an annotated "Suggested Reading" list, and the entire New Revised Standard Version (NRSV) text under discussion are the hallmarks of all volumes in the series.

ALSO IN THE SERIES
Revelation, Ben Witherington III

FORTHCOMING VOLUMES
Genesis, Bill T. Arnold
Exodus, Carol Meyers
Deuteronomy, Brent Strawn
Joshua, Douglas A. Knight
1–2 Chronicles, William M. Schniedewind
Psalms 1–72, Walter Brueggemann and Patrick D. Miller
Psalms 73–150, Walter Brueggemann and Patrick D. Miller
Isaiah 1–39, David Baer
Jeremiah, Baruch Halpern
Hosea, Joel, and Amos, J. J. M. Roberts
The Gospel of Matthew, Craig A. Evans
The Gospel of Luke, Amy-Jill Levine and Ben Witherington III
The Gospel of John, Jerome H. Neyrey
Paul's Letters to the Corinthians, Craig S. Keener
The Letters of James and Jude, William F. Brosend
The Letters of John, Duane F. Watson

Judges and Ruth

Victor H. Matthews
Southwest Missouri State University

CAMBRIDGE
UNIVERSITY PRESS

PUBLISHED BY THE PRESS SYNDICATE OF THE UNIVERSITY OF CAMBRIDGE
The Pitt Building, Trumpington Street, Cambridge, United Kingdom

CAMBRIDGE UNIVERSITY PRESS
The Edinburgh Building, Cambridge CB2 2RU, UK
40 West 20th Street, New York, NY 10011-4211, USA
477 Williamstown Road, Port Melbourne, VIC 3207, Australia
Ruiz de Alarcón 13, 28014 Madrid, Spain
Dock House, The Waterfront, Cape Town 8001, South Africa

http://www.cambridge.org

First published 2004

Printed in the United States of America

Typeface Minion 10.5/13 pt.   *System* LaTeX 2ε [TB]

A catalog record for this book is available from the British Library.

Library of Congress Cataloging in Publication Data
Matthews, Victor Harold.
Judges and Ruth / Victor H. Matthews.
    p.   cm. – (New Cambridge Bible commentary)
Includes bibliographical references and index.
ISBN 0-521-80606-2 – ISBN 0-521-00066-1 (pbk.)
1. Bible. O.T. Judges – Commentaries.   2. Bible. O.T. Ruth – Commentaries.   I. Title.   II. Series.
BS1305.53.M27   2003
222′.3077 – dc21   2003053218

ISBN 0 521 80606 2 hardback
ISBN 0 521 00066 1 paperback

*To Bill Arnold, Lorene Stone, and Carol Matthews,
who contributed in their own way to the
completion of this volume*

Contents

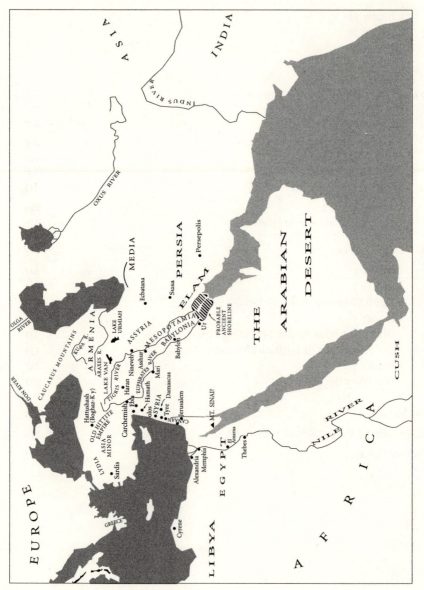

THE ANCIENT NEAR EAST

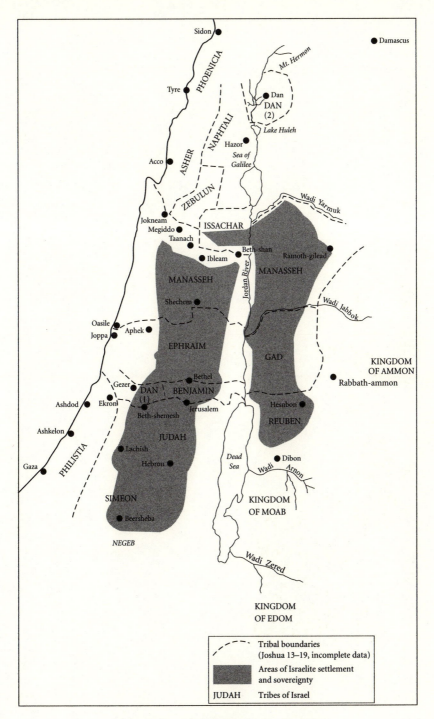

PREMONARCHIC TRIBAL ALLOTMENTS

A Word about Citations

*A*ll volumes in the New Cambridge Bible Commentary include foot-notes, with full bibliographical citations included in the note when a source text is first mentioned in each chapter. Subsequent citations include the author's initial or initials, full last name, abbreviated title for the work, and date of publication. Most readers prefer this citation system to endnotes, which require searching through pages at the back of the book.

The Suggested Reading lists, also included in all NCBC volumes after the introductions, are not a part of this citation apparatus. Annotated and organized by publication type, the self-contained Suggested Reading lists are intended to introduce and briefly review some of the most well-known and helpful literature on the biblical text under discussion.

Features of the Commentary

A commentary is designed to be a companion to the biblical text. It provides a discussion of literary, philological, and cultural features in the narrative and helps to direct the serious reader to a better understanding of the stories, their place within the canon of Scriptures, and the ways in which these materials speak to the modern world. The biblical story was composed thousands of years ago, but the universality of its message has been one of the contributing factors to its survival and continued use by faith communities and scholars today.

To assist the reader, this commentary includes the following features:

1. A general introduction is included at the beginning of each book. These are designed to provide basic information on the content of Judges and Ruth, highlighting specific literary features and providing enough historical and cultural background so that the reader will feel comfortable with the mention of events and customs as they appear later in the commentary.

2. The full text of the NRSV of Judges and Ruth prefaces analysis sections. In most cases large segments are provided followed by commentary, but there are a few instances in which the text has been broken up to highlight particularly important sections or pericopes.

3. Displayed lists are interspersed throughout the commentary. These are designed to provide additional information, extra-biblical texts, or outlines of literary features in the text.

4. Sections entitled "A Closer Look" provide in-depth examination of an event, an important person or group, or a particularly crucial theological point.

5. At the end of each major literary section, a feature entitled "Bridging the Horizons" gives some clues on how the material could be taught or preached to a contemporary audience, or offers illustrations that amplify the meaning of the text.

Abbreviations

AB	Anchor Bible
ANET	*Ancient Near Eastern Texts Relating to the Old Testament* (ed. J. B. Pritchard)
ARM	Archives Royales de Maris (Paris)
ATANT	Abhandlungen zur Theologie des Alten und Neuen Testaments (Zurich)
BA	*Biblical Archaeologist*
BAR	*Biblical Archaeology Review*
BASOR	*Bulletin of the American Schools of Oriental Research*
BBB	Bonner Biblische Beiträge (Bonn)
Bib	*Biblica*
BibInt	*Biblical Interpretation*
BRev	*Bible Review*
BTB	*Biblical Theology Bulletin*
BZAW	Beihefte zur *ZAW*
CB	Cambridge Bible for Schools and Colleges
CBQ	*Catholic Biblical Quarterly*
CH	Code of Hammurabi
COS	*The Context of Scripture*
CTA	*Corpus des tablettes en cunéi formes alphabétiques découvertes à Ras Shamra-Ugarit de 1929 à 1939* (A. Herdner; Paris)
HAR	*Hebrew Annual Review*
HUCA	*Hebrew Union College Annual*
ICC	International Critical Commentary on the Holy Scriptures of the Old and New Testaments
IEJ	*Israel Exploration Journal*

Int	*Interpretation*
IOS	*Israel Oriental Studies*
JAAR	*Journal of the American Academy of Religion*
JANES	*Journal of the Ancient Near Eastern Society*
JANESCU	*Journal of the Ancient Near Eastern Society of Columbia University*
JBL	*Journal of Biblical Literature*
JCS	*Journal of Cuneiform Studies*
JETS	*Journal of the Evangelical Theological Society*
JNES	*Journal of Near Eastern Studies*
JNSL	*Journal of Northwest Semitic Languages*
JSNTSup	Supplements of *Journal for the Study of the New Testament*
JSOT	*Journal for the Study of the Old Testament*
JSOTSup	Supplements of *Journal for the Study of the Old Testament*
JSS	*Journal of Semitic Studies*
JSSEA	*Journal of the Society for the Study of Egyptian Antiquity*
JTS	*Journal of Theological Studies*
KHCAT	Kurzer Hand-Commentar zum AT
KTU	*Die Keilalphabetischen Texte aus Ugarit* (M. Dietrich, O. Loretz, and J. Sanmartin; Kevelaer)
LAB	Liber antiquitatum biblicarum (Pseudo-Philo)
LXX	Septuagint
MAL	Middle Assyrian Laws
MT	Massoretic text 230
NEA	*Near Eastern Archaeology* (formerly *Biblical Archaeologist*)
NICOT	New International Commentary on the Old Testament
NRSV	New Revised Standard Version
OBO	Orbis Biblicus et Orientalis
OTL	Old Testament Library
PEQ	*Palestine Exploration Quarterly*
PRSt	*Perspectives in Religious Studies*
ResQ	*Restoration Quarterly*
RTR	*Reformed Theological Review*
SBJT	*Southern Baptist Journal of Theology*
SBL	Society of Biblical Literature
Sir	Sirach Bensira or Ecclesiasticus
SJOT	*Scandinavian Journal of the Old Testament*
TynBul	*Tyndale Bulletin*

UF	*Ugarit-Forschungen*
USQR	*Union Seminary Quarterly Review*
VT	*Vetus Testamentum*
VTSup	Supplements to *Vetus Testamentum*
ZAW	*Zeitschrift für die alttestamentlich Wissenschaft*
ZTK	*Zeitschrift für Theologie und Kirche*

PART ONE

The Book of Judges

1. Introduction

⚜

The stories compiled in the Book of Judges are filled with dynamic and at times enigmatic characters. They sometimes jump off the pages, like the tales of Gideon or Samson, surprising the reader with actions or words that are completely unexpected. There are also occasions when the reader is left wondering where the rest of the story has gone or why only certain details have been included in the narrative. For, although some of these tales contain fairly well-developed plots and fleshed-out characters, some are quite sketchy and beg to be completed or to have rough edges smoothed out (see the tales of Othniel and Ehud). In fact, some characters are barely there (only a couple of verses – like Shamgar), and the information provided about them is so enigmatic that the purpose for including them is unclear. But that is the way it is with the Book of Judges. It is filled with irony, both earthy and dark comedy, very human situations, great danger, and a continual plea for stability that always seems to elude the people of the Israelite tribes.

It is quite likely that much of the received text of the Book of Judges was drawn from oral tradition – especially "hero" stories – based on the cultural memories of each of the tribes or regions of ancient Israel. Some of it is fragmentary, and that may be a reflection of an incomplete survival of traditions or an editor's decision-making process, which drew the stories into a set literary or theological framework and eliminated those features that were not part of this agenda. Much of it is entertaining, but there are episodes that are incredibly violent, and some characters perform acts in the name of national liberty that modern readers would consider scandalous or frightening (see Ehud's murder of Eglon or Jael's driving a tent peg through Sisera's brow). There are also some remarkable gaps in what might be expected of a people who have made a covenant with Yahweh (see Exod 24). For instance, the Ark of the Covenant, so prominent in the stories about Moses and Joshua (e.g., Exod 25:10–22; Num 10:33–36; Josh 3:3–6; 6:8–16),

3

is missing from most of the Book of Judges (see only 20:27). In addition, there is no mention of the Ten Commandments (Exod 20:1–17) except in the speech of an unnamed prophet in the Gideon narrative (Judg 6:10), and very little compliance with any of these statutes.

The Book of Judges does not mention a central shrine where Israelite worship took place (see the use of Shiloh in 1 Sam 1:3). In most cases the acts of worship take place at village "high places" that may be dedicated to Baal and Asherah (Judg 6:25–26) or used to honor various gods, including Yahweh (Judg 13:15–16). There also is no mention of a high priest like Aaron or one of his descendants (see Exod 29) – only solitary Levites who are answerable to no higher authority and seem unconcerned with anything other than personal employment or personal welfare (Judg 17:7; 19:1).

Even more evident is the lack of cooperation between the various tribes. This can of course be explained to a certain extent by the absence of political unity during this period and the disorganized nature of isolated settlements scattered throughout the hill country. However, the text makes a real point of noting those instances in which some tribes actually refuse a call to arms (Judg 5:13–18), and those in which tribes (especially Ephraim) engage in intimidation and spark open warfare with other tribes (Judg 12:1–7). Crowning this anarchic situation is the general civil war between Benjamin and all of the other tribes over the rape of the Levite's concubine (Judg 19–21). Although it may be a true reflection of frontier literature, it seems more likely that the editors constructed the narrative in such a way that it becomes an intentional caricature of events and thus an argument for law and order. The Judges material therefore is supposed to be rough, uncouth, and in places very exciting and comical.

The settlement period prior to the establishment of the Israelite monarchy forms the background to the Book of Judges (ca. 1100–1000 BCE). Unlike the more idealized accounts of the conquest of Canaan in the Book of Joshua (e.g., Josh 11:16–12), the episodes in Judges provide a somewhat more realistic portrayal of life in the Central Hill Country and in the Transjordanian area of Gilead before the monarchy (see Judg 1:19–36). There is more attention to the military failures of the Israelites as well as to the aspects of everyday life of individuals and families (see Deborah judging cases in 4:5, Gideon's ploy to save his grain in 6:11, and the distrait woman in 9:53 who fled with her grindstone and then cast it down on Abimelech's head).

As noted in Josh 13:2–3, the Philistines control the area of the Shephelah, a fertile plateau region extending from the southern coastal plain inland to the Judean Hill Country. The five major cities of these people were founded by a portion of the Sea People invaders sometime after 1200 BCE, and their superior organization and technology gave them the edge needed to enforce their hegemony over much of the rest of Canaan (1 Sam 13:19–21). In what could be considered a face-saving piece of political rhetoric, Pharaoh Rameses III describes how he defeated contingents of Sea Peoples and other tribes while allowing some to settle in Canaan (*ANET*, 262): "I slew the Denyen in their islands, while the Tjeker and the Philistines [Peleset] were made ashes. The Sherden and the Weshesh of the Sea were made nonexistent. . . . I settled them in strongholds, bound in my name." It seems that the Egyptians lost control over Canaan and that new peoples including the Philistines and the Israelites were able to settle and carve out portions of the land for themselves.

Thus the settlement period, as portrayed in the Book of Judges, presents a time of political opportunism, internecine warfare between various tribes and peoples, temporary chiefdoms ruled or led by warlords, and a generally lawless, anarchic era. What has come down to us in written form is a compilation of episodes by an editor or a group of editors, referred to as the Deuteronomistic Historian, that originally circulated in the monarchic period in oral form. The Deuteronomistic History is the term commonly employed to refer to the material in the Book of Deuteronomy as well as Joshua, Judges, 1–2 Samuel, and 1–2 Kings in the Hebrew Bible. Many scholars concur that this body of literature is the product of an editing process that utilized oral tradition, court histories, and other literary materials, and thereby shaped the emphasis and presentation of the biblical text to create a distinct theological perspective. The primary aim of the Deuteronomistic History is to emphasize the importance of obedience to the covenant and the dire consequences of failure to adhere to the law and to God's pronouncements. A common structure and vocabulary is identified by scholars, and it is generally dated to the latter portion of the sixth century BCE.[1]

The disparate stories in the Book of Judges by these late editors describe the difficulties of life as the Israelites begin to settle in Canaan and the attempt to meet the challenge of creating a group identity. From the very beginning the editors try to create a coherent sense of the history of this long-ago period in a plausible manner while at the same time speaking more directly to a

---

[1] See Steven L. McKenzie, "Deuteronomistic History." Pages 160–68 of vol. 2 in *The Anchor Bible Dictionary*. Edited by David N. Freedman. New York: Doubleday, 1992, for a more complete discussion of the origins and history of scholarly opinion on the Deuteronomistic History.

much later audience living in the Babylonian exile and, like the people of the Judges period, lacking a king or political control over events that affect their lives.[2]

The narrative in Judges begins with the announcement of Joshua's death, and the people are immediately thrown into the uncertainties attendant with a lack of strong leadership. As a result one of the main themes in the book is the search or desire for "legitimate leadership,"[3] articulated in the final chapters in the recurrent phrase, "in those days there was no king in Israel; all the people did what was right in their own eyes" (Judg 18:1; 21:25). Given the likelihood that much of this material was edited no earlier than the late seventh century BCE by the Deuteronomistic Historian, the agenda of the editors may have been to legitimize Josiah's administration (640–609 BCE) in Judah. Another possibility, based on statements in 1 Samuel 12, would be their effort to demonstrate that the true king of the Israelites is Yahweh and that without divine direction the people fall into political and social chaos.[4]

LITERARY ANALYSIS

The most distinctive literary feature of the Book of Judges is that the various and unrelated stories have been compiled and systematically arranged and edited into a coherent whole.[5] A three-part division provides (1) an introductory and explanatory narrative (1:1–3:6), (2) a collection of tales about the judges (3:7–16:31), and (3) four episodes that accentuate the anarchic character of the time period (17:1–21:25). Such an easily defined structure indicates conscious editing and a specific theological emphasis on the part of one[6] or possibly two[7] late monarchic or postexilic groups. This is not to say that the stories can be put aside as totally secondary to the theological

---

2   Baruch Halpern, *The First Historians: The Hebrew Bible and History.* San Francisco: Harper & Row, 1988b: 138–39.
3   E. Theodore Mullen Jr., "The 'Minor Judges': Some Literary and Historical Considerations," *CBQ* 44 (1982): 194.
4   Marc Z. Brettler, "The Book of Judges: Literature as Politics," *JBL* 108 (1989): 395–418; William J. Dumbrell, " 'In Those Days There Was No King in Israel; Every Man Did What Was Right in His Own Eyes': The Purpose of the Book of Judges Reconsidered," *JSOT* 25 (1983): 31–32.
5   See the chart in Marvin A. Sweeney, "Davidic Polemic in the Book of Judges," *VT* 47 (1997): 529.
6   Hans D. Hoffmann, *Reform und Reformen: Untersuchungen zu einem Grundthema der deuteronomistischen Geschichtsschreibung.* ATANT 66. Zurich, Switz.: Theologischer Verlag, 1980; John Van Seters, *In Search of History: Historiography in the Ancient World and the Origins of Biblical History.* New Haven, Conn.: Yale University Press, 1983.
7   Andrew D. H. Mayes, *The Story of Israel between Settlement and Exile: A Redactional Study of the Deuteronomistic History.* London: SCM, 1983: 58–80; Mark A. O'Brien,

agenda of the Deuteronomistic Historian. They existed first, and from them come the real character and tone of the book, however they may have been packaged by later redactors.[8]

The Book of Judges begins with a general introduction, which provides a transition from the orderly period of Joshua's leadership to the chaotic conditions that necessitate the "raising" of judges. These first two chapters explain why the Israelite tribes were not able to complete their conquest of the Canaanites and other inhabitants of the Promised Land. One example appears in Judg 1:19, where it states that Yahweh, the divine warrior, gave the Israelite tribe of Judah a victory in the hill country, but the Israelites were not able to defeat the people of the plain because they had "iron chariots." This is an unusual admission of failure considering the victories over chariot armies described in Josh 11:6–9 and Judg 4:13–16. It provides, however, a more balanced appraisal of the Israelites' ability to conquer occupied territory than does the idealized narrative in the first twelve chapters of the Book of Joshua. It also emphasizes the differences in material culture between the Israelites and the indigenous inhabitants of Canaan.

The explanatory material contains as well two competitive statements concerning the retention of some of these enemy peoples in Canaan.[9] The more theological of the two declares that Yahweh has decided to allow them to survive (i.e., God would not drive them out) in order "to test Israel, whether or not they would take care to walk in the way of the Lord as their ancestors did" (Judg 2:22). Curiously, in the other explanation God chooses to use these people "to teach those [Israelites] who had no experience of [war]" warfare's methods (Judg 3:2). Rationalizations such as these, the latter of which is placed in parentheses by the New Revised Standard Version (NRSV) translators to show it was not part of the original story, represent later commentary on the narrative material. It is unlikely that the Israelites during the Judges period would appreciate the value of having Canaanites as test subjects or military drill instructors, especially while they were being oppressed by them. However, the Deuteronomistic Historian views these events from hindsight and can therefore present them in a manner to illustrate the point that the people had brought their punishment on themselves and that only Yahweh could remove their oppressors.[10]

The Deuteronomistic History Hypothesis: A Reassessment. OBO 92. Göttingen, Ger.: Vandenhoeck & Ruprecht, 1989: 82–98.

8 B. Halpern, *The First Historians* (1988b): 124–30.

9 Marc Z. Brettler, *The Book of Judges.* London and New York: Routledge, 2002: 79.

10 Robert H. O'Connell, *The Rhetoric of the Book of Judges.* VTSup 63. Leiden, Neth.: Brill, 1996: 76–79.

The stories in the middle portion of the book (3:7–16:31) are progressively chaotic. Othniel (3:7–11), the first judge, is a paragon of virtue who is raised by God to serve the people and is filled with the spirit of the Lord. He responds to the needs of the people, provides them with a military victory, and then provides them with forty years of rest without claiming the title of king or imposing any strictures on them. From there on, however, it is a swift decline in moral standards and authoritative leadership. From Ehud's role as a bloody-handed assassin, to Gideon's uncertainties in his own abilities, to Samson's lustful romp through the Philistine cities, the world in the stories in chapters 3–16 borders on being totally anarchic. However, the biblical editors made a very conscious effort to tie these episodes into an apparently chronological narrative. In addition, the stories present a polemical view of this period of Israelite history, with the general intention of promoting the political importance of the tribe of Judah (see Judg 1:2; although contrast Judg 15:9–13). In particular, they enhance the importance of later stability of the Davidic dynasty versus the failures of Saul and the Benjaminites.[11] The stories are not arranged chronologically, however, and they share only the disorder of the times. The cycle or framework that is used to tie the stories together gives a sense of literary and theological unity.

The framework used by the biblical editors is quite simple, following a consistent pattern of events (Judg 2:11–19). It emphasizes, in its repeated usage, that the Israelites, despite having a judge raised to assist them, always resume the pattern of disobedience that caused God's displeasure in the first place:[12]

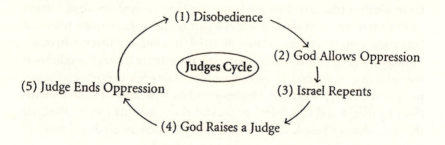

(1) Disobedience

Judges Cycle

(2) God Allows Oppression

(5) Judge Ends Oppression

(3) Israel Repents

(4) God Raises a Judge

[11] M. A. Sweeney, "Davidic Polemic" (1997): 517; Andrew D. H. Mayes, "Deuteronomistic Royal Ideology in Judges 17–21," *BibInt* 9 (2001): 252–53.

[12] Michael K. Wilson, "'As You Like It': The Idolatry of Micah and the Danites (Judges 17–18)," *RTR* 54 (1995): 75.

1. The people of Israel sin by violating the covenant (doing "evil in the sight of the Lord," turning away from Yahweh, and worshipping other gods [3:7]).

2. A disappointed Yahweh becomes angry and allows the Israelites to be oppressed by their neighbors. This is an excellent example of a theodicy, an explanation for why God allows bad things to happen to the chosen people. It is not unique to the Israelites. In the ninth century BCE "Stele of Mesha," King Mesha of Moab, explains why his people have been oppressed by the Israelites, saying, "Omri, the King of Israel controlled Moab for many years because Chemosh, our chief god, was angry at his people."[13]

3. The Israelites repent and call upon Yahweh to deliver them from their oppressors. This step in the framework provides the Israelites with proof that repentance on their part is necessary to regain God's favor toward them. It does not justify their previous actions and is not a quid pro quo requiring Yahweh to help them, but it is the only way they can return to compliance with the terms of the covenantal agreement.

4. Yahweh responds by raising up a judge to deal with the crisis. In several cases this includes an infusion of God's spirit into the judges impelling them to action and giving them greater authority. In most cases the task of the judge takes the form of military activity within a defined area, although it is not always organized warfare.

5. A period of peace and order (usually in increments of twenty, forty, or eighty years), coinciding with the career of the judge, is almost immediately followed by a return to the sin that had precipitated the original crisis, and the cycle resumes. This resumption of their "failed" condition is the catalyst for moving on to the next episode.

The basic features of this structure begin to break down in Judg 9 with the violent story of Abimelech and his attempt to seize the kingship that his father Gideon had rejected. From that point on, none of the judges will be entirely successful, and none will be described as having brought peace to the land. Jephthah is raised to his position as judge by members of his own tribe, and although he is successful in defeating the Ammonites, he does not remove all of the oppressing nations, and he violates a basic tenet of Israelite religious practice when he sacrifices his daughter after attempting

[13] Victor H. Matthews and Don C. Benjamin, *Old Testament Parallels: Laws and Stories from the Ancient Near East.* Mahwah, N.J.: Paulist Press, 1997: 158.

to blackmail God into giving him a military victory (Judg 11:29–40). Samson, the last major judge, never leads his people in battle but instead engages in a private war that centers more on a series of women in his life, and he dies in the suicidal action of pulling a Philistine temple down on a huge crowd (Judg 16:28–31).

The final five chapters (Judg 17–21) are distinct because they do not contain any mention of a judge. They are filled with the same sorts of anarchic events occurring in other portions of the book – lawlessness, civil war, and idolatry – but no judge arises to meet the problems. Instead there is a tale of a rogue Levite who assists an idolater by officiating in a shrine in Micah's home and then performs the same duties for the migrating tribe of Dan after it confiscates the idols and creates a shrine in the new capital. Topping off the theme of reckless behavior is a fantastic tale of brutal rape and civil war involving all of the tribes. While it is tempting to say that these stories were appended to the end of the book because of their similarity to other Judges material, it is more likely that they were added to provide a final literary transition for the opening of the monarchy period that begins in 1 Sam. The theme that "in those days there was no king in Israel; all the people did what was right in their own eyes" (Judg 21:25) is best exemplified in these final chapters.

This concluding section also provides a crowning argument for the establishment of the monarchy and lays the foundation for the anointing of Saul and David as the first national leaders of Israel. In addition, the Deuteronomistic Historian may have hoped to underscore the importance of a "righteous" king like Josiah, who cleansed the Jerusalem temple, destroyed the false altars in Bethel, and restored the Passover celebration (2 Kings 22:3–23:27). In this way a direct contrast is made to polemicize Josiah's sons Jehoiakim and Zedekiah, who came to the throne with the political assistance of foreign powers and eventually brought the wrath of Nebuchadnezzar and Babylon upon Jerusalem (2 Kings 23:36–24:20).[14]

OUTLINE OF THE JUDGES

| Othniel | Raised by God to defeat Cushan-rishathaim of Aram-naharaim, resulting in 40 years of rest (3:7–11) |
| Ehud | Assassinates Eglon of Moab, resulting in 80 years of rest (3:12–30) |

---

[14] E. Aydeet Mueller, *The Micah Story: A Morality Tale in the Book of Judges.* New York: Peter Lang, 2001: 15.

Shamgar	Kills 600 Philistines with an ox goad, thereby "delivering" Israel (3:31)
Deborah	A prophetess and local judge who incites Barak to raise an army among the tribes to defeat Jabin and Sisera (4–5)
Gideon	Invested with God's spirit to deliver Israel from Midian in a series of military campaigns, resulting in 40 years of rest (6–8)
Abimelech	Gideon's son, but not a judge, who kills 70 brothers, becomes a warlord with help of the city of Shechem, and is killed in battle after 3 years (9)
Tola	Minor judge of Issachar who served for 23 years (10:1–2)
Jair	Minor judge of Gilead with 30 sons who served for 22 years (10:3–5)
Jephthah	Bandit chief invited by elders of Gilead to deliver them from Ammonites, who also fights a civil war with Ephraim and sacrifices his daughter to fulfill a vow (10:6–12:7)
Ibzan	Minor judge of Bethlehem with 30 sons and 30 daughters who served 7 years (12:8–10)
Elon	Minor judge of Zebulun who served 10 years (12:11–12)
Abdon	Minor judge of Pirathon in Ephraim with 40 sons and 30 grandsons who served for 8 years (12:13–15)
Samson	Nazirite with superhuman strength whose personal adventures involve a series of Philistine women, slaughter of thousands of Philistines, and a tragic end. He judged Israel for 20 years (13–16) [15]

CULTURAL ANALYSIS

To understand the Judges material it is necessary to try to comprehend the intention of the authors of these stories and the later editors who compiled them into an extended narrative. Every nation has its "wild" period, a time that some would like to forget but that was very important in the development of the people into a nation. Tribal Israel was at best a loose confederation of tribal territories made up primarily of an agriculturally based village

---

[15]   This outline is a revised version of that found in J. Maxwell Miller and John H. Hayes, *A History of Ancient Israel and Judah*. Philadelphia: Westminster, 1986: 88.

culture.[16] The tribes cooperated occasionally, but as the "song of Deborah" (Judg 5:12–18) and the feud between Jephthah and the Ephraimites (Judg 12:1–6) demonstrate, that cooperation was never universal or long-lasting. Rules of law and allegiance to a covenant that bound the people into a single political unit came later in Israelite history. It might well have been impossible for that union to take place without the chaos of the Judges period to serve as the example of what they had escaped and into which they never wished to sink again. In this way a case is made, however propagandistic, for law and order and the establishment of a government to ensure stability. These stories also function as a reminder, especially to the people of the postexilic era who also had no king, that chaos – cultural and political – is to be equated with a failure to obey the covenant.

In approaching the Book of Judges, it may be most useful to imagine a period in history when lawlessness and disregard for tradition were rampant, such as in twelfth-century England, when the heirs of Henry I (Matilda and Stephen) and their followers ravaged the country and legal constraints were abandoned, or during the colonial period in Canada, when French trappers were known for their trailbreaking exploits and a desire to stay as far away from civilization as possible. A similar period of North American frontier life occurred during the latter half of the nineteenth century CE, when the man with the most firepower and the ability to trick, cajole, or threaten his way through every situation was heralded as a hero or at least an antihero. Names like Billy the Kid, Jessie James, and Wild Bill Hickok come to mind, and their excesses and flaunting of the law have become just as legendary as some of the figures described in Judges. They are bigger than life, and the exaggerations about their lives and accomplishments set the tone for an era rather than chronicle its history.

This period of Israelite history was a time of new settlements and of the struggle to survive both social and physical environments. As yet no evidence has been uncovered that proves a discernible ethnic difference between the Canaanites and those people who would eventually become the Israelites.[17] In fact, many of the "Israelite" villages were probably made up of Canaanites who had fled their former homes to escape the warfare, famine, and disease plaguing Syria-Palestine between 1200 and 1000 BCE. New population groups

---

[16]   Victor H. Matthews and Don C. Benjamin, *The Social World of Ancient Israel*. Peabody, Mass.: Hendrickson, 1993: 96–97.

[17]   Kurt L. Noll, *Canaan and Israel in Antiquity: An Introduction*. London: Sheffield Academic Press, 2001: 140–45.

that entered the area during this time of chaos then may have joined them.[18] It is during this period, when the incursions of the Sea Peoples dissolved Egyptian control over the area, that new social groups were founded on a common need to pool their labor to produce crops and to establish new settlements in quieter regions of the country. The struggle to survive within a kin-based, egalitarian village community forged a sense of cooperation and care for each other, which is also reflected in the covenantal obligations imposed on them by the law and by their God (see especially the statutes designed to protect widows, orphans, and strangers in Deut 24:17–21).[19]

The culture that does develop in the hill country is initially based on former Canaanite models, but it will eventually take on a distinctive character.[20] These pioneers will have to be tougher and more resourceful to survive in the more marginal environment they have been forced to settle. Most of the sites identified by archaeologists are located in previously uninhabited areas of the hill country of Judah, an indication that the better sites were taken by the Philistines. Thus the pragmatism of village life, directed by elders and emphasizing the ideals of hard work and shared responsibility, had to become the norm. In addition, the ideals of an egalitarian society marked by the virtues of trust, honor, and a hatred of slavery contribute to the creation of a distinct people that will become Israelite. The Israelite credo expressing this attitude is found repeatedly in the legal statutes of the Deuteronomic Law Code (Deut 5:15; 15:15; 16:12; 24:18, 22): "Remember that you were a slave in Egypt."

Life in these small villages (75–100 inhabitants) therefore would have been dependent on the available natural resources, such as arable land, grazing area, and water sources. It would have been driven by the forces of nature that may or may not have provided sufficient rain in season, and the people's concerns would be to protect themselves and their crops and animals from killing winds and plagues of locust (see Deut 28:38–39). The people worked extremely hard in their fields, and when they made sacrifices they did so in thanks to Yahweh and also, apparently, to the Canaanite gods (Judg 6:25–30) in the expectation of continued good fortune and sustained fertility. Their villages were mapped out not in grids but according to the households of

---

[18] Volkmar Fritz, "Israelites and Canaanites: You Can Tell Them Apart," *BAR* 28 (4, 2002): 30–31.

[19] Frank Crüsemann, *The Torah: Theology and Social History of Old Testament Law*. Minneapolis: Fortress Press, 1996: 225–34.

[20] Victor H. Matthews, *A Brief History of Ancient Israel*. Louisville, Ky.: Westminster/John Knox, 2002: 30–32.

each villager. Cottage industry was a part of the responsibilities of each family, but there may have been some families able to specialize as potters, tanners, or dye makers, with their shops attached to their houses. These "specialists" offered simple wares while also working their own farming plots or vineyards.

Village law and assembly of the people would have been conducted on the centrally located threshing floor (Judg 6:37; Ruth 3:3–6). Here, where grain was processed and distributed, disputes were settled and the needs of the poor were ascertained and addressed. In this way the village cared for its own and managed its harvest to the benefit and survival of the entire community. This shared system works best on a small scale. Later it will be tapped and exploited by the monarchy (1 Sam 8:14–15), and eventually the community's resources will be drained by taxes, and the sense of egalitarianism will be weakened. Once the monarchy is established, a structured, multilevel social system will replace the simpler village culture.

The material culture of the hill country settlements during the settlement period could therefore be described as environmentally focused. Survival required risk-taking strategies and a mixed economy that did not concentrate on a single crop or resource.[21] Often just enough grain was produced to maintain the population and perhaps provide a small surplus that could be used for trade or stored against the inevitable bad years. Population growth could provide a larger work force, but it would also drain, at least temporarily, the food supply. In other words, life was a gamble, and for the Israelites to master their new environment and eventually to expand beyond the hill country they would have to do two things: (1) increase their population and (2) borrow many of the useful aspects of the material culture of the Canaanite cities of the plains. It was this latter requirement, however, that was the principal danger.

When one culture borrows from another (a process known as syncretism) the temptation is to become "just like" that other culture and to allow the distinctive aspects of the borrowing culture to be submerged or lost. The biblical writers continually argue against syncretism, especially with regard to the worship of foreign gods. But, the stories in the Book of Judges clearly suggest that many of the Israelites were true neither to Yahweh nor to the covenant made at Sinai. These people strongly resembled their neighbors, working and worshiping in much the same way and drawing what they could from the land. The struggle for survival, however, also provided them with

---

[21]   David C. Hopkins, *The Highlands of Canaan.* Sheffield, Eng.: Almond Press, 1985: 267–69.

an incentive to seek out God's help and draw on the covenant to define both their relationship with Yahweh and with each other. Although the judges, for the most part, are not good role models, they do act in the name of Yahweh and are empowered with the spirit of God. Thus their stories add to the cultural foundation of ancient Israel and serve as one of the developmental steps leading to the establishment of the monarchy and a more unified people.

ARCHAEOLOGICAL ANALYSIS

Because this period is not well documented except in the Bible, most of what we can learn about life during the early Iron Age is based on archaeological remains.[22] The pattern of new settlements in the hill country (at present over 300 excavated or surveyed) suggests a migration of the population to this previously underpopulated region during the period between 1200 and 1000 BCE.[23] In their examination of these village sites, archaeologists try to identify patterns of culture based on pottery types, architectural styles, and technologies.[24] Very often a new people entering an area will bring in a distinctive culture, evidenced by its possessions, such as pottery, jewelry, and weapons, and even its burial styles.

Although it would be helpful if there were startling differences between Israelite and Canaanite material cultures, that does not seem to be the case. New housing styles, such as the four-room house, do indicate a change, but this may be due to the environment of the hill country, where most new settlements had a mixed agricultural and pastoral economy.[25] These standardized structures contained a central courtyard that was flanked by a room on either side and a broad room at one end. This arrangement, with access to each of the rooms by way of the courtyard, provided shared living and storage space for the extended family that dwelt there as well as shelter for the animals. A sense of unity may have been created by this

[22] Lawrence E. Stager, "The Archaeology of the Family in Ancient Israel," *BASOR* 260 (1985): 25–28.

[23] William G. Dever, "Excavating the Hebrew Bible, or Burying It Again?" *BASOR* 322 (2001): 71; idem, "Will the Real Israel Please Stand Up? Archaeology and Israelite Historiography: Part I," *BASOR* 297 (1995): 72; Israel Finkelstein, "The Emergence of the Monarchy in Israel: The Environmental and Socio-Economic Aspects," *JSOT* 44 (1989): 53–59.

[24] See the discussion in Philip J. King and Lawrence E. Stager, *Life in Biblical Israel.* Louisville, Ky.: Westminster/John Knox, 2001: 9–19.

[25] L. E. Stager, "The Archaeology of the Family" (1985): 17; Shlomo Bunimovitz and Avraham Faust, "Ideology in Stone: Understanding the Four-Room House," *BAR* 28 (4, 2002): 36.

architectural design, communicating a sense of inward or familial strength and egalitarian ethos that could successfully struggle against the chaos of the outside world.[26]

Identification of pottery types and styles is one of the most universally accepted means of determining entrance of new cultures into an area. This method, however, is of little help during the settlement period in identifying uniquely Israelite ceramics. Other than the Aegean-style Philistine one-handled cooking jugs and craters decorated with birds, the ceramics of this portion of the early Iron Age remain the same as the older Canaanite forms. They used two-handled cooking pots, collared-rim storage jars, and a variety of undecorated bowls and jugs.[27]

Other innovations produced in these villages, such as the terracing of hill-sides for farming and the plastering of cisterns to prevent seepage of water into the porous limestone, seem to be a matter more of the natural developments of life in the hill country than of inventions that radically changed their world. Still these simple methods of shaping their environment and preserving precious natural resources add to the sense of communal life.[28] People in small villages without walls or a means of defense saw their struggle with nature rather than with their neighbors. Certainly, they could be harassed by raiders (Judg 6:2–6) and claimed as part of a larger political unit for taxation purposes (Judg 3:12–13), but their real strength was to be found in their sense of community. They formed nonstratified, close-knit, kinship-based villages and were dependent on each other and on living from harvest to harvest.

What has come out of the ground in the last two decades of archaeological investigation is a fuller understanding of the Philistine presence in Canaan. Sites like Gezer and Tell Miqne-Ekron reveal well-established urban cultures. They maintained large-scale industry, especially in the rendering of olive oil, and established trade contacts from Egypt to Phoenicia. Their purported widespread use of iron technology, however, appears to be exaggerated. They possessed a knowledge of iron, but bronze continued to be the principal metal used for weapons, farm implements, and industrial tools. The statement in 1 Sam 13:19 that there was "no smith to be found throughout all the land of Israel" and that the Israelites were forced to rely upon the

---

[26] S. Bunimovitz and A. Faust, "Ideology in Stone," *BAR* 28 (2002): 40–41.
[27] P. J. King and L. E. Stager, *Life in Biblical Israel* (2001): 139.
[28] William G. Dever, "The Identity of Early Israel: A Rejoinder to Keith W. Whitelam," *JSOT* 72 (1996): 15–16.

Philistines to sharpen their farm implements suggests not a monopoly on iron technology but on metal working in general.[29] Intensive specialization of labor would have been less likely in the Israelite villages where most efforts had to be directed to farming. They would most likely have produced their own common ware pottery, tanned their own hides, and woven their own cloth for clothing, but a blacksmith is a dedicated profession, not one that can be done part-time.

One can trace the place names mentioned in the biblical text. The Philistine cities of Ashkelon, Ashdod, Ekron, Gaza, and Gezer, as well as the Canaanite and Phoenician cities of Megiddo, Acco, Sidon, Beth-shemesh, Jebus (Jerusalem), and Hazor have all been located, and it can be ascertained that they existed and were inhabited during the early Iron Age. It is more difficult to authenticate the social and religious practices of this period. Some cultic sites (temples, shrines, etc.) have been excavated, images discovered, and sacrifices described in documents written in later eras (such as the Stele of Mesha of the late ninth century BCE). These kinds of archaeological data, however, must be examined with caution. Mute artifacts obviously have their limitations, and drawing conclusions or parallels based on similar but later social customs may be misleading. As is the case with other poorly documented periods of biblical history, the age of Judges must, for now, remain more tentative than concrete. What remains is an examination of the received text of the Book of Judges, which is an artifact that, like pottery or architecture, can be analyzed in an attempt to reconstruct the society of ancient Israel.

---

29   Paula McNutt, *Reconstructing the Society of Ancient Israel.* Louisville, Ky.: Westminster/ John Knox, 1999: 74–75.

2. Suggested Reading

*T*here is a vast amount of scholarly attention paid to the Book of Judges, but much of it is written specifically for scholars and therefore assumes command of the ancient languages and an intimate familiarity with the history and cultures of the ancient Near East. For those who are coming fresh to this material I would suggest first reading the Book of Judge carefully with some basic reference tools at hand. For example, for basic information on the time period, archaeological data, and characters found in Judges, consult the articles in any one of the recently published one-volume Bible dictionaries, such as Paul Achtemeier, ed., *HarperCollins Bible Dictionary,* rev. ed. (San Francisco: Harper & Row, 1996) or David N. Freedman, ed., *Eerdmans Dictionary of the Bible* (Grand Rapids, Mich.: Eerdmans, 2000), or a specialized Bible commentary, such as John H. Walton, Victor H. Matthews, and Mark W. Chavalas, eds., *IVP Bible Background Commentary: Old Testament* (Downers Grove, Ill.: InterVarsity, 2000). More extensive articles and information can be found in the multivolume *Anchor Bible Dictionary* (New York: Doubleday, 1992), edited by David N. Freedman. Written by hundreds of scholars, this reference work provides the full range of data on the ancient Israelite world.

COMMENTARIES ON JUDGES

To more fully investigate the linguistic and theological issues raised by the Hebrew texts of Judges and Ruth, the serious reader should consult major biblical commentaries. While it is still profitable to consult the early works in this genre, such as those by George F. Moore, *A Critical and Exegetical Commentary on Judges,* ICC (New York: Charles Scribner's Sons, 1895 [1923]), K. Budde, *Das Buch der Richter,* KHCAT (Freiburg, Ger.: G. Ragoczy, 1897), and G. A. Cooke, *Judges,* CB (Cambridge: The University Press, 1913), the more recent commentaries provide sufficient and reliable reference. The standard works reflecting scholarship during the 1960s–1980s include the excellent commentary by Robert Boling, *Judges: A New Translation with Introduction and Commentary,* AB (Garden City, N.Y.: Doubleday, 1975) and the historical-critical treatment of the text by J. A. Soggin, *Judges,* OTL (Philadelphia: Westminster, 1981). Boling's linguistic insights are still the most cited by scholars, and his acceptance of the Deuteronomistic redaction of the text is still accepted by many scholars. Soggin's extensive reference to European scholarship is an aid to those less familiar with the writings from the German academy and with ancient Near Eastern texts.

Among the more current works, the commentary by Tammi J. Schneider, *Judges,* Berit Olam (Collegeville, Minn.: Liturgical Press, 2000), is perhaps the most useful in drawing out the theme of "degenerative progression," in which each story contributes to a downward spiral of social chaos and disobedience to the covenant. She skillfully points out the use of irony in many of these stories and links many of the events to aspects of the social world of ancient Israel. A similar treatment of the theological situation portrayed in the text is found in Clint McCann, *Judges,* Interpretation (Louisville, Ky.: Westminster/John Knox, 2002). For a more diachronic, redactional approach to the text, the reader is directed to Yairah Amit, *The Book of Judges: The Art of Editing* (Leiden, Neth.: Brill, 1999). The unfinished commentary by Barnabas Lindars, *Judges 1–5* (Edinburgh: T & T Clark, 1995), is also an excellent resource for the literary aspects of the early section of Judges.

Other commentaries making significant contributions include

Burney, C. F. *The Book of Judges,* 2nd ed. London: Rivingtons, 1920.
Cundall, Arthur E. *Judges: An Introduction and Commentary.* Leicester, Eng.: InterVarsity Press, 1968.
Gray, John. *Joshua, Judges, Ruth.* New Century Bible Commentary. Grand Rapids, Mich.: Eerdmans, 1986.
Hamlin, E. John. *Judges: At Risk in the Promised Land.* International Theological Commentary. Grand Rapids, Mich.: Eerdmans, 1990.
Mayes, A. D. H. *Judges.* Sheffield, Eng.: JSOT Press, 1985.

LITERARY STUDIES

The "Bible as Literature" movement that began in the 1970s, represented by the work of Robert Alter, *The Art of Biblical Narrative* (New York: Basic

Books, 1981), has sparked a variety of literary theories and methods. The fragmentation of critical interpretation has in turn led to a host of new approaches in analyzing the Book of Judges. For instance, a structural approach, examining the narrative meaning of the text of Judges, is provided by Barry G. Webb, *The Book of Judges: An Integrated Reading* (Sheffield, Eng.: JSOT Press, 1987). His intent is to explore the interaction of characters within the narrative and to distinguish the unfolding plot without specific regard to possible historical context. Another quite helpful treatment is the rhetorical analysis provided in Robert H. O'Connell, *The Rhetoric of the Book of Judges*, VTSup 63 (Leiden, Neth.: Brill, 1996). He defines rhetoric as "the ideological purpose or agenda of the Judges compiler/redactor with respect to the implied readers of the book."[1] Thus he identifies and deals with formal structures and patterns that appear in the deliverer stories and suggests that the purpose or intent of the redactors was to "endorse a divinely appointed Judahite king." A somewhat broader, postmodern literary paradigm is suggested by Jacobus Marais, *Representation in Old Testament Narrative Texts* (Leiden, Neth.: Brill, 1998). He deems "representation" as a relational concept that is indicative of the relationship between a text and reality, which is "mediated" by such factors as language, semiotics, the writing conventions of storytelling, and literary genres. With regard to Judges, he points to juxtaposition as the principal convention of narration, with characters, scenes, and actions juxtaposed as a means of expressing their sense of reality.[2] Marc Brettler, *The Book of Judges* (New York: Routledge, 2001) takes a more eclectic approach, employing what he calls a literary-historical method, allowing these apparently competing methods to stand side by side and thereby provide a sort of synthesis of interpretation. This allows him to speak of Judges as a unity, not just as a collection of disparate stories or episodes.

Among the many other literary studies on Judges, I have found the following most helpful in my analysis of the text:

Alter, Robert. "Biblical Type-Scenes and the Uses of Convention." *Critical Inquiry* 5 (2, 1978): 355–68.

    "How Convention Helps Us Read: The Case of the Bible's Annunciation Type-Scene." *Prooftexts* 3 (1983): 115–30.

---

[1]   Robert H. O'Connell, *The Rhetoric of the Book of Judges*. VTSup 63. Leiden, Neth.: Brill, 1996: 1.
[2]   Jacobus Marais, *Representation in Old Testament Narrative Texts*. Leiden, Neth.: Brill, 1998: 145–46.

Bauer, Uwe F. W. "Judges 18 as an Anti-Spy Story in the Context of an Anti-Conquest Story: The Creative Usage of Literary Genres." *JSOT* 88 (2000): 37–47.

Berlin, Adele. *Poetics and Interpretation of Biblical Narrative*. Sheffield, Eng.: Almond Press, 1983.

Blenkinsopp, Joseph. "Ballad Style and Psalm Style in the Song of Deborah: A Discussion." *Bib* 42 (1961): 61–76.

"Structure and Styles in Judges 13–16." *JBL* 82 (1963): 65–76.

"Will the Real Gideon Please Stand Up? Narrative Style and Intention in Judges 6–9." *JETS* 40 (1997a): 353–66.

Brenner, Athalya. "A Triangle and a Rhombus in Narrative Structure: A Proposed Integrative Reading of Judges iv and v." *VT* 40 (1990): 129–38.

Craig, Kenneth M. "Bargaining in Tov (Judges 11, 4–11): The Many Directions of So-Called Direct Speech." *Bib* 79 (1998): 76–85.

Crenshaw, James L. "The Samson Saga: Filial Devotion or Erotic Attachment?" *ZAW* 86 (1974): 470–504.

Samson, A Secret Betrayed, a Vow Ignored. Atlanta: Mercer University Press, 1978.

Emerton, John A. "Some Comments on the Shibboleth Incident (Judges XII 6)." Pages 149–57 in *Mélanges bibliques et orientaux en l'honneur de M. Mathias Delcor*. Edited by André Caquot, S. Légasse, and M. Tardieu. Neukirchen-Vluyn: Verlag Butzon & Bercker Kevelaer, 1985.

Exum, J. Cheryl. "Promise and Fulfillment: Narrative Art in Judges 13." *JBL* 99 (1980): 43–59.

Aspects of Symmetry and Balance in the Samson Saga." *JSOT* 19 (1981): 3–29.

"The Tragic Vision and Biblical Narrative: The Case of Jephthah." Pages 59–83 in *Signs and Wonders: Biblical Texts in Literary Focus*. Edited by J. Cheryl Exum. Atlanta: Scholars Press, 1989a.

"The Centre Cannot Hold: Thematic and Textual Instabilities in Judges." *CBQ* 52 (1990): 410–31.

Tragedy and Biblical Narrative: Arrows of the Almighty. Cambridge: Cambridge University Press, 1992.

"Harvesting the Biblical Narrator's Scanty Plot of Ground: A Holistic Approach to Judges 16:4–22." Pages 39–46 in *Tehillah le-Moshe: Biblical and Judaic Studies in Honor of Moshe Greenberg*. Edited by Mordechai Cogan, et al. Winona Lake, Ind.: Eisenbrauns, 1997.

Fewell, Danna N. "Deconstructive Criticism: Achsah and the (E)rased City of Writing." Pages 119–45 in *Judges and Method: New Approaches in Biblical Studies*. Edited by Gale Yee. Minneapolis: Fortress Press, 1995.

Fishbane, Michael. *Text and Texture: Close Reading of Selected Biblical Texts*. New York: Schocken Books, 1979.

Globe, Alexander. "The Text and Literary Structure of Judges 5,4–5." *Bib* 55 (1974): 168–78.

Hess, Richard S. "Judges 1–5 and Its Translation." Pages 142–60 in *Translating the Bible: Problems and Prospects*. Edited by Simon E. Porter and Richard S. Hess. JSNTSup 173. Sheffield, Eng.: Sheffield Academic Press, 1999.

Jobling, David. "Structuralist Criticism: The Text's World of Meaning." Pages 91–118 in *Judges and Method: New Approaches in Biblical Studies*. Edited by Gale A. Yee. Minneapolis: Fortress Press, 1995.

Kim, Jichan. *The Structure of the Samson Cycle*. Kampen, Neth.: Kok Pharos, 1993.

Klein, Lillian R. *The Triumph of Irony in the Book of Judges*. JSOTSup 68, Sheffield, Eng.: Almond Press, 1989.

Lee, Bernon. "Fragmentation of Reader Focus in the Preamble to Battle in Judges 6.1–7.14." *JSOT* 97 (2002): 65–86.

Marcus, David. *Jephthah and His Vow*. Lubbock: Texas Tech Press, 1986.

Matthews, Victor H. "Freedom and Entrapment in the Samson Narrative: A Literary Analysis." *PRSt* 16 (1989): 245–57.

Mueller, E. Aydeet. *The Micah Story: A Morality Tale in the Book of Judges*. New York: Peter Lang, 2001.

Murray, Donald F. "Narrative Structure and Technique in the Deborah-Barak Story, Judges iv 4–22." Pages 155–89 in *Studies in the Historical Books of the Old Testament*. Edited by John A. Emerton. Leiden, Neth.: Brill, 1979.

Niditch, Susan. *Underdogs and Tricksters. A Prelude to Biblical Folklore*. San Francisco: Harper & Row, 1987.

"Reading Story in Judges 1." Pages 193–208 in *The Labour of Reading: Desire, Alienation, and Biblical Interpretation*. Edited by Fiona C. Black et al. Atlanta: SBL, 1999.

Ogden, Graham S. "Jotham's Fable: Its Structure and Function in Judges 9." *Bible Translator* 46 (1995): 301–8.

Olson, Dennis T. "Dialogues of Life and Monologues of Death: Jephthah and Jephthah's Daughter in Judges 10:6–12:7." Pages 43–54 in *Postmodern Interpretations of the Bible: A Reader*. Edited by A. K. M. Adam. St. Louis, Mo.: Chalice Press, 2001.

Penchansky, David. "Staying the Night: Intertextuality in Genesis and Judges." Pages 77–88 in *Reading between Texts: Intertextuality and the Hebrew Bible*. Edited by Danna N. Fewell. Louisville, Ky.: Westminster/John Knox, 1992.

Satterthwaite, Philip. "Narrative Artistry in the Composition of Judges XX 29FF." *VT* 42 (1992): 80–89.

———. "'No King in Israel': Narrative Criticism and Judges 17–21." *TynBul* 44 (1993): 75–88.

Sternberg, Meir. *The Poetics of Biblical Narrative: Ideological Literature and the Drama of Reading*. Bloomington: Indiana University Press, 1985.

Waldman, Nahum M. "Concealment and Irony in the Samson Story." *Dor le Dor* 13 (1984–85): 71–79.

REDACTION STUDIES

Many scholars have taken the position that Judges is a composite piece of literature, a collection of unrelated stories that have been edited into a single book by a body of editors or redactors during the late monarchic or early exilic period. This process would involve not only editorial decisions based on a theological or political agenda but the insertion of details or story elements to provide a sense of continuity or unity to the whole. The so-called Deuteronomistic Historian is the term most often applied to the editor(s) of Judges, and this would place the formation of the text in the troubled period encompassing the end of the monarchy in Judah, the deportation of the people to Mesopotamia, and a redefinition of Israelite values and institutions based around the covenant with Yahweh. There is also embedded within the text a political polemic against the northern kingdom (Ephraim) and an exaggerated justification for the idealized monarchy in Judah. Building on the earlier work of Martin Noth, *The Deuteronomistic History*, JSOTSup 15 (Sheffield, Eng.: JSOT Press, 1981), the best surveys and analyses of the work of the Deuteronomistic Historian can be found in Robert Polzin, *Moses and the Deuteronomist: A Literary Study of the Deuteronomic History. Part One: Deuteronomy, Joshua, Judges* (New York: Seabury, 1980); Wolfgang Richter, *Traditionsgeschichtliche Untersuchungen zum Richterbuch*, 2nd ed., BBB 18 (Bonn, Ger.: Peter Hanstein, 1966); and Baruch Halpern, *The First Historians: The Hebrew Bible and History* (San Francisco: Harper & Row, 1988b). The latter work does an excellent job of reconstructing the process utilized by the Deuteronomistic Historian in piecing together the materials that comprised the Former Prophets (Josh through 2 Kings).

Amidst the scholarship that investigates the redaction of the text of Judges and its relationship to the Deuteronomistic Historian I have found the following most helpful:

Amit, Yairah. "Literature in the Service of Politics: Studies in Judges 19–21." Pages 28–40 in *Politics and Theopolitics in the Bible and Postbiblical Literature*. Edited by H. G. Reventlow, Y. Hoffman, and B. Uffenheimer. JSOTSup 171. Sheffield, Eng.: Sheffield Academic Press, 1994.

Becker, Uwe. *Richterzeit und Königtum: Redaktionsgeschichtliche Studien zum Richterbuch*. BZAW 192. Berlin and New York: Walter de Gruyter, 1990.

Benjamin, Don C. *Deuteronomy and City Life*. Lanham, N.Y.: University Press of America, 1983.

Block, Daniel I. "Deborah among the Judges: The Perspective of the Hebrew Historian." Pages 229–53 in *Faith, Tradition and History*. Edited by Alan R. Millard et al. Winona Lake, Ind.: Eisenbrauns, 1994.

Brettler, Marc Z. "The Book of Judges: Literature as Politics." *JBL* 108 (1989): 395–418.

Daube, David. "The Culture of Deuteronomy." *Orita* 3 (1969): 27–52.

Dragga, Sam. "In the Shadow of the Judges: The Failure of Saul." *JSOT* 38 (1987): 39–46.

Dumbrell, William J. " 'In Those Days There Was No King in Israel; Every Man Did What Was Right in His Own Eyes': The Purpose of the Book of Judges Reconsidered." *JSOT* 25 (1983): 23–33.

Hoffmann, Hans D. *Reform und Reformen: Untersuchungen zu einem Grundthema der deuteronomistischen Geschichtsschreibung*. ATANT 66. Zurich, Switz.: Theologischer Verlag, 1980.

Malamat, Abraham. "The Danite Migration and the Pan-Israelite Exodus-Conquest: A Biblical Narrative Pattern." *Bib* 51 (1970): 1–16.

"Deuteronomistic Royal Ideology in Judges 17–21." *BibInt* 9 (2001): 241–58.

Mayes, Andrew D. H. *The Story of Israel between Settlement and Exile: A Redactional Study of the Deuteronomistic History*. London: SCM, 1983.

Mullen, E. Theodore. *Narrative History and Ethnic Boundaries*. Atlanta: Scholars Press, 1993.

O'Brien, Mark A. *The Deuteronomistic History Hypothesis: A Reassessment*. OBO 92. Göttingen, Ger.: Vandenhoeck & Ruprecht, 1989.

Sweeney, Marvin A. "Davidic Polemic in the Book of Judges." *VT* 47 (1997): 517–29.

Van Seters, John. *In Search of History: Historiography in the Ancient World and the Origins of Biblical History.* New Haven, Conn.: Yale University Press, 1983.

FEMINIST STUDIES

In recent years, the stories found in the Book of Judges have sparked a very large number of articles and monographs that examine the text from a feminist perspective. The primary aim of these works is to throw greater light on both the strong female characters in the stories and to provide a more sympathetic, less androcentric interpretation of the victimization of women in the ancient world and in modern critical analysis. Among the most seminal of these works is that of Phyllis Trible, *Texts of Terror: Literary-Feminist Readings of Biblical Narratives* (Philadelphia: Fortress Press, 1984), and the groundbreaking treatments of the Deborah and Samson narratives by Mieke Bal, *Lethal Love: Feminist Literary Readings of Biblical Love Stories* (Bloomington: Indiana University Press, 1987), *Murder and Difference: Gender, Genre, and Scholarship on Sisera's Death* (Bloomington: Indiana University Press, 1988a), and *Death and Dissymmetry: The Politics of Coherence in the Book of Judges* (Bloomington: Indiana University Press, 1988b). Tikva Frymer-Kensky, *In the Wake of the Goddesses: Women, Culture and the Biblical Transformation of Pagan Myth* (New York: Free Press, 1992), provides a broader perspective on the role and restrictions placed on women in ancient Near Eastern culture. Other scholars, who do not consider themselves to be feminist critics but who take an active interest in the treatment of women in these stories, include Daniel Block, "Unspeakable Crimes: The Abuse of Women in the Book of Judges," *SBJT* 2–3 (1998): 46–55, and Victor H. Matthews, "Female Voices: Upholding the Honor of the Household," *BTB* 24 (1994a): 8–15.

Also of importance to the study of ancient Israelite women are the volume by Susan Ackerman, *Warrior, Dancer, Seductress, Queen: Women in Judges and Biblical Israel* (New York: Doubleday, 1998), and the volumes in the Feminist Companion to the Bible series edited by Athalya Brenner, which contain articles by many younger female scholars and a very fresh analysis of the material. In addition, J. Cheryl Exum has for many years published studies of the Judges episodes with particular emphasis on a feminist understanding of these stories. Two collections of these articles are *Fragmented Women: Feminist, (Sub)versions of Biblical Narratives,* JSOTSup 163 (Sheffield, Eng.: JSOT Press, 1993) and *Plotted,*

Shot, and Painted, JSOTSup 215 (Sheffield, Eng.: Sheffield Academic Press, 1996).

Other articles and books that follow this particular interpretative path generally center on the Deborah narrative (Judg 4–5), the story of Jephthah's daughter (Judg 11), Samson's women (Judg 13–16), and the tragic tale of the Levite's concubine in Judg 19:

Amit, Yairah. "Judges 4: Its Contents and Form." *JSOT* 39 (1987): 89–111.

"'Manoah Promptly Followed His Wife' (Judges 13.11): On the Place of the Woman in Birth Narratives." Pages 146–56 in *A Feminist Companion to Judges.* Edited by Athalya Brenner. Sheffield, Eng.: JSOT Press, 1993.

"Literature in the Service of Politics: Studies in Judges 19–21." Pages 28–40 in *Politics and Theopolitics in the Bible and Postbiblical Literature.* Edited by H. G. Reventlow, Y. Hoffman, and B. Uffenheimer. JSOTSup 171. Sheffield, Eng.: Sheffield Academic Press, 1994.

Bach, Alice. "Rereading the Body Politic: Women and Violence in Judges 21." *BibInt* 6 (1998): 1–19.

Bal, Mieke. "A Body of Writing: Judges 19." Pages 208–30 in *A Feminist Companion to Judges.* Edited by Athalya Brenner. Sheffield, Eng.: Sheffield Academic Press, 1993.

Bos, Johanna W. H. "Out of the Shadows: Genesis 38; Judges 4:17–22; Ruth 3." *Semeia* 42 (1988): 37–67.

Brenner, Athalya. "A Triangle and a Rhombus in Narrative Structure: A Proposed Integrative Reading of Judges iv and v." *VT* 40 (1990): 129–38.

"Naomi and Ruth." Pages 70–84 in *A Feminist Companion to Ruth.* Edited by Athalya Brenner. Sheffield, Eng.: Sheffield Academic Press, 1993.

"The Food of Love: Gendered Food and Food Imagery in the Song of Songs." *Semeia* 86 (1999a): 101–12.

"Ruth as a Foreign Worker and the Politics of Exogamy." Pages 158–62 in *Ruth and Esther: A Feminist Companion to the Bible,* 2nd series. Edited by Athalya Brenner. Sheffield, Eng.: Sheffield Academic Press, 1999b.

Exum, J. Cheryl. "Promise and Fulfillment: Narrative Art in Judges 13." *JBL* 99 (1980): 43–59.

Aspects of Symmetry and Balance in the Samson Saga." *JSOT* 19 (1981): 3–29.

"The Theological Dimension of the Samson Saga." *VT* 33 (1983): 30–45.

"The Tragic Vision and Biblical Narrative: The Case of Jephthah." Pages 59–83 in *Signs and Wonders: Biblical Texts in Literary Focus*. Edited by J. Cheryl Exum. Atlanta: Scholars Press, 1989a.

"Murder They Wrote: Ideology and the Manipulation of Female Presence in Biblical Narrative." *USQR* 43 (1989b): 19–39.

"The Centre Cannot Hold: Thematic and Textual Instabilities in Judges." *CBQ* 52 (1990): 410–31.

Tragedy and Biblical Narrative: Arrows of the Almighty. Cambridge: Cambridge University Press, 1992.

"Feminist Criticism: Whose Interests Are Being Served?" Pages 65–90 in *Judges and Method: New Approaches in Biblical Studies*. Edited by Gale Yee. Minneapolis: Fortress Press, 1995.

"Harvesting the Biblical Narrator's Scanty Plot of Ground: A Holistic Approach to Judges 16:4–22." Pages 39–46 in *Tehillah le-Moshe: Biblical and Judaic Studies in Honor of Moshe Greenberg*. Edited by Mordechai Cogan et al. Winona Lake, Ind.: Eisenbrauns, 1997.

Fewell, Danna N., and David Gunn. "Controlling Perspectives: Women, Men, and the Authority of Violence in Judges 4 and 5." *JAAR* 58 (1990a): 389–411.

Guest, Pauline D. "Dangerous Liaisons in the Book of Judges." *SJOT* 11 (1997): 241–69.

Janzen, J. G. "A Certain Woman in the Rhetoric of Judges 9." *JSOT* 38 (1987): 33–37.

Jones-Warsaw, Koala. "Toward a Womanist Hermeneutic: A Reading of Judges 19–21." Pages 172–86 in *A Feminist Companion to Judges*. Edited by Athalya Brenner. Sheffield, Eng.: Sheffield Academic Press, 1993.

Keefe, Alice A. "Rapes of Women/Wars of Men." *Semeia* 61 (1993): 79–97.

Klein, Lillian R. "The Book of Judges: Paradigm and Deviation in Images of Women." Pages 55–71 in *A Feminist Companion to Judges*. Edited by Athalya Brenner. Sheffield, Eng.: JSOT Press, 1993.

"Achsah: What Price This Prize?" Pages 18–26 in *Judges: A Feminist Companion to the Bible*, 2nd series. Edited by Athalya Brenner. Sheffield, Eng.: Sheffield Academic Press, 1999.

Niditch, Susan. "The 'Sodomite' Theme in Judges 19–20: Family, Community, and Social Disintegration." *CBQ* 44 (1982): 365–78.

Pressler, Carolyn. *The View of Women Found in the Deuteronomic Family Laws*. BZAW 216. Berlin: Walter de Gruyter, 1993.

Reinhartz, Adele. "Samson's Mother: An Unnamed Protagonist." *JSOT* 55 (1992): 25–37.

Reis, Pamela T. "Spoiled Child: A Fresh Look at Jephthah's Daughter." *Proof* 17 (1997): 279–98.

Van der Kooij, Arie. "On Male and Female Views in Judges 4 and 5." Pages 135–52 in *On Reading Prophetic Texts.* Edited by Bob Becking and Meindert Dijkstra. Leiden, Neth.: Brill, 1996.

Williams, James G. "The Beautiful and the Barren: Conventions in Biblical Type-Scenes." *JSOT* 17 (1980): 107–19.

  Women Recounted: Narrative Thinking and the God of Israel. Sheffield, Eng.: Almond Press, 1982.

Yee, Gale A. "By the Hand of a Woman: The Metaphor of the Woman Warrior in Judges 4." *Semeia* 61 (1993): 99–132.

  "Ideological Criticism: Judges 17–21 and the Dismembered Body." Pages 146–70 in *Judges and Method: New Approaches in Biblical Studies.* Edited by Gale A. Yee. Minneapolis: Fortress Press, 1995.

SOCIAL WORLD AND ARCHAEOHISTORICAL STUDIES

Because so much of the material found in Judges is set in the village context, many scholars have chosen to concentrate on the various aspects of tradition and custom evidenced in the text. While it is difficult to provide a firm historical foundation for these stories, the comparisons made with other ancient Near Eastern and traditional cultures are helpful in reconstructing the settlement period of ancient Israel. One recently published general study of manners and customs is by Philip J. King and Lawrence E. Stager, *Life in Biblical Times* (Louisville, Ky.: Westminster/John Knox, 2002); it marshals a large amount of the archaeological data and presents it in a fashion usable for both scholars and laypersons. More detailed studies that center on the environmental conditions, specific aspects of ancient farming and herding techniques, and life in the marginal world of the Central Hill Country of ancient Canaan include David Hopkins, *The Highlands of Canaan* (Sheffield, Eng.: Almond Press, 1985) and Oded Borowski, *Agriculture in Iron Age Israel* (Winona Lake, Ind.: Eisenbrauns, 1987). A more recent monograph dealing with this archaeological and historical reconstruction of the period is Paula McNutt, *Reconstructing the Society of Ancient Israel* (Louisville, Ky.: Westminster/John Knox, 1999). Her attention to ancient Israel's social structure, politics, economics, material culture, and law make her volume an excellent resource for social world studies.

For more specific and technical studies on archaeology and Iron Age Israel, see

Bloch-Smith, Elizabeth, and Beth Nakhai, "A Landscape Comes to Life: The Iron Age I." *NEA* 62 (1999): 62–92, 101–27.

Bunimovitz, Shlomo, and Avraham Faust. "Ideology in Stone: Understanding the Four-Room House." *BAR* 28 (4, 2002): 32–41, 59–60.

Dever, William G. "Will the Real Israel Please Stand Up? Archaeology and Israelite Historiography: Part I." *BASOR* 297 (1995): 61–80.

"The Identity of Early Israel: A Rejoinder to Keith W. Whitelam." *JSOT* 72 (1996): 3–24.

"Excavating the Hebrew Bible, or Burying It Again?" *BASOR* 322 (2001): 67–77.

Dothan, Trude. "The 'Sea Peoples' and the Philistines of Ancient Palestine." Pages 1267–79 of vol. 1 in *Civilizations of the Ancient Near East*. Edited by Jack M. Sasson. Peabody, Mass.: Hendrickson, 1995.

Finkelstein, Israel. *The Archaeology of the Settlement of Israel*. Jerusalem: Israel Exploration Society, 1988.

"The Emergence of the Monarchy in Israel: The Environmental and Socio-Economic Aspects." *JSOT* 44 (1989): 43–74.

Fritz, Volkmar. "Israelites and Canaanites: You Can Tell Them Apart." *BAR* 28 (4, 2002): 28–31, 63.

Halpern, Baruch. "The Assassination of Eglon: The First Locked-Room Murder Mystery." *BRev* 4 (6, 1988a): 33–41, 44.

Gitin, Seymour. "Philistia in Transition: The Tenth Century BCE and Beyond." Pages 162–83 in *Mediterranean Peoples in Transition: Thirteenth to Early Tenth Centuries BCE*. Edited by Seymour Gitin et al. Jerusalem: Israel Exploration Society, 1998.

Mazar, Amihai. *Archaeology of the Land of the Bible: 10,000–586 B.C.E.* New York: Doubleday, 1990.

Paul, Shalom, and William C. Dever. *Biblical Archaeology*. Jerusalem: Keter, 1973.

Stager, Lawrence E. "The Archaeology of the Family in Ancient Israel." *BASOR* 260 (1985): 1–35.

Archaeology, Ecology, and Social History: Background Themes to the Song of Deborah," VTSup 40 (Leiden, Neth.: Brill, 1986): 221–34.

"Forging an Identity: The Emergence of Ancient Israel." Pages 123–75 in *The Oxford History of the Biblical World*. Edited by Michael D. Coogan. New York: Oxford University Press, 1998.

Turkowski, Lucian. "Peasant Agriculture in the Judean Hills." *PEQ* 101
(1969): 101–12.

SOCIAL SCIENTIFIC STUDIES

The aim of social scientific criticism, as a subfield of biblical exegesis, is to
study biblical materials as a reflection of their cultural setting. The meaning
and/or the social background of the text are thus more fully illumined by
the exercise of sociological and anthropological methods and theories. Since
the 1970s the emphasis of social scientific critics has been on a variety of sociological and anthropological methods, in conjunction with the emerging
field of ethnoarchaeology. While some studies choose to look at isolated
cultural phenomena, it is more common to find comparative studies. The
principal methods center on structural-functional traditions, conflict theories of social development, and cultural materialist perspectives, which
examine subsistence strategies or economic patterns. It is also quite common for scholars to employ multiple methods that complement each other.[3]
An excellent summary of this approach as it relates to Judges is found in
Naomi Steinberg, "Social Scientific Criticism: Judges 9 and Issues of Kinship," Pages 45–64 in *Judges and Method.* Edited by Gale A. Yee. Minneapolis:
Fortress Press, 1995.

For studies that use the social scientific approach in their analysis of
Judges, I would recommend the following as very helpful:

Bechtel, Lyn M. "Shame as a Sanction of Social Control in Bibli-
     cal Israel: Judicial, Political, and Social Shaming." *JSOT* 49 (1991):
     47–76.
Bohmbach, Karla G. "Conventions/Contraventions: The Meanings of
     Public and Private for the Judges 19 Concubine." *JSOT* 83 (1999): 83–98.
Guest, Pauline D. "Dangerous Liaisons in the Book of Judges." *SJOT* 11
     (1997): 241–69.
Handy, Lowell. "Uneasy Laughter: Ehud and Eglon as Ethnic Humor." *JSOT*
     6 (1992): 233–46.
Hobbs, T. Raymond. "Hospitality in the First Testament and the 'Teleological
     Fallacy.'" *JSOT* 95 (2001): 3–30.

---

[3] Charles E. Carter, "A Discipline in Transition: The Contributions of the Social Sciences to
     the Study of the Hebrew Bible." Pages 3–36 in *Community, Identity, and Ideology: Social
     Science Approaches to the Hebrew Bible.* Edited by Charles E. Carter and Carol L. Meyers.
     Winona Lake, Ind.: Eisenbrauns, 1996.

Lasine, Stuart. "Guest and Host in Judges 19: Lot's Hospitality in an Inverted World." *JSOT* 29 (1984): 38–59.

Matthews, Victor H. "Hospitality and Hostility in Judges 4." *BTB* 21 (1991): 13–21.

"Hospitality and Hostility in Genesis 19 and Judges 19." *BTB* 22 (1992): 3–11.

Matthews, Victor H., and Don C. Benjamin. *Social World of Ancient Israel 1250–587 BCE*. Peabody, Mass.: Hendrickson, 1993.

Niditch, Susan. "Samson as Culture Hero, Trickster, and Bandit: The Empowerment of the Weak." *CBQ* 52 (1990): 608–24.

Olyan, Saul M. "What Do Shaving Rites Accomplish and What Do They Signal in Biblical Ritual Contexts?" *JBL* 117 (1998): 611–22.

Stone, Kenneth A. "Gender and Homosexuality in Judges 19: Subject-Honor, Object-Shame?" *JSOT* 67 (1995): 87–107.

HISTORICAL-CRITICAL STUDIES

For those interested in historical-critical issues and in a basic sense of how Israel and its neighbors fit into ancient Near Eastern history, the best place to start is with a history of ancient Israel, such as J. Maxwell Miller and John H. Hayes, *A History of Ancient Israel and Judah* (Philadelphia: Westminster, 1986) or Victor H. Matthews, *A Brief History of Ancient Israel* (Louisville, Ky.: Westminster/John Knox, 2002). These works provide a foundation for historical reconstruction without forcing the reader into a single interpretation of the settlement period. Because it is not possible to place the Judges period into a specific time or tie it to historical events, Marc Brettler[4] points to storytelling in Judges as a means of "reinventing the past." Thus the emphasis on entertainment and the need to illustrate aspects of social morality may often take precedence over what we would consider to be history writing today.

Other sources that provide some historical-critical aspects of the Judges period include

John McKenzie, *The World of the Judges*. Englewood Cliffs, N.J.: Prentice-Hall, 1966.

---

[4] Marc Z. Brettler, *The Book of Judges*. London and New York: Routledge, 2002: 8.

Malamat, Abraham. "The Period of the Judges." Pages 129–63 in *The World History of the Jewish People*. Vol. 3: *Judges*. Edited by Benjamin Mazar. New Brunswick, N.J.: Rutgers University Press, 1971a.

    Mari and the Early Israelite Experience. Oxford: Oxford University Press, 1989.

Noll, Kurt L. *Canaan and Israel in Antiquity: An Introduction*. London: Sheffield Academic Press, 2001.

Snell, D. C. *Life in the Ancient Near East*. New Haven, Conn.: Yale University Press, 1997.

Weinfeld, Moshe. "Judge and Officer in the Ancient Near East." *IOS* 7 (1977): 65–88.

    "Divine Intervention in War in Ancient Israel and in the Ancient Near East." Pages 121–47 in *History, Historiography and Interpretation*. Edited by Hayim Tadmor and Moshe Weinfeld. Jerusalem: Magnes Press, 1983.

    "Judges 1.1–2.5: The Conquest under the Leadership of the House of Judah." Pages 388–400 in *Understanding Poets and Prophets*. Edited by A. Graeme Auld. JSOTSup 152. Sheffield, Eng.: Sheffield Academic Press, 1993.

Willis, Timothy M. "The Nature of Jephthah's Authority." *CBQ* 59 (1997): 33–44.

Younger, K. Lawson. "Heads! Tails! Or the Whole Coin?! Contextual Method and Intertextual Analysis: Judges 4 and 5." Pages 109–46 in *Scripture in Context, IV : The Biblical Canon in Comparative Perspective*. Edited by K. Lawson Younger et al. Lewiston, N.Y.: Edwin Mellen Press, 1991.

    "Judges 1 in Its Near Eastern Context." Pages 207–27 in *Faith, Tradition, and History: Old Testament Historiography in Its Near Eastern Context*. Edited by Alan R. Millard et al. Winona Lake, Ind.: Eisenbrauns, 1994.

ADDITIONAL ARTICLES AND MONOGRAPHS OF INTEREST

Rather than continue to create categories for each method or type of investigatory style, I simply provide here a list of additional articles and monographs that I found helpful in preparing this commentary.

Auld, A. Graeme. "Gideon: Hacking at the Heart of the Old Testament." *VT* 39 (1989): 257–67.

Bauer, Uwe F. W. "Judges 18 as an Anti-Spy Story in the Context of an Anti-Conquest Story: The Creative Usage of Literary Genres." *JSOT* 88 (2000): 37–47.

Beem, Beverly. "The Minor Judges: A Literary Reading of Some Very Short Stories." Pages 147–72 in *The Biblical Canon in Comparative Perspective: Scripture in Context IV*. Edited by K. Lawson Younger et al. Lewiston, N.Y.: Edwin Mellen Press, 1991.

Block, Daniel I. "Deborah among the Judges: The Perspective of the Hebrew Historian." Pages 229–53 in *Faith, Tradition and History*. Edited by Alan R. Millard et al. Winona Lake, Ind.: Eisenbrauns, 1994.

"Will the Real Gideon Please Stand Up? Narrative Style and Intention in Judges 6–9." *JETS* 40 (1997a): 353–66.

"Empowered by the Spirit of God: The Holy Spirit in the Historiographic Writings of the Old Testament." *SBJT* 1 (1997b): 42–61.

Boogaart, Thomas A. "Stone for Stone: Retribution in the Story of Abimelech and Shechem." *JSOT* 32 (1985): 45–56.

Brooks, Simcha S. "Was There a Concubine at Gibeah?" *Bulletin of the Anglo-Israel Archaeological Society* 15 (1996–97): 31–40.

Cartledge, Tony W. "Were Nazirite Vows Unconditional?" *CBQ* 51 (1989): 409–22.

Cline, E. H. *The Battles of Armageddon*. Ann Arbor: University of Michigan Press, 2000.

Cross, Frank M. *Canaanite Myth and Hebrew Epic*. Cambridge, Mass.: Harvard University Press, 1973.

Crüsemann, Frank. *The Torah: Theology and Social History of Old Testament Law*. Minneapolis: Fortress Press, 1996.

Day, John. *Yahweh and the Gods and Goddesses of Canaan*. JSOTSup 265. Sheffield, Eng.: Sheffield Academic Press, 2000.

Eissfeldt, Otto. *Die Quellen des Richterbuches*. Leipzig, Ger.: Hinrichs, 1925.

Emerton, John A. "Gideon and Jerubbaal." *JTS* 27 (1976): 289–312.

Exum, J. Cheryl. "The Theological Dimension of the Samson Saga." *VT* 33 (1983): 30–45.

Fritz, Volkmar. "Abimelech und Sichem in Jdc. IX." *VT* 32 (1982): 129–44.

Frymer-Kensky, Tikva. "Virginity in the Bible." Pages 79–96 in *Gender and Law in the Hebrew Bible and the Ancient Near East*. Edited by Victor H. Matthews et al. JSOTSup 262. Sheffield, Eng.: Sheffield Academic Press, 1998.

Gese, Hartmut. "Die ältere Simsonüberlieferung (Richter c. 14–15)." *ZTK* 82 (1985): 261–80.

Globe, Alexander. "The Text and Literary Structure of Judges 5,4–5." *Bib* 55 (1974): 168–78.

Good, Robert M. "The Just War in Ancient Israel." *JBL* 104 (1985): 385–400.

Gray, John. *I and II Kings.* Philadelphia: Westminster, 1970.

Greene, Mark. "Enigma Variations: Aspects of the Samson Story Judges 13–16." *Vox Evangelica* 21 (1991): 53–79.

Greengus, Samuel. "Old Babylonian Marriage Ceremonies and Rites." *JCS* 20 (1966): 55–72.

"Sisterhood Adoption at Nuzi and the 'Wife-Sister' in Genesis." *HUCA* 46 (1975): 5–31.

Greenspahn, Frederick E. "The Theology of the Framework of Judges." *VT* 36 (1986): 385–96.

Greenstein, Edward L. "The Riddle of Samson." *Proof* 1 (1981): 237–60.

Gunn, David M. "The 'Battle Report': Oral or Scribal Convention?" *JBL* 93 (1974): 513–18.

"Samson of Sorrows: An Isaianic Gloss on Judges 13–16." Pages 225–53 in *Reading between Texts: Intertextuality and the Hebrew Bible.* Edited by Danna N. Fewell. Louisville, Ky.: Westminster/John Knox Press, 1992.

Habel, Norman. "The Form and Significance of the Call Narratives." *ZAW* 77 (1965): 297–323.

Hallo, William W., and K. Lawson Younger Jr. *The Contexts of Scripture,* 3 vols. Leiden, Neth.: Brill, 1997–2002.

Hallpike, C. R. "Social Hair." *Man* 4 (1969): 256–64.

Halpern, Baruch. "Levitic Participation in the Reform Cult of Jeroboam I." *JBL* 95 (1976): 31–42.

Hauser, Alan J. "The 'Minor Judges': A Re-evaluation." *JBL* 94 (1975): 190–200.

"Unity and Diversity in Early Israel before Samuel." *JETS* 22 (1979): 289–303.

"Two Songs of Victory: Exodus 15 and Judges 5." Pages 265–84 in *Directions in Biblical Hebrew Poetry.* Edited by Elaine R. Follis. JSOTSup 40. Sheffield, Eng.: JSOT Press, 1987.

Hostetter, Edwin. *Nations Mightier and More Numerous.* Berkeley, Calif.: Bibal, 1995.

Janzen, Waldemar. *Old Testament Ethics: A Paradigmatic Approach.* Louisville, Ky.: Westminster/John Knox Press, 1994.

Jull, Tom A. "*Mqrh* in Judges 3: A Scatological Reading." *JSOT* 81 (1998): 63–75.

Jungling, Hans W. *Richter 19 - Ein Pladoyer für das Königtum: Stilistische Analyse der Tendenzerzählung Ri 19, 1–30a; 21, 25.* AB 84, Rome: Pontifical Biblical Institute, 1981.

Macintosh, Andrew A. "The Meaning of *MKLYM* in Judges XVIII 7." *VT* 35 (1985): 68–77.

Marcus, David. "The Bargaining between Jephthah and the Elders (Judges 11:4–11)." *JANES* 19 (1989): 95–100.

"Ridiculing the Ephraimites: The Shibboleth Incident (Judg 12:6)." *MAARAV* 8 (1992): 95–105.

Margalith, Othniel. "Samson's Foxes." *VT* 30 (1980): 224–29.

"Samson's Riddle and Samson's Magic Locks." *VT* 36 (1986): 229–34.

"The Legends of Samson/Heracles." *VT* 37 (1987): 63–70.

Matthews, Victor H. "The Social Context of Law in the Second Temple Period." *BTB* 28 (1998): 7–15.

"The Unwanted Gift: Implications of Obligatory Gift Giving in Ancient Israel." *Semeia* 87 (1999): 91–104.

Old Testament Themes. St. Louis, Mo.: Chalice Press, 2000.

Matthews, Victor H., and Don C. Benjamin. *Old Testament Parallels: Laws and Stories from the Ancient Near East*, 2nd ed. Mahwah, N.J.: Paulist Press, 1997.

Mobley, Gregory. "The Wild Man in the Bible and the Ancient Near East." *JBL* 116 (1997): 217–33.

Moyer, James C. "Weapons and Warfare in the Book of Judges," Pages 42–50 in *Discovering the Bible: Archaeologists Look at Scripture*. Edited by T. Dowley. Grand Rapids, Mich.: Eerdmans, 1986.

Mullen, E. Theodore, Jr. "The 'Minor Judges': Some Literary and Historical Considerations." *CBQ* 44 (1982): 185–201.

Otzen, Benedikt. "Heavenly Visions in Early Judaism: Origin and Function." Pages 199–215 in *In the Shelter of Elyon*. Edited by William B. Barrick and John R. Spencer. JSOTSup 31. Sheffield, Eng.: JSOT Press, 1984.

Parker, Simon B. "The Vow in Ugaritic and Israelite Narrative Literature." *UF* 11 (1979): 693–700.

Patrick, Dale A. "Epiphanic Imagery in Second Isaiah's Portrayal of a New Exodus." *HAR* 8 (1984): 125–41.

Ramras-Rauch, Gila. "Fathers and Dauthers: Two Biblical Narratives." Pages 158–69 in *Mappings of the Biblical Terrain*. Edited by Vincent Tollers and Johann Maier. Lewisburg, Pa.: Bucknell University Press, 1990.

Revell, E. John. "The Battle with Benjamin (Judges XX 29–48) and Hebrew Narrative Techniques." *VT* 35 (1985): 417–33.

The Designation of the Individual: Expressive Language in Biblical Narrative. Kampen, Neth.: Kok Pharos, 1996.

Reviv, Hanoch. *The Elders in Ancient Israel*. Jerusalem: Magnes Press, 1989.

Sasson, Jack M. "Who Cut Samson's Hair? (And Other Trifling Issues Raised by Judges 16)." *Proof* 8 (1988): 333–46.

Schley, Donald G. *Shiloh: A Biblical City in Tradition and History.* JSOTSup 63. Sheffield, Eng.: JSOT Press, 1989.

Schniedewind, William M. "The Geopolitical History of Philistine Gath." *BASOR* 309 (1998): 69–77.

Segert, Stanislav. "Paronomasia in the Samson Narrative in Judges xiii–xvi." *VT* 34 (1984): 454–61.

Shearman, Susan L., and John B. Curtis. "Divine-Human Conflicts in the Old Testament." *JNES* 28 (1969): 235–40.

Shupak, Nili. "New Light on Shamgar ben 'Anath." *Bib* 70 (1989): 517–25.

Smith, Carol. "Samson and Delilah: A Parable of Power?" *JSOT* 76 (1997): 45–57.

Van Selms, A. "Judge Shamgar." *VT* 14 (1964): 294–309.

van der Toorn, Karel. *Family Religion in Babylonia, Syria and Israel.* Leiden, Neth.: Brill, 1996.

Vickery, John. "In Strange Ways: The Story of Samson." Pages 58–73 in *Images of Man and God: Old Testament Stories in Literary Focus.* Edited by B. O. Long. Sheffield, Eng.: Almond Press, 1981.

Webb, Barry G. "The Theme of the Jephthah Story (Judges 10:6–12:7)." *RTR* 45 (1986): 34–43.

Weinberg, Werner. "Language Consciousness in the Old Testament." *ZAW* 92 (1980): 185–204.

Wharton, James A. "The Secret of Yahweh: Story and Affirmation in Judges 13–16." *Int* 27 (1973): 48–66.

Wilson, Michael K. " 'As You Like It': The Idolatry of Micah and the Danites (Judges 17–18)." *RTR* 54 (1995): 73–85.

Zevit, Ziony. *The Religions of Ancient Israel.* New York: Continuum, 2001.

I have also created and continue to update an on-line bibliography of sources related to Judges and Ruth. It can be accessed on the web at: http://courses.smsu.edu/vhm970f/bib/JUDGES.html.

3. Commentary

CHAPTER 1

(1) After the death of Joshua, the Israelites inquired of the Lord, "Who shall go up first for us against the Canaanites, to fight against them?" (2) The Lord said, "Judah shall go up. I hereby give the land into his hand." (3) Judah said to his brother Simeon, "Come up with me into the territory allotted to me, that we may fight against the Canaanites; then I too will go with you into the territory allotted to you." So Simeon went with him. (4) Then Judah went up and the Lord gave the Canaanites and the Perizzites into their hand; and they defeated ten thousand of them at Bezek. (5) They came upon Adonibezek at Bezek, and fought against him, and defeated the Canaanites and the Perizzites. (6) Adonibezek fled; but they pursued him, and caught him, and cut off his thumbs and big toes. (7) Adonibezek said, "Seventy kings with their thumbs and big toes cut off used to pick up scraps under my table; as I have done, so God has paid me back." They brought him to Jerusalem, and he died there. (8) Then the people of Judah fought against Jerusalem and took it. They put it to the sword and set the city on fire. (9) Afterward the people of Judah went down to fight against the Canaanites who lived in the hill country, in the Negeb, and in the lowland. (10) Judah went against the Canaanites who lived in Hebron (the name of Hebron was formerly Kiriath-arba); and they defeated Sheshai and Ahiman and Talmai. (11) From there they went against the inhabitants of Debir (the name of Debir was formerly Kiriath-sepher). (12) Then Caleb said, "Whoever attacks Kiriath-sepher and takes it, I will give him my daughter Achsah as wife." (13) And Othniel son of Kenaz, Caleb's younger brother, took it; and he gave him his daughter Achsah as wife. (14) When she came to him, she urged him to ask her father for a field. As she dismounted from her donkey, Caleb said to her, "What do you wish?" (15) She said to him, "Give me a present;

since you have set me in the land of the Negeb, give me also Gulloth-mayim.
So Caleb gave her Upper Gulloth and Lower Gulloth.

POST-JOSHUA CONQUEST STORIES

The stage is set for the settlement period of Israelite history (1200–1000 BCE)
by the simple statement that Joshua has died. There will be more detailed
references later (Judg 2:7–9, 21, 23) to add substance to this report,[1] but unlike
Joshua 1:1, there is to be no direct transition of leadership for the people.
Instead the editor(s) of the Book of Judges initially moves away from a single
military commander to the tribal level, as seen especially in v. 2, "Judah shall
go up." The repeated sense of leaderlessness will set a tone for the rest of
the book and will be most evident in its final chapters, when all law and any
concept leadership have broken down.[2] As a result none of the judges in the
cyclic section (Judg 3:7–16:31) will serve as a national leader, nor will they
be able to pass their authority on to family members. Ultimately, as seen
in the final set of narratives (Judg 17–21), it will be the failure of the tribes
to unite that will become the grand argument for the establishment of the
monarchy as a solution to their political and military weaknesses (Judg 18:1;
19:1; 21:25).

Some consider this chapter evidence of the pro-Judahite position of the
editor(s), which attempts to make Judah prominent to justify Judah's later
political role as the center of Davidic power.[3] In fact, David's ties to Hebron
as his first capital city are framed in a phrase quite similar to that in Judg 1:1,
"Shall I go up into any of the cities of Judah?" (2 Sam 2:1). The alliance with
Simeon might be compared to the role Simeon and Judah play in the Joseph
narrative (Gen 42:24–43:10) but more likely is an indicator of the political
submersion of Simeon within the tribe of Judah early in Israelite history.
The alliance represents a violation of divine instructions since Judah was not
told to seek allies in the military campaign and serves as the first of many
errors by the Israelites in these narratives.[4]

---

[1]   Jacobus Marais, *Representation in Old Testament Narrative Texts*. Leiden, Neth.: Brill,
      1998: 73.

[2]   E. Theodore Mullen Jr., "The 'Minor Judges': Some Literary and Historical Considera-
      tions," *CBQ* 44 (1982): 190.

[3]   Marc Z. Brettler, "The Book of Judges: Literature as Politics," *JBL* 108 (1989): 395–418;
      Marvin A. Sweeney, "Davidic Polemic in the Book of Judges," *VT* 47 (1997): 526–27.

[4]   Richard S. Hess, "Judges 1–5 and Its Translation." Pages 143–44 in *Translating the Bible:
      Problems and Prospects*. Edited by Simon E. Porter and Richard S. Hess. JSNTSup 173.
      Sheffield, Eng.: Sheffield Academic Press, 1999.

The same question regarding military strategy will be asked during the civil war when the tribes swear to attack the tribe of Benjamin after the sexual assault at Gibeah (Judg 20:18), and in both cases Judah is chosen. While the Book of Judges is essentially episodic, this is one of several clear editorial attempts to provide a sense of cohesion to the stories. That Judah is so prominent in these two narratives and yet is portrayed as weak, even cowardly, elsewhere (Judg 15:9–13) indicates the editor(s)' willingness to describe less favorable events without whitewashing the account.

Note the similarities between this battle chronicle and the Assyrian Annals.[5] In both the enemy king or commander is said to have fled before the victorious army, and both describe the capture and mutilation of this enemy king. It is possible that Adonibezek's role is simply to indicate the principle of reciprocity, "those who live by the sword die by the sword," or in this case suffer humiliation and crippling injury.[6] The Assyrian Annals are filled with descriptions of mutilating prisoners of war as a means of psychological intimidation.[7] However, as in this case, the act is designed not to kill but to maim. Adonibezek, king of Jerusalem (Josh 10:1–5), will never be able to rule again in his crippled condition. As he shuffles across the floor or awkwardly tries to pick up or hold an object, he will serve as an example to other rulers who oppose the Israelites. Similarly, if the men of Jabesh-gilead had agreed to Nahash's terms, they would have been partially blinded, unable to fight, but still able to work and thus produce yearly tribute for their Ammonite masters (1 Sam 11:2 [hamstringing horses was a means of limiting the enemy's chariotry (2 Sam 8:4)]).

Battle reports are consistently favorable for Judah in this opening section. In that sense they follow the pattern set in Joshua, where the only battle lost by the Israelites is at Ai when one man (Achan) breaks the law of *ḥērem* (holy war) and steals from the loot set aside for God after the capture of Jericho (Josh 7). Later acknowledgment in the text that Benjamin was assigned to attack Jerusalem and that this tribe failed to drive out its Jebusite inhabitants (Judg 1:21) stands independent of the Judah account. It is essential to the

5   K. Lawson Younger, "Judges 1 in Its Near Eastern Context." Page 226 in *Faith, Tradition, and History: Old Testament Historiography in Its Near Eastern Context.* Edited by Alan R. Millard et al. Winona Lake, Ind.: Eisenbrauns, 1994.

6   Susan Niditch, "Reading Story in Judges 1." Page 196 in *The Labour of Reading: Desire, Alienation, and Biblical Interpretation.* Edited by Fiona C. Black et al. Atlanta: SBL, 1999.

7   Erika Bleibtreu, "Grisly Assyrian Record of Torture and Death," *BAR* 17 (1, 1991): 52–61, 75; A. K. Grayson, *Assyrian Royal Inscriptions, Part 2: Tiglath-pileser I to Ashur-nasir-apli II.* Wiesbaden, Ger.: Otto Harrassowitz, 1976: 120–27.

editor(s) to tie the conquest of Jerusalem and Hebron to Judah (see 2 Sam 2:1–7; 5:6–9) because both cities are of extreme importance to the Davidic monarchy.[8] The statement "they put it to the sword and set the city on fire" does not imply that Judah maintained control over the city. It seems clear, both from David's need to conquer Jerusalem in 2 Sam 5:6–10 and from his subsequent occupation and expansion of it, that Judah's action in the Judges account might be better understood as a raid.

The continued recital of conquests now (1:11) includes a city whose name suggests that it is a seat of learning, "City of Scribes," an easy target for invading bands of warriors and one that may well promise rich loot.[9] The loss of knowledge associated with its destruction can be lamented,[10] but it falls naturally into the cycle of emergent civilization, maturing culture, and destructive waves of invaders that typified ancient Near Eastern history from its outset.

Distinct individuals in the Judges account begin with Caleb and his daughter Achsah (1:12–15). Achsah also appears in a similar story in Josh 15:13–19. In both she is offered as a prize to the hero who can capture the city of Debir (compare Saul's offer of a daughter in 1 Sam 17:25). When Othniel prevails, Achsah publicly confronts her father over the quality of the dowry he supplies her since it consists only of arid land in the Negeb. Leaving her new husband behind, she forces her father to ask her "What do you wish?" by returning to his encampment and dismounting from her donkey, an act suggesting that their business is not complete and requiring him to respond.[11] She then points out the poor nature of the land grant, describing herself as "Negeb land" (i.e, a woman without a suitable dowry), and asks for the Gulloth springs as well.[12] Her socially subversive action resists the social stereotype that daughters should simply accept what is given,[13] and her pointed speech,

8   Moshe Weinfeld, "Judges 1.1–2.5: The Conquest under the Leadership of the House of Judah." Page 392 in *Understanding Poets and Prophets*. Edited by A. Graeme Auld. JSOTSup 152. Sheffield, Eng.: Sheffield Academic Press, 1993.

9   Lillian R. Klein, "Achsah: What Price This Prize?" Page 20 in *Judges: A Feminist Companion to the Bible*, 2nd series. Edited by Athalya Brenner. Sheffield, Eng.: Sheffield Academic Press, 1999.

10 Danna N. Fewell, "Deconstructive Criticism: Achsah and the (E)rased City of Writing." Pages 131–32 in *Judges and Method: New Approaches in Biblical Studies*. Edited by Gale Yee. Minneapolis: Fortress Press, 1995.

11 Tammi J. Schneider, *Judges*. Berit Olam. Collegeville, Minn.: Liturgical Press, 2000: 14–15.

12 Tikva Frymer-Kensky, *In the Wake of the Goddesses: Women, Culture and the Biblical Transformation of Pagan Myth*. New York: Free Press, 1992: 131.

13 Lila Abu-Lughod, "The Romance of Resistance: Tracing Transformations of Power through Bedouin Women," *American Ethnologist* 17 (1990): 44–46.

which required her father to respond, shames him. This engenders a guilt reaction in Caleb that can be described as a "shame-anger sequence in which the anger is directed back at the self."[14] Subsequently, he provides an additional land grant as a way to relinquish his self-directed, angry emotions and restore his honor. Achsah thereby demonstrates the proper role of the wife, or even the betrothed woman, whose loyalties are immediately transferred to the household of their husband (compare Rebekah in Gen 24:52–59 and Michal in 1 Sam 19:12–17).

A CLOSER LOOK AT ANCIENT WARFARE

Warfare in the ancient Near East is commonly thought to be the clash of national armies whose masses of sword- and spear-carrying infantry are matched against each other and whose horse-drawn war chariots flit about the battlefield carrying messengers and harassing the flanks with arrows.[15] The use of locusts as a metaphor for the devastation caused by invading armies (Judg 6:5; 7:12; Jer 46:23; Joel 1:4) is quite apt given that these soldiers were not paid a salary and therefore engaged in looting to gain recompense for their service. This was such a common practice that the eighteenth-century BCE Mari texts from Mesopotamia chronicle how seriously the men and their commanders took the traditional distribution of the spoils of war.[16] Such a tradition makes it that much more unusual that the Israelites are commanded to engage in *ḥērem* at Jericho (Josh 6:17–19), because it meant that all the people and their property were to be "dedicated" as sacrifices to God and looting was absolutely forbidden.

There are some massive battles involving thousands of combatants in ancient Near Eastern history. For instance, the Battle of Kadesh between the Egyptians of Rameses II and the Hittite forces of Muwatallis ca. 1285 BCE involved four divisions of Egyptian troops plus mercenaries and 20,000 Hittites, and it covered a wide expanse along the Orontes River. Although the outcome of the battle was inconclusive, both sides claimed victory in

---

14 Thomas J. Scheff and Suzanne M. Retzinger, *Emotions and Violence: Shame and Rage in Destructive Conflicts.* Lexington, Mass.: D. C. Heath, 1991: 13.

15 See Yigael Yadin, *The Art of Warfare in Biblical Lands in the Light of Archaeological Discovery.* London: Weidenfeld and Nicolson, 1963, for a compendium of information on weapons, tactics, and battle strategies.

16 Jack M. Sasson, *The Military Establishment at Mari.* Rome: Pontifical Biblical Institute, 1969: 37.

their official accounts and touted their claims to control over the important city of Kadesh and the area of Syria and Canaan (see *COS* 2.2.5:32–40).

Realistically, however, many conflicts were more local and involved a few hundred men at most, and the area being claimed was generally only a small piece of territory with its towns and villages. The soldiers were not heavily armed, and many employed farm implements (Shamgar's oxgoad in Judg 3:31) or chance weapons (jawbone used by Samson in Judg 15:15). As farmers and herders, the Israelites would not have been trained warriors nor would they have had a need for mail coats, swords, or spears. This made them easy targets when better-equipped troops swept through their villages. Gideon's temerity when called to lead his people in battle (Judg 6:11–15) can easily be explained by this disparity in skills and military technology. It would have been very difficult to face "iron chariots" (Judg 1:19) with willowing forks, axes, and clubs.[17]

When battles occur in the Judges account, they are usually determined by a strategy of trickery. Ehud, for example, does not lead his Ephraimites into battle with the Moabites until he has murdered their king, Eglon (3:16–29).[18] Similarly, Gideon uses a night attack and the confusion caused by the crashing of pots, waving of torches, and blasting of trumpets to take advantage of an Ammonite encampment (7:16–22). Capitalizing on the topography and the elements of nature also helped the Israelites to overcome the greater numbers and weapons of their foes (see Deborah's and Barak's rout of Sisera's army on the slopes of Mt. Tabor during a rainstorm that swells the Wadi Kishon [5:19–21]).

Implicit in these conflicts is the involvement of Yahweh and the gods of Canaan. God is described as manipulating the forces of nature to provide the Israelites with a military victory in Josh 6:15–21 (Jericho) and 10:12–13 (Gibeon) and Judg 5:19–21 (Mt. Tabor), or as planting the seeds of fear in dreams in Judg 7:9–15. Citing God's command to go to war and then giving God credit for the victory is a common theme throughout the Bible, but it is also a part of the official annals of ancient Near Eastern kings, who see themselves and their people as servants of the gods.[19] The conflict is laid at

---

[17]   See James C. Moyer, "Weapons and Warfare in the Book of Judges." Pages 42–50 in *Discovering the Bible: Archaeologists Look at Scripture*. Edited by T. Dowley. Grand Rapids, Mich.: Eerdmans, 1986.

[18]   Susan Niditch, *War in the Hebrew Bible: A Study in the Ethics of Violence*. New York: Oxford University Press, 1993: 117–18.

[19]   Ibid., 125; Bustenay Oded, *War, Peace and Empire: Justifications for War in Assyrian Royal Inscriptions*. Wiesbaden, Ger.: Ludwig Reichert Verlag, 1992: 10.

the feet of a higher authority, and defeat can be blamed on a failure to obey strictly the commands or instructions of the deity.

(16) The descendants of Hobab the Kenite, Moses' father-in-law, went up with the people of Judah from the city of palms into the wilderness of Judah, which lies in the Negeb near Arad. Then they went and settled with the Amalekites. (17) Judah went with his brother Simeon, and they defeated the Canaanites who inhabited Zephath, and devoted it to destruction. So the city was called Hormah. (18) Judah took Gaza with its territory, and Ekron with its territory. (19) The Lord was with Judah, and he took possession of the hill country, but could not drive out the inhabitants of the plain, because they had chariots of iron. (20) Hebron was given to Caleb, as Moses had said; and he drove out from it the three sons of Anak. (21) But the Benjaminites did not drive out the Jebusites who lived in Jerusalem; so the Jebusites have lived in Jerusalem among the Benjaminites to this day. (22) The house of Joseph also went up against Bethel; and the Lord was with them. (23) The house of Joseph sent out spies to Bethel (the name of the city was formerly Luz). (24) When the spies saw a man coming out of the city, they said to him, "Show us the way into the city, and we will deal kindly with you." (25) So he showed them the way into the city; and they put the city to the sword, but they let the man and all his family go. (26) So the man went to the land of the Hittites and built a city, and named it Luz; that is its name to this day. (27) Manasseh did not drive out the inhabitants of Beth-shean and its villages, or Taanach and its villages, or the inhabitants of Dor and its villages, or the inhabitants of Ibleam and its villages, or the inhabitants of Megiddo and its villages; but the Canaanites continued to live in that land. (28) When Israel grew strong, they put the Canaanites to forced labor, but did not in fact drive them out. (29) And Ephraim did not drive out the Canaanites who lived in Gezer; but the Canaanites lived among them in Gezer. (30) Zebulun did not drive out the inhabitants of Kitron, or the inhabitants of Nahalol; but the Canaanites lived among them, and became subject to forced labor. (31) Asher did not drive out the inhabitants of Acco or the inhabitants of Sidon, or of Ahlab, or of Achzib, or of Helbah, or of Aphik, or of Rehob; (32) but the Asherites lived among the Canaanites, the inhabitants of the land; for they did not drive them out. (33) Naphtali did not drive out the inhabitants of Beth-shemesh, or the inhabitants of Beth-anath, but lived among the Canaanites, the inhabitants of the land; nevertheless the inhabitants of Beth-shemesh and of Beth-anath became subject to forced labor for them. (34) The Amorites pressed the Danites back into the hill country; they did not allow them to come down to the plain. (35) The Amorites continued

to live in Har-heres, in Aijalon, and in Shaalbim, but the hand of the house of Joseph rested heavily on them, and they became subject to forced labor. (36) The border of the Amorites ran from the ascent of Akrabbim, from Sela and upward.

*T*he recital of tribal activity resumes in this second segment of the first chapter with the story of the tribe of Judah's campaign. The "city of the palms" is a euphemism for Jericho (Deut 34:3), located at the north end of the Dead Sea in an oasis studded with palm trees and serving as an entry point into central Canaan (see Josh 2:1) and a trading center for the region. There is some confusion in the biblical sources between Kenites and Midianites. Moses' father-in-law in Exod 2:16–18 is named Reuel, but he is named Jethro in Exod 3:1, and in both cases these men are referred to as "the priest of Midian." In this passage in Judges and again in Judg 4:11, Hobab the Kenite is named as Moses' father-in-law but is not given a priestly title. Some explain this by identifying the Kenites as a subtribe or clan of the Midianite coalition.[20] Others see this as an attempt on the part of the Deuteronomistic Historian to deal with claims made by the Aaronide priesthood and the priestly writer, which transform the Midianites from an Israelite ally into a corrupting force that makes them, like the Amalekites, the archenemies of Israel (see Num 25:6–15; 31:1–12). By separating the Kenites from the Midianites and their somewhat suspect priestly function, the Deuteronomistic editor in Judges upholds the image of Moses as the ideal leader of the people and spokesperson for Yahweh.[21] What are demonstrated in the Judges passage, however, are the apparently fluctuating loyalties of the Kenites. Despite their early connection with the Israelites through Moses, they never formally affiliate with the Israelites. Instead they appear alongside traditional enemies (Amalekites – see Exod 17:8–16; Arameans – see Judg 4:11, 17) and thus could be considered political neutrals who deserved some consideration but were not treated as kin (1 Sam 15:6).

The one anomaly in this list of Judah's conquests is found in the simple statement that they could not defeat the people of the plains because they had "chariots of iron" (i.e., chariots with iron fittings or décor). These engines of war had not stopped the Israelites in Josh 11:1–9 in their war against

---

[20] William J. Dumbrell, "Midian – A Land or a League?" *VT* 25 (1975): 323–37.
[21] Baruch Halpern, "Kenites." Pages 17–22 in vol. 4 of *The Anchor Bible Dictionary*. Edited by David N. Freedman. New York: Doubleday, 1992.

the king of Hazor. However, that the chariots were burnt and the horses hamstrung is an indication that the Israelites had no intention of using them; rather, they only prevented their enemies from employing them in the future. In addition, the willingness of the editor to admit this failure in the complete conquest of the land stands as an element of historical reality amid what to this point has been a series of easy victories on the part of the Israelites. The iron chariots of Judg 1:19 reflect the physical reality of a higher material culture enjoyed by the Philistines (contrast the technology found in 1 Sam 13:19–22). Although iron technology was not generally introduced until the tenth century (the likely time when these narratives were edited), the reference here could be as much to political and economic organization as to a deciding factor in the success of the people of the plain to resist Israelite incursions.[22] As long as they continued to have this technological/cultural edge, the Philistines and their Canaanite allies would remain in control of the Shephelah and coastal plain and the Israelites would be relegated to the hill country.

The tribe of Judah is credited with capturing the city of Jerusalem in Judg 1:8, but Benjamin is faulted for the tribe's failure to expel the Jebusites from that city (compare Josh 15:63, where Judah is the one at fault). In this way the Judahite editors of this text allows the tribe of Judah to retain its long-standing authority as the masters of Jerusalem. In contrast the editors of the Joshua material wished to credit the success of the conquest to the Joseph tribes who later ruled the northern kingdom of Israel.[23]

The Joshua conquest account does not describe the capture of Bethel, although it is assigned to the Josephites in Josh 16:1, and Luz is mentioned as a point on the border of Benjaminite territory in Josh 18:13. Bethel appears most often as a geographical marker in relation to the city of Ai, another site that is captured through stealth (Josh 8:9, 12; 12:9). There are some similarities between this story in Judg 1:22–26 and the story of Rahab in Joshua 2:12–14, including the use of the phrase "deal kindly" (Hebrew: *ḥesed*), a covenant-related term.[24] In both cases residents of the targeted city are willing to aid the Israelites in exchange for the safety of their families. The origin story for a new city of Luz in the "land of the Hittites" resembles the founding of cities in the primordial history in Genesis (Enoch – 4:17; Nimrod's

---

22 Paula McNutt, *Reconstructing the Society of Ancient Israel*. Louisville, Ky.: Westminster/John Knox, 1999: 74–75.
23 M. Weinfeld, "Judges 1.1–2.5," in *Understanding Poets and Prophets* (1993): 392, 396.
24 Trent C. Butler, *Joshua*. Waco, Tex.: Word Books, 1983: 34.

cities – 10:10–12). Since Syria continued to be referred to as Hatti-land (i.e., the "land of the Hittites") in eighth-century Neo-Assyrian texts, it is likely that this is the area meant in this story.[25]

The final section of this chapter includes the list of cities in the Jezreel Valley and along the coastal plain left unconquered by the Israelite tribes. It stands in contrast to the statement of total victory found in Josh 12:7–24, but it seems to correspond to the political situation faced by Saul, whose territory lay south and east of these important Canaanite cities (1 Sam 31:10).[26] The difficulties faced by the Danites in dealing with their neighbors may stand as a premise for the story of their migration in Judg 18:1–2, 27–31. If the Danites could not coexist as the other tribes do with their Canaanite neighbors, and if no new territory could be allotted to them (Josh 19:40–48), then it could be said that they had no choice but to seek a territory for themselves. The idea of forcing the Canaanites to perform labor service is similar to the situation imposed on the Gibeonites in Josh 9:22–27, but in this case it probably refers to conditions during the period of the Israelite monarchy (see 1 Kgs 9:20–21). The road to power and economic prosperity in the ancient Near East was often paved with the labor of subject peoples. They had been either conquered, placed in vassalage, or intimidated into paying tribute from their crops and herds and into providing men to build roads and fortresses for their masters.[27]

The recurring phrase "the Canaanites [or Amorites] continued to live in..." is a subtle acknowledgement of Israel's failure to conquer the Promised Land and serves as a counterpoint to Joshua's exuberant accounts of total victory. The sober reality of Israel's inability to conquer and occupy territories beyond the central highlands explains much of the nation's subsequent history and fits the archaeological record. One can trace this theme in Judg 1 by noting the recurring Hebrew terms for these developments. Thus the subjugating tribe "did not drive out" ($y^e r\check{e}\check{s}$) the inhabitants (vv. 19, 21, 27, 29, 30, 31), and the Canaanites and Amorites "lived among" ($y^e \check{s}eb$) them (vv. 21, 29, 30, 32, 33). Such constant reiteration of a phrase serves

[25] Barnabas Lindars, *Judges 1–5*. Edinburgh: T & T Clark, 1995: 55.
[26] Eric H. Cline, *The Battles of Armageddon*. Ann Arbor: University of Michigan Press, 2000: 66–74.
[27] Daniel C. Snell, *Life in the Ancient Near East*. New Haven, Conn.: Yale University Press, 1997: 83. For mention of this practice in the villages associated with the ancient seaport of Ugarit, see John Gray, *I & II Kings*. Philadelphia: Westminster Press, 1970: 134. Gray (pp. 155–56) draws a distinction between Solomon's practice of forced labor (1 Kings 5:13) for non-Israelite "serfs" and Israelites, who were occasionally recruited for the corvée and the military but were not subject to permanent serfdom.

both as a mnemonic and as a didactic element reinforcing the conclusion of the Deuteronomistic Historian that the failures of the settlement period contributed to the eventual failures of the monarchy.

CHAPTER 2

(1) Now the angel of the Lord went up from Gilgal to Bochim, and said, "I brought you up from Egypt, and brought you into the land that I had promised to your ancestors. I said, 'I will never break my covenant with you. (2) For your part, do not make a covenant with the inhabitants of this land; tear down their altars.' But you have not obeyed my command. See what you have done! (3) So now I say, I will not drive them out before you; but they shall become adversaries to you, and their gods shall be a snare to you." (4) When the angel of the Lord spoke these words to all the Israelites, the people lifted up their voices and wept. (5) So they named that place Bochim, and there they sacrificed to the Lord. (6) When Joshua dismissed the people, the Israelites all went to their own inheritances to take possession of the land. (7) The people worshiped the Lord all the days of Joshua, and all the days of the elders who outlived Joshua, who had seen all the great work that the Lord had done for Israel. (8) Joshua son of Nun, the servant of the Lord, died at the age of one hundred ten years. (9) So they buried him within the bounds of the hill country in Timnath-heres, in the hill country of Ephraim, north of Mount Gaash. (10) Moreover, that whole generation was gathered to their ancestors, and another generation grew up after them, who did not know the Lord or the work that he had done for Israel. (11) Then the Israelites did what was evil in the sight of the Lord and worshiped the Baals; (12) and they abandoned the Lord, the God of their ancestors, who had brought them out of the land of Egypt; they followed other gods, from among the gods of the peoples who were all around them, and bowed down to them; and they provoked the Lord to anger. (13) They abandoned the Lord, and worshiped Baal and the Astartes. (14) So the anger of the Lord was kindled against Israel, and he gave them over to plunderers who plundered them, and he sold them into the power of their enemies all around, so that they could no longer withstand their enemies. (15) Whenever they marched out, the hand of the Lord was against them to bring misfortune, as the Lord had warned them and sworn to them; and they were in great distress. (16) Then the Lord raised up judges, who delivered them out of the power of those who plundered them. (17) Yet they did not listen even to their judges; for they lusted after other

gods and bowed down to them. They soon turned aside from the way in which their ancestors had walked, who had obeyed the commandments of the Lord; they did not follow their example. (18) Whenever the Lord raised up judges for them, the Lord was with the judge, and he delivered them from the hand of their enemies all the days of the judge; for the Lord would be moved to pity by their groaning because of those who persecuted and oppressed them. (19) But whenever the judge died, they would relapse and behave worse than their ancestors, following other gods, worshiping them and bowing down to them. They would not drop any of their practices or their stubborn ways. (20) So the anger of the Lord was kindled against Israel; and he said, "Because this people has transgressed my covenant that I commanded their ancestors, and have not obeyed my voice, (21) I will no longer drive out before them any of the nations that Joshua left when he died." (22) In order to test Israel, whether or not they would take care to walk in the way of the Lord as their ancestors did, (23) the Lord had left those nations, not driving them out at once, and had not handed them over to Joshua.

JUDGES CYCLE EXPLAINED

Comment or commentary on the obligations of the covenant with Yahweh often includes the statement "I brought you up from Egypt" (see Exod 16:32; 19:4; 20:2; 29:46; Lev 25:38; Num 15:41). It serves both as a reminder of the saving act of God in delivering the Israelites from bondage and as a reinforcement of legal pronouncements or the sentencing of the people to judgment for their failure to obey God's command. This section is an appropriate follow-up to the list of cities and peoples that the Israelites had failed to drive out and now functions as the preface for the cycle of stories that appear in chapters 3–16. The divine warrior, so prominent in the Joshua conquest account (Josh 6:16; 10:12–13; 11:6), now deserts them and allows the Israelites to be defeated and subjected to the temptations of economic and cultural syncretism. The justice of this condemnation is acknowledged by the Israelites in their weeping and expiatory sacrifice and is certified by naming the place where this happens for their sorrow. Similar etiological stories explaining the origin of place names can be found in Gen 16:13–14; 21:31; 50:11 and Judg 15:19.

A short aside is inserted in the text at vv. 6–10 for what appears to be at first glance an editorial gloss. This segment harkens back to an epitaph for Joshua and his faithful generation found in Josh 24:29–31. By comparing the settings of both appearances, however, it becomes clear that this is an example of irony employed by the editor of the Judges text. At the end of the book of Joshua, the Israelite leader calls the people together at Shechem, performs a covenant renewal ceremony, and dismisses them to their allotted inheritances. His death and burial are then recounted, and there is a note describing the burial of Joseph's bones near Shechem (Josh 24:32), thereby giving the Joseph tribes pride of place as the last groups mentioned in a glorious conquest and settlement of the promised land. The purpose of the Judges passage, with its verbatim reiteration of Josh 24:29–31, is to reinforce the judgment placed on the people in vv. 1–5. That the Joseph tribes are the last mentioned in the recitation of Israelite failures (Judg 2:35) reverses the acclaim they had achieved in Joshua and serves as a political polemic favoring the house of David and the kingdom of Judah.[28] The text then draws a distinct line in v. 10 between those who had witnessed the divine warrior in action and those who fell into error in the generation after the settlement of the land.[29] The readers are thus prepared for the beginning of a spiraling decay in Israelite obedience and fortunes throughout the remainder of the Book of Judges.

Having made this point, the editor then lays out quite systematically the cycle of disobedience, oppression, and divine pity that will serve as the literary framework and theodicy for the stories of the judges. According to this formula God, expressing compassion for his repentant people, raises a judge, who, with the assistance of the divine warrior, removes the oppression. However, the judge's influence quickly wanes after his/her death, which results in more idolatry and disobedience to divine command. This cycle, which has similarities to the raising up of prophets in later Israelite history (Jer 1:14–19; Ezek 2:3–3:11), will serve as the basic structure for the stories of the judges. A careful contrast is made here between the God who had delivered them from Egypt and the false gods of the Canaanites to whom the people had turned. One could ask why they made this unwise choice. Following are two interrelated ways of speaking to this issue:

■ From a literary standpoint, the Judges cycle is an editorial projection imposed on the stories of the judges. It reflects the Deuteronomistic view of history and provides a basis for later claims that the people have always been "stubborn" (Deut 9:6; 31:27), "stiff-necked" (Exod 33:5), and disobedient. The later difficulties faced by the nation during the monarchy

---

28 T. J. Schneider, *Judges* (2000): 29; M. A. Sweeney, "Davidic Polemic," *VT* 47 (1997): 526.
29 L. R. Klein, *The Triumph of Irony in the Book of Judges*. JSOTSup 68. Sheffield, Eng.: Almond Press, 1989: 32, emphasizes the weight placed on the distinction between the generation that "knows" and "saw" Yahweh's deed and those who do "not know" and therefore have fallen away into idolatry.

period (as the political superpowers in Egypt and Mesopotamia jockeyed for control of Syria-Palestine) were a direct result of the failure of the Israelites to obey the covenant. This theodicy placed the blame squarely on the people for the oppression they experienced. The Judges cycle thus demonstrates that God is willing to intervene and save the people from their oppressors, but there is a danger that they will quickly forget the source of their aid and fall back into the pattern of behavior that had caused God to punish them in the first place.

■ The Israelites during the settlement and much of the monarchy period were little different culturally from their Canaanite neighbors. They were polytheistic and served many gods, collectively referred to in the biblical text as the Baals and the Astartes (or Asherah). Since their lives and fortunes depended upon the fertility of their crops, herds, and families, they divided their devotions by making sacrifices on their local high places and by engaging in rituals designed to gain them the favor of these gods and thereby obtain bountiful harvests, healthy children, and success in battle. If they had sworn allegiance at some point to Yahweh (see Exod 24:3–8), many of them would have felt it unwise to put all of their trust into a single deity. If Yahweh were to fail, to whom would they then turn for help? The writers of the Judges cycle are thus playing off of a cultural reality. To draw the people away from polytheism and the borrowing of Canaanite rituals, they point out that the original covenant agreement with Yahweh is binding and that failure to uphold its stipulations, as would be the case with any other treaty, would lead to definite consequences due not to God but to the disobedient people.[30] In the monarchic period this struggle to demonstrate "who really is God" plays out in the prophet Elijah's contest on Mt. Carmel with the 450 prophets of Baal and the 400 prophets of Asherah (1 Kings 18:19–40). This also will be the theme of the later prophets, who like Isaiah can speak of enemy nations like Assyria as "the rod of my [God's] anger" (Isa 10:5) and thereby demonstrate Yahweh's supremacy over other gods and nations.

The Israelites were in a treaty or covenant relationship with Yahweh. This placed obligations on both parties and also stipulated specific penalties for

---

[30] The vassal treaties of Esarhaddon (680–669 BCE) contain a list of gods, who serve as witnesses and co-signers of treaties between the Assyrian monarch and lesser states, and several explicit clauses listing the obligations of the vassals, followed by curses on all violators (*ANET*, 534–41).

failure to abide by the terms of the treaty. It can therefore be concluded that when the phrase "the anger of the Lord" occurs in the text (v. 20) it functions as a theological explanation for God's justified response based on the Israelites' violation of the covenant. Additional examples of this response can be found in the following:

Exod 4:14   Moses incurs God's anger because he failed to circumcise his son.

Deut 6:14–15   The people are warned that idolatry will incur God's wrath.

Deut 29:19–28   Failure to obey the covenant leads to a destroyed land.

Although this final section of chapter 2 (vv. 20–23) is an abbreviated summary of 2:11–19, it may actually be an independent source, which is not as elaborate and does not create a literary cycle, to encompass the stories of the judges. This simpler form probably reflects an older tradition while still providing a theodicy explaining why these nations coexist with the Israelites in Canaan. The theological explanation thus allows for a physical reality and makes use of it for God's purposes.

Finally, the idea in v. 22 of God "testing" the people's obedience is quite common.[31] For instance, the provision of manna in the wilderness becomes a test to see if the people will obey the instructions on its gathering and thereby preserve the Sabbath rest (Exod 16:4; compare Deut 8:11–16). In Jer 6:27–30, the Babylonian threat is referred to as a means of testing a "stubbornly rebellious" people, and a similar allusion to testing the people is found in the apocalyptic vision of Zech 13:9, where the prophet refers to the refining of precious metals and the separation of impurities.

CHAPTER 3

(1) Now these are the nations that the Lord left to test all those in Israel who had no experience of any war in Canaan (2) (it was only that successive generations of Israelites might know war, to teach those who had no experience

---

[31] The testing of Abraham in the *Aqedah* (Gen 22) differs in the sense that it deals with a single individual rather than the "people" as a whole. There is also the matter of a precedent being set that allows for the substitution of animal sacrifice for human sacrifice.

of it before): (3) the five lords of the Philistines, and all the Canaanites, and the Sidonians, and the Hivites who lived on Mount Lebanon, from Mount Baalhermon as far as Lebohamath. (4) <mark>They were for the testing of Israel,</mark> to know whether Israel would obey the commandments of the Lord, which he commanded their ancestors by Moses. (5) So the Israelites lived among the Canaanites, the Hittites, the Amorites, the Perizzites, the Hivites, and the Jebusites; (6) and they took their daughters as wives for themselves, and their own daughters they gave to their sons; <mark>and they worshiped their gods.</mark>

*A*s a preface to the stories of the judges, a list of enemy peoples is included to serve as a reference or "program" of villains. This list is an abbreviated form of the genealogy of Canaan found in Gen 10:15–18. It is augmented by the inclusion of the five Philistine city-states that established themselves after 1150 BCE along the southern coastal plain, extended east into the Shephelah and north along the Mediterranean coast as far as Tell Qasile (in what is now a northern suburb of Tel Aviv) and east through the Jezreel Valley to Beth-shean. The reference to the Sidonians may reflect both the Sea People's successor kingdoms (mentioned in the eleventh-century Egyptian "Tale of Wenamon" [*COS* 1.41: 89–93]) as well as the Phoenicians who came to dominate the Lebanon coast and commercial shipping in the Mediterranean.

<mark>The connection drawn between intermarriage, cultural assimilation, and idolatry is also made in the ancestral stories</mark> (see Gen 26:34–35) but is most prominent in the story of Solomon's apostasy (1 Kings 11), the story of Jezebel's control over Ahab (1 Kings 17), and the very aggressive anti-intermarriage campaigns of Ezra and Nehemiah in the postexilic period (Ezra 9–10:19; Neh 13:23–27). While this sets the stage for the corruption of the Israelites during the settlement period (see the parental disapproval of Samson's Philistine wife in Judg 14:1–3), it is quite likely that the editor has added greater emphasis on it here to draw comparisons with similar practices during the monarchy period. Its importance during the postexilic period, as could be said of the settlement period, is based on <mark>the need to establish and maintain cultural identity in the face of other cultures that dominate them culturally and politically.</mark>[32] *still true today.*

---

[32] Victor H. Matthews, "The Social Context of Law in the Second Temple Period," *BTB* 28 (1998): 10–11; David L. Smith-Christopher, "The Mixed Marriage Crisis in Ezra 9–10 and Nehemiah 13: A Study of the Sociology of the Post-Exilic Judean Community." Pages 245–50 in *Second Temple Studies*, 2. Edited by Tamara C. Eshkenazi and Kent Richards. Atlanta: Scholars Press, 1994.

BRIDGING THE HORIZONS

Having come to the end of this first major literary unit in the book of Judges, it is helpful to consider some possible ways in which this material can be used for personal reflection, teaching, and preaching. I would suggest the following issues or topics for discussion:

(1) Everyone is left without clear leadership at times. Just as the Israelites felt lost after the death of Joshua, so too do we when a national leader dies or is assassinated or even when a manager leaves for a new job and there is uncertainty for the near future. One way of coping with this situation is to recognize the source of true power. Just as the Israelites turned to God to ask "who should go up first" (1:1) as they prepared to take the Promised Land, we should prayerfully consider our options and seek council before taking actions that may have long-term, undesirable consequences.

(2) If everyone shared the same beliefs and everyone was committed to obey God's commands, there would be little temptation to violate that trust. However, there would also be no measure of comparison and no real sense of struggle. When God resolved not to drive out the inhabitants of Canaan, leaving them in place as adversaries and their gods as snares for the Israelites, it made the task of obedience more of a challenge (2:3). It thus became the Israelites' choice to remain faithful to the covenant and to resist the slide into syncretism and idolatry.

(3) God's decision to "raise up" judges (2:16–19) to deliver the Israelites when they cried out for help demonstrates the commitment of Yahweh to the covenant, even in the face of repeated disobedience on the part of the people. The cycle of violation, oppression, repentance, deliverance, and a return to violation is not just a literary device imposed on the stories to hold them together. It meshes with the familiar struggle of most believers to maintain a consistent faith. In this way the Judges cycle is a form of wisdom literature, playing on the universalism of human frailty and the constancy of divine promise. *yes. makes sense.*

SUCCESSION OF JUDGES TALES BEGINS

A CLOSER LOOK AT THE "JUDGE" IN JUDGES

The most fundamental characteristic of the judge/deliverer figures in the book of Judges is that each is "raised" to the position of *šôpēṭ* by God. Without that measure of authority embodied in several cases with a physical infusion of the "spirit of God," they would be nothing but warlords like Gideon's son Abimelech. Despite being given a title of judge or administrator (see the more normal usage in 1 Sam 7:15 and 2 Sam 15:4),[33] most of the judges in the Book of Judges are not portrayed as legal officials. Only Deborah actively functions in this role, hearing the cases of the Israelites as she sat under the palm tree at Ramah (4:5). In general their role is that of military chief, leading the tribes in battle and delivering them from their oppressors. Othniel, Ehud, Gideon, and Jephthah fit this description. Because these individuals are invested with God's spirit, there is little discussion in the stories of any special qualifications they may have had. Only Jephthah has previous military experience as an exiled bandit chief (11:1–4). In this way it is made clearer that the true savior or deliverer of the people is Yahweh and that the judges are simply instruments of divine power.[34]

Furthermore, there is no attempt by the judges to become kings or civil administrators, even when urged to do so (see Judg 8:22–23), to unify the nation under their rule.[35] In no case can they obtain a pledge from all the tribes to act, and in some cases (5:12–18; 12:1–6) their authority is challenged by tribes other than their own. As a result it is best to describe them as individual heroes, who appear in times of crisis, perform a specific task with the aid of God, and then after a period of time disappear from the scene, leaving no legacy or heir and opening the door for a new crisis to spring up.

Curiously, on only one occasion is a judge (Gideon) called on to uphold the covenant and restore proper worship (6:28–35). While Samson's pulling down the temple of Dagon might be compared with Gideon's demolishing the altar of Baal in his village, Gideon is instructed by God to rebuild the altar and make a sacrifice, while Samson's destructive act is his own idea and the sacrifice is his own life and that of his Philistine victims (16:28–30). The lack of religious activities may be a reflection of the editor's desire to demonstrate how out of compliance the Israelites are in this period. This accentuates the Deuteronomistic theme that Israel cannot ignore its obligations to God and must be in compliance with the covenant or face the consequences.

[33] Temba L. J. Mafico, "Judge, Judging." Pages 1104–6 of vol. 3 in *The Anchor Bible Dictionary*. Edited by David N. Freedman. New York: Doubleday, 1992, provides a summary of the use of *šôpēt* in the Hebrew Bible as well as in Akkadian texts from Mari (using *'apitum*).

[34] John McKenzie, *The World of the Judges*. Englewood Cliffs, N.J.: Prentice-Hall, 1966: 16–17.

[35] J. Alberto Soggin, *Judges: A Commentary*. OTL. Philadelphia: Westminster, 1981 (2nd ed., 1987): 3.

OTHNIEL

(7) The Israelites did what was evil in the sight of the Lord, forgetting the Lord their God, and worshiping the Baals and the Asherahs. (8) Therefore the anger of the Lord was kindled against Israel, and he sold them into the hands of King Cushan-rishathaim eight years. (9) But when the Israelites cried out to the Lord, the Lord raised up a deliverer for the Israelites, who delivered them, Othniel son of Kenaz, Caleb's younger brother. (10) The spirit of the Lord came upon him and he judged Israel; he went out to war, and the Lord gave King Cushan-rishathaim of Aram into his hand; and his hand prevailed over Cushan-rishathaim. (11) So the land had rest forty years. Then Othniel son of Kenaz died.

*H*aving outlined the pattern that will characterize the appearance of the judges and demonstrate the glorification of Yahweh's power, the narrative now provides its first example, using Othniel, known as a hero related to the tribe of Judah in Josh 15:17. In this way the sequence of judges begins with an almost stereotypical character. Othniel, in fact, is the only judge who has a completely sterling character. He is chosen for his job and with the aid of the divine warrior quickly completes it and returns the land to its "rest" until he passes from the scene. Such a successful beginning, however, simply provides the start of a long slide into ineffective leadership – from a perfect role model (Othniel) to a self-centered, self-indulgent judge (Samson).

The threat to the Israelites in this instance comes from a king with a Hurrian name, Cushan-rishathaim of Aram (v. 10). This suggests that among the peoples who had settled in Canaan during the period after the Sea People's disruption of the old political order were remnants of that former Mitanni Empire (located in eastern Syria and the Habur triangle of the upper Euphrates region). The ease with which Othniel brushes him aside with God's help is typical of this abbreviated account.

Clearly, there is a formulaic character to this initial short story,[36] using set phrases and themes that will appear in subsequent examples in Judges:

1. They forgot their God and worshiped the Baals and Asherahs.
2. The anger of the Lord was kindled against Israel _____ (fill in the enemy's name).

---

[36] Yairah Amit, *The Book of Judges: The Art of Editing*. Leiden, Neth.: Brill, 1999: 161–63; Marc Z. Brettler, *The Book of Judges*. London and New York: Routledge, 2002: 26–27.

3. The Lord raised up a deliverer for the Israelites _____ (fill in the judge's name).
4. The spirit of the Lord came upon him . . . and he went out to war.
5. The land had rest for _____ years and _____ (fill in the numbers) died.

Perhaps the most important aspect of this formula is the reference to the "spirit of the Lord" (*rûᵃḥ Yahweh*) that "came upon" Othniel (see similar usage in 11:29 for Jephthah). This infusion of divine power is also found in instances of prophetic speech (Balaam in Num 24:2; Ezekiel in Ezek 11:5) or frenzy (Saul's messengers in 1 Sam 11:20 and Saul in v. 23), and as a sign of divine favor (David in 1 Sam 16:13).[37] Thus the selection of the judge is tied to a divine act, thereby adding authority to the judge's subsequent actions as the mobilizer of tribal forces to conduct a war of liberation in the name of Yahweh.[38] Variations on this theme and phrasing appear in the Gideon narrative (6:34) and the cycle of stories about Samson (14:6, 19; 15:14), and these will be discussed in more detail. It also should be noted that only Othniel benefits without qualification from receiving a measure of God's spirit. While the other judges are able to perform remarkable military and personal feats, their accomplishments seem to lead them into excess and error that will cloud their careers or lead to their demise.[39]

A CLOSER LOOK AT THE "SPIRIT OF GOD" IN JUDGES

The "spirit of God" commonly appears in the Old Testament at those points when Yahweh steps in and affects the history/destiny of the Israelites. Thus the spirit impels the judges to deeds that might have otherwise been beyond them and that serve to deliver their people from oppression. Slightly later in time, Saul is also infused with God's spirit and is able to deliver the besieged city of Jabesh-gilead (1 Sam 11:6, 13). In each of these cases, however, the presence of the spirit is a transitory feature of the story. It is only when the monarchy is established and the kings become permanent leaders that the spirit reposed in the person of the monarch (1 Sam 16:13). As a result there

---

[37] G. F. Moore, *A Critical and Exegetical Commentary on Judges*. ICC. New York: Charles Scribner's, 1895 [1923]: 87–88, provides a fuller listing of the instances in which the spirit of the Lord empowers or takes possession of a human to initiate military action, prophetic speech, or artistic endeavor (see Exod 31:3; 36:1; 2 Sam 23:2).

[38] Barry G. Webb, *The Book of Judges: An Integrated Reading*. Sheffield, Eng.: JSOT Press, 1987: 227, n. 47.

[39] T. J. Schneider, *Judges* (2000): 41.

is less frequent mention of individual acts based on the injection of God's spirit into that person.[40]

There are a number of different ways in which spirit ($rû^a ḥ$) is used in the historiographic writings of the biblical text,[41] including metaphorical usage for "wind" (2 Sam 22:11; 1 Kings 17:45) and anthropological usage for "breath" (1 Kings 10:5; 2 Chron 9:4). There is also theological usage indicating the agency or agent of Yahweh instructing (Deut 34:9), transporting (1 Kings 18:12), conscripting (Judg 3:10), or inspiring ecstatic prophecy (1 Sam 10:6).

In the Book of Judges, God's spirit or agency is used to signal the raising of a judge and the empowerment of that person to lead or engage in remarkable acts. The Hebrew phrases used include

(1) "the $rû^a ḥ$ $yhwh$ came upon _____" (Othniel – 3:10; Jephthah – 11:29).

(2) $rû^a ḥ$ $yhwh$ $lābĕšâ$ 'et _____: "the spirit of Yahweh clothed _____" (Gideon – 6:34)

(3) $wattislah$ 'al _____ $rû^a ḥ$ $yhwh$: "and the spirit of Yahweh rushed upon _____" (Samson – 14:6, 19; 15:14)

These varied phrases may simply serve to illustrate the artistry of the story-teller, but a closer look at the episodes demonstrates a clear intent for each one. There is also a downward progression in the sequential occurrences that parallels or shadows that same cyclic dive toward societal corruption and disobedience found in the Judges narratives.[42] The simplest example in 3:10 marks Othniel as divinely chosen for his task. The story in Judg 1:12–13 provides authentication of his abilities as a military leader, just as Judg 11:3 contains a mention of Jephthah's previous experience as a warlord. Thus the infusion of God's spirit does not require elaboration for these individuals. Its presence is a signal that the conscript is prepared for the task of mobilizing the people to war against the enemy nations.[43] In Gideon's case, however, an investiture ceremony (see the comment later on 6:34) "clothes" the reluctant and self-effacing conscript and empowers him to take on the mantle of leadership (compare Luke 24:49 and Jesus' admonition to disciples to wait until they are "clothed with power from on high").

---

[40] John McKenzie, "Aspects of Old Testament Thought." Page 1290.77:35 in *The New Jerome Biblical Commentary*. Edited by Raymond E. Brown et al. Englewood Cliffs, N.J.: Prentice-Hall, 1990.

[41] See Table 1 in Daniel I. Block, "Empowered by the Spirit of God: The Holy Spirit in the Historiographic Writings of the Old Testament," *SBJT* 1 (1997b): 60.

[42] J. Clinton McCann, *Judges*. Louisville, Ky.: Westminster/John Knox, 2002: 43.

[43] B. G. Webb, *Book of Judges* (1987): 61–62.

The most pronounced variation takes place in the Samson narrative. Like Gideon, the self-indulgent Samson did not see himself as a leader of his people, and like Jephthah, he is an unlikely choice to serve God's purposes. Thus, as Block suggests,[44] he is thrust into action by the inrushing of God's spirit. However, it is not to be construed that Samson is without volition of his own.[45] He accomplishes great feats of strength, which the editor acknowledges are designed to give him the opportunity to act against the Philistines (14:4). While Samson may have enjoyed the "rush" and expected it to come to his assistance whenever he was in danger, his failure to keep his Nazirite vow led to his capture and the loss of God's spirit within him (16:20).

One other cautionary note concerns the use of the term *šôpēt* (judge). As it appears in these stories, the title of judge seldom refers to legal activity or to the settling of disputes (with the exception of Deborah in Judg 4:4–5). Instead most of these figures' energies are given to military endeavors. Their activities are also confined to local rather than national crises, and in no case are they able to transfer their authority to their sons or daughters.

EHUD

(12) The Israelites again did what was evil in the sight of the Lord; and the Lord strengthened King Eglon of Moab against Israel, because they had done what was evil in the sight of the Lord. (13) In alliance with the Ammonites and the Amalekites, he went and defeated Israel; and they took possession of the city of palms. (14) So the Israelites served King Eglon of Moab eighteen years. (15) But when the Israelites cried out to the Lord, the Lord raised up for them a deliverer, Ehud son of Gera, the Benjaminite, a left-handed man. The Israelites sent tribute by him to King Eglon of Moab. (16) Ehud made for himself a sword with two edges, a cubit in length; and he fastened it on his right thigh under his clothes. (17) Then he presented the tribute to King Eglon of Moab. Now Eglon was a very fat man. (18) When Ehud had finished presenting the tribute, he sent the people who carried the tribute on their way. (19) But he himself turned back at the sculptured stones near Gilgal, and said, "I have a secret message for you, O King." So the king said, "Silence!" and all his attendants went out from his presence. (20) Ehud came to him, while he was sitting alone in his cool roof chamber, and said, "I have a message from God for you." So he rose from his

44 D. I. Block, "Empowered by the Spirit of God," *SBJT* 1 (1997b): 45.
45 Robert G. Boling, *Judges: Introduction, Translation and Commentary*. AB 6A. Garden City, N.Y.: Doubleday, 1975: 25–26.

seat. (21) Then Ehud reached with his left hand, took the sword from his right thigh, and thrust it into Eglon's belly; (22) the hilt also went in after the blade, for he did not draw the sword out of his belly; and the dirt came out. (23) Then Ehud went out into the vestibule, and closed the doors of the roof chamber on him, and locked them. (24) After he had gone, the servants came. When they saw that the doors of the roof chamber were locked, they thought, "He must be relieving himself in the cool chamber." (25) So they waited until they were embarrassed. When he still did not open the doors of the roof chamber, they took the key and opened them. There was their lord lying dead on the floor. (26) Ehud escaped while they delayed, and passed beyond the sculptured stones, and escaped to Seirah. (27) When he arrived, he sounded the trumpet, in the hill country of Ephraim; and the Israelites went down with him from the hill country, having him at their head. (28) He said to them, "Follow after me; for the Lord has given your enemies the Moabites into your hand." So they went down after him, and seized the fords of the Jordan against the Moabites, and allowed no one to cross over. (29) At that time they killed about ten thousand of the Moabites, all strong, able-bodied men; no one escaped. (30) So Moab was subdued that day under the hand of Israel. And the land had rest eighty years.

*H*aving established a literary framework for describing the deeds of the judges, the writer now provides a more detailed literary creation that presents a hero who is less idealized than Othniel and who fits the role of underdog that will be a part of Israel's folklore throughout much of its history.[46]

There are a number of comic elements employed in this finely crafted story that may be best described as an example of "ethnic humor."[47] To begin with, the reader is informed that Eglon, a powerful king who has expanded his domain to include Jericho and other Israelite territory in the area assigned to Ephraim, is a very fat man. Immediately, his power is diminished as the reader conjures up an image of a gross figure, more a caricature than a real person.[48] His adversary in this story, Ehud, also has a distinct physical

---

[46]   Susan Niditch, *Underdogs and Tricksters. A Prelude to Biblical Folklore.* San Francisco: Harper & Row, 1987.

[47]   Lowell Handy, "Uneasy Laughter: Ehud and Eglon as Ethnic Humor," *SJOT* 6 (1992): 233–46, comments on the literary and the ethnic character of this story while concluding that it probably is not representative of actual historical events.

[48]   Robert Alter, *The Art of Biblical Narrative.* New York: Basic Books, 1981: 38–41, emphasizes the use of punning and the dual meanings attached to personal names. Thus the fat Eglon, whose name is a word play on *'égel* (calf) becomes the "fatted calf" fit for slaughter.

characteristic – he is left-handed or, more likely, ambidextrous.[49] Thus two physical anomalies come into play: one to make the enemy vulnerable and the other to provide the hero of the tale with a means of tricking his opponent. This trickster component is a common feature in the Book of Judges, especially in the stories of Gideon and Samson.[50] It allows characters to behave in what might otherwise be considered antisocial or criminal behavior and still be viewed as heroes. In this case Ehud engages in political assassination to demoralize his enemies and to gain the freedom of his people. As a result the Israelites, for whom this story is written, must have viewed his actions as both necessary and courageous.

Two other unusual elements in the story now draw us toward its conclusion. Ehud fashions a double-edged dagger (one cubit = eighteen inches) that he straps beneath his robes on his right thigh. Such a slim weapon (placed awkwardly for anyone who is right-handed since it must be drawn across the body to be *en garde*) would be more likely to pass the inspection of the guards to Eglon's palace. Once Ehud has paid his tribute, he then goes back (presumably the guards grew used to seeing him) and, on the pretext that he has a message for the king from God, is cloistered with the ruler in his cool roof chamber. The Hebrew word for upper chamber (*'aliyyâ*) refers to a structure placed on beams, and its companion term for the area under the beams of the chamber (*misdārôn*) appears only in this passage. The general consensus is that it is a private toilet, set in a room above an accessible latrine that could be periodically cleaned by servants.[51] Given the hot climate of Jericho ("city of palms"), an oasis at the northern tip of the Dead Sea whose temperatures often reach above 110°F, an elevated room is less likely to have been cooler. It is more likely that the toilet was simply a small, enclosed area in one corner of the throne room.[52] Although it provided the two men with privacy, it also gave Ehud an escape route down through the toilet and out

---

49 The same quality is assigned to all of the members of the tribe of Benjamin in Judg 20:16, suggesting that it is a training strategy for their young men to give them an edge in battle against those who are strictly right-handed. Naturally, if Ehud is left-handed, then he will have the opportunity to conceal his weapon and make an unexpected move to strike down Eglon.

50 Victor H. Matthews, "Freedom and Entrapment in the Samson Narrative: A Literary Analysis," *PRSt* 16 (1989): 245–57; Susan Niditch, "Samson as Culture Hero, Trickster, and Bandit: The Empowerment of the Weak," *CBQ* 52 (1990): 608–24.

51 Baruch Halpern, "The Assassination of Eglon: The First Locked-Room Murder Mystery," *BRev* 4 (6, 1988a): 33–41, 44; T. J. Schneider, *Judges* (2000): 50.

52 Tom A. Jull, "*Mqrh* in Judges 3: A Scatological Reading," *JSOT* 81 (1998): 64–66, 69, argues for a euphemistic meaning for the name of the king's privy tied to other usage of *qrh* in the impurity law of Deut 23:10–15.

the service entrance. Once in this small room, it was a simple matter to kill Eglon, thrusting his knife upward into the king's belly where it may have struck his heart. The trauma associated with the wound would have caused his anal sphincter to explode (i.e., "and the dirt came out").[53] The blade is enveloped by the overhanging flesh, capping the wound so that there was little or no blood to seep under the door of the chamber. The very private nature of the king's privy compounded by the pungent smell created by the evacuation of Eglon's bowels would have kept the guards at bay.[54] This, in turn, gives Ehud time to escape and rally his Ephraimite troops, to secure control of the fords across the Jordan River (compare Judg 12:1–6), and thus to defeat the "able-bodied"[55] and leaderless Moabites.

This is the first example of three in which the Ephraimites are described as contributing to a military campaign by controlling the fords of the Jordan River (see Judg 7:24–8:3; 12:1–6). As is the case in so many other recurring events/themes in the Book of Judges, the perception of the Ephraimites progresses from positive action (in the Ehud narrative), to tardy support (Gideon account), and finally to divisive and antagonistic behavior (Jephthah episode). The conflict between the Ephraimites and the judge in the latter two passages may serve as a literary indicator of the internal struggles during the settlement period or the conflict between tribal groups "inside" Canaan and those in Transjordan.[56]

Finally, the question could be raised why the king of Moab would believe that Ehud had a "secret message" for him from God. This may be connected to the mention of the "sculptured stones" at Gilgal (compare the idols in Judg 17:3–4), which probably sat at a cultic site as well as on the border between Moab and Benjaminite territory.[57] This reference could therefore serve as both a geographic marker as well as a revelatory basis for Ehud's claim of having received a divine message. Notably, he makes two statements to

---

[53] M. Z. Brettler, *Book of Judges* (2002): 30–32, ties the symbolism of Eglon as a "sacrificial calf" to the use of Ehud's dagger as a "sacrificial knife" and also notes a theme of sexual domination of the Moabites in a euphemistic "penetration" of the king by Ehud.

[54] Note the euphemism in v. 24 is better translated "covering his feet" and can be compared to other instances in which the character may be assumed to be emptying his bowels (1 Sam 24:3).

[55] This term completes the pun on Eglon's name since both refer to fatted calves. Thus the Moabite soldiers, like their king, are "fat" and easily defeated in their panic.

[56] David Jobling, "Structuralist Criticism: The Text's World of Meaning." Pages 110–14 in *Judges and Method: New Approaches in Biblical Studies*. Edited by Gale A. Yee. Minneapolis: Fortress Press, 1995.

[57] J. A. Soggin, *Judges* (1987): 51. The combination of a border and a cultic site can also be found in Gen 31:43–54.

Eglon. The first could be interpreted as a reference to a military or state secret, and thus the king clears his audience chamber as he might for the report of a spy. Having taken Ehud into the upper room/toilet, the Benjaminite leader then states that his message is from God, and this causes Eglon to rise, perhaps being agitated by the possibilities of such a message.[58] In the process of shifting his considerable weight, Eglon presented an easy target for the assassin's knife.

SHAMGAR

(31) **After him came Shamgar son of Anath, who killed six hundred of the Philistines with an oxgoad. He too delivered Israel.**

*A*ppended to the end of Ehud's story is what in modern parlance might be referred to as a sound bite about Shamgar ben Anath. Many commentators uphold that this verse was added to the Judges material late in its editing, demonstrating an interpretative process that responded to portions of the older narratives. Thus the mention of Shamgar in Judg 5:6, where he is described as a contemporary of Deborah and Jael, becomes the basis for the creation of this brief note.[59] While this interpretation is possible, there is also evidence, based on Egyptian inscriptions, that ben Anath was a common name used by the 'Apiru/Habiru mercenaries employed by the Egyptians during the twelfth–tenth centuries BCE. They took on the name of the Canaanite goddess of war to mark both their ferocity in battle and their membership in a military cadre.[60] Shamgar's mention in the Jael story could therefore reflect the activities of Pharaoh Rameses III (1198–1190 BCE) against the Philistines in northern Canaan. While his weapon, an "oxgoad," may be reference to Anath's staff, it more likely functions as evidence of

---

[58] Y. Amit, *Book of Judges* (1999): 186–88. T. A. Jull, "*Mgrh* in Judges 3," *JSOT* 81 (1998): 70–71, argues that Eglon stands up because he is shocked that Ehud would intrude into his private chamber. The king could have gone into the toilet to relieve himself or just to think privately about the possibility of Ehud's message, and Ehud might be making an excuse for entering, saying he has a "message from God." In either case, a startled victim is more vulnerable to attack.

[59] B. Lindars, *Judges 1–5* (1995): 156; M. Z. Brettler, *Book of Judges* (2002): 24, also notes that the creation of Shamgar's exploits against the Philistine may be a response to the mention in Judg 10:11 that Yahweh had previously freed the Israelites from the oppression of many enemies, including the Philistines.

[60] Nili Shupak, "New Light on Shamgar ben 'Anath," *Bib* 70 (1989): 517–25.

the use of unconventional weapons by the Israelite heroes.[61] Thus, like the non-Israelite Jael, Shamgar, whose own ethnic origins may be Hurrian or Canaanite,[62] is easily added to the roster of Israelite heroes because he defeats their enemies.

CHAPTER 4

DEBORAH

(1) The Israelites again did what was evil in the sight of the Lord, after Ehud died. (2) So the Lord sold them into the hand of King Jabin of Canaan, who reigned in Hazor; the commander of his army was Sisera, who lived in Harosheth-hagoiim. (3) Then the Israelites cried out to the Lord for help; for he had nine hundred chariots of iron, and had oppressed the Israelites cruelly twenty years. (4) At that time Deborah, a prophetess, wife of Lappidoth, was judging Israel. (5) She used to sit under that palm of Deborah between Ramah and Bethel in the hill country of Ephraim; and the Israelites came up to her for judgment. (6) She sent and summoned Barak son of Abinoam from Kedesh in Naphtali, and said to him, "The Lord, the God of Israel, commands you, 'Go, take position at Mount Tabor, bringing ten thousand from the tribe of Naphtali and the tribe of Zebulun. (7) I will draw out Sisera, the general of Jabin's army, to meet you by the Wadi Kishon with his chariots and his troops; and I will give him into your hand.' " (8) Barak said to her, "If you will go with me, I will go; but if you will not go with me, I will not go." (9) And she said, "I will surely go with you; nevertheless, the road on which you are going will not lead to your glory, for the Lord will sell Sisera into the hand of a woman." Then Deborah got up and went with Barak to Kedesh. (10) Barak summoned Zebulun and Naphtali to Kedesh; and ten thousand warriors went up behind him; and Deborah went up with him.

The intrusive nature of the Shamgar reference at the end of chapter 3 is reinforced by the resumption of the narrative with the death of Ehud. The standard pattern of the Judges cycle then continues, although there

---

[61] J. C. Moyer, "Weapons and Warfare," in *Discovering the Bible* (1986): 42–50, discusses the use of a tent peg (Judg 4:21), trumpets, jars, and torches (Judg 7:19), and the jawbone of a donkey (Judg 15:15).

[62] A. van Selms, "Judge Shamgar," *VT* 14 (1964): 294–309.

is no direct statement that Deborah is raised up to become a judge. Her judicial function is already established, and it will be upon that authority and her role as prophet that she will summon Barak to take military action. The conflict with Jabin, king of Hazor, parallels the story in Josh 11:1–15, although that account includes a coalition of northern kings and Joshua as the Israelite hero. There is also a reference in both accounts to a large number of chariots (iron chariots only in Judges), an indicator of the technological superiority of the Canaanites that is overcome by the intervention of Yahweh, the divine warrior. Sisera and his territory of Harosheth-Hagoiim (probably the forested area of the Galilee region) appear only in the Judg 4–5 accounts.[63] Since his name is non-Semitic, he may be related to the Sea Peoples who are known to have settled along the northern coast of Canaan and up into the Lebanon area.

As introduced in the text, Deborah is a liminal female, which means that she does not fit into the normal categories assigned to women in her society. Although she is identified as the "wife of Lappidoth," there is no male household mentioned in the narrative. She appears to be operating completely on her own initiative as judge and prophet.[64] This probably indicates that she is a postmenopausal female, who, like the "wise women" of the David narrative (2 Sam 14:2–20; 20:15–22), functions as an elder. Gender, once women have become postmenopausal, no longer disqualifies them from serving in an authoritative role.

Based on the scene so briefly sketched here, it is possible to describe Deborah as the only character in the Book of Judges who actually functions in a judicial position; hearing and deciding cases for those who choose to come and consult her.[65] However, this does not directly parallel Moses' actions at Mt. Sinai, when he "sat as judge for the people . . . from morning until evening" (Exod 18:13). Instead Deborah's prestige appears to be based on her oracular role. Given the corrupt nature of the priesthood during

---

[63] Benjamin Mazar, "Beth-She'arim, Gaba, and Harsheth of the Peoples," *HUCA* 24 (1952): 81–84.

[64] The description of "the prophetess Huldah the wife of Shallum son of Tikvah, son of Harhas, keeper of the wardrobe" in 2 Kings 22:14 is quite similar. In both cases the women are identified with a particular household but are consulted to discover God's intent/judgment, and both are considered to be authoritative figures.

[65] J. A. Soggin, *Judges* (1987): 71, describes her role as "forensic," seeing her service to the people already established on the legal plane prior to this example of a political and religious inquiry. The description of her "court" is similar to that found in the Ugaritic epic of Aqhat (ca. 1500 BCE), which depicts King Danil sitting on a threshing floor before the city gates, judging the cases of the widows and orphans (*COS* 1.103: 346; Aqhat III.i.20–25).

the Judges/settlement period (Judg 17:7–13; 1 Sam 2:12–17), it is quite likely
that the people as well as military leaders like Barak chose to "come up" to
consult her as a prophetic voice of God.[66]

Deborah's palm apparently served as a landmark for the tribal territory
of Benjamin on a well-traveled route between Ramah (identified with er-
Ram, three miles north of Jerusalem) and Bethel (Beitin, four miles north
of Ramah along the road into Ephraimite territory). Thus her authority was
based on her credibility as a true prophet, her presence at a site associated
with oracular performance, and her ability to summon leaders to carry out
the instructions of Yahweh.[67]

Deborah's status as a prophet as well as a judge is found in this portrait
of her summoning a military leader. Similar scenes for other prophets are
found in Deut 31:7, where Moses summons Joshua to lead the people into
conquest of the Promised Land, and in 1 Sam 15:2–3, where Samuel summons
Saul to carry out a *ḥērem* (holy war) with the aim of totally annihilating the
Amalekites.

The exchange between Barak and Deborah suggests the warrior's concern that no tribe would rally to his call without the presence of a divine
representative. There is no precedent for this request by Barak, but Moses
does function as the spokesperson of the divine warrior in the exodus and
wilderness narratives (Exod 17:8–13; Num 16), and Elisha is described as
accompanying the army of Jehoram and Jehoshaphat in 2 Kings 3:11–20.
Deborah's prediction that a woman will be the basis for the Israelite victory
provides a direct response to Barak's demure in carrying out the divine command (compare Samuel's condemnation of Saul for his failure to complete
the *ḥērem* against the Amalekites in 1 Sam 15:10–33). It also sets up an ironic
twist since the reader would initially believe that Deborah is referring to
herself. In addition, that a woman could tip the scales against the enemy
plays into the underdog theme common in Israelite tradition and can be
compared to a theme found in the Ugaritic epic of Aqhat, in which a woman
takes on the male role and slays a villain.[68]

---

[66] Daniel I. Block, "Deborah among the Judges: The Perspective of the Hebrew Historian."
Pages 246–47 in *Faith, Tradition and History*. Edited by Alan R. Millard et al. Winona
Lake, Ind.: Eisenbrauns, 1994.

[67] See Bruce Lincoln, *Authority*. Chicago: University of Chicago Press, 1994: 4–13, for discussion of the discourse authority that is demonstrated by the reaction of the audience
to both speech and iconic images (in this case the palm tree).

[68] This theme also appears in the story of Judith's murder of Holofernes in the Deutero-
canonical literature (see Carey A. Moore, "Judith: The Case of the Pious Killer," *BRev* 6
[1, 1990]: 26–36). In the Ugaritic epic, Aqhat's sister Paghat avenges his murder by dressing

Their exchange also provides the basis for a theme running throughout this narrative in which the male characters are shamed by their failure to take initiative or by their supersession by the dominant female characters.[69] It could even be said that these male characters put aside the hero stereotype (courageous, forceful, and direct) and take on either the role of little boys dependent upon their mother for support or stereotypical female characteristics (uncertain, frightened) as part of the theme of social reversal.[70] The volatile situation may also demand that the female take on an uncharacteristic warrior role, at least temporarily, to meet the needs of the people and to help ensure their survival.[71]

Cf. Queen Esther!

JAEL AND SISERA

(11) Now Heber the Kenite had separated from the other Kenites, that is, the descendants of Hobab the father-in-law of Moses, and had encamped as far away as Elon-bezannaim, which is near Kedesh. (12) When Sisera was told that Barak son of Abinoam had gone up to Mount Tabor, (13) Sisera called out all his chariots, nine hundred chariots of iron, and all the troops who were with him, from Harosheth-hagoim to the Wadi Kishon. (14) Then Deborah said to Barak, "Up! For this is the day on which the Lord has given Sisera into your hand. The Lord is indeed going out before you." So Barak went down from Mount Tabor with ten thousand warriors following him. (15) And the Lord threw Sisera and all his chariots and all his army into a panic before Barak; Sisera got down from his chariot and fled away on foot, (16) while Barak pursued the chariots and the army to Harosheth-hagoiim. All the army of Sisera fell by the sword; no one was left. (17) Now Sisera had fled away on foot to the tent of Jael wife of Heber the Kenite; for there was peace between King Jabin of Hazor and the clan of Heber the Kenite. (18) Jael came out to meet Sisera, and said to him "Turn

---

herself in male garments and then further disguising herself as a barmaid so that she can slay the murderer Yatpan. In this way she ritually transforms herself into the "male" avenger while retaining the outward appearance of a female (*CTA* 19.205–21; *COS* 1.103: 350–56).

[69]   Arie van der Kooij, "On Male and Female Views in Judges 4 and 5." Page 139 in *On Reading Prophetic Texts*. Edited by Bob Becking and Meindert Dijkstra. Leiden, Neth.: Brill, 1996.

[70]   J. Cheryl Exum, "Feminist Criticism: Whose Interests Are Being Served?" Pages 71–72 in *Judges and Method: New Approaches in Biblical Studies*. Edited by Gale A. Yee. Minneapolis: Fortress Press, 1995; Meir Sternberg, *The Poetics of Biblical Narrative: Ideological Literature and the Drama of Reading*. Bloomington: Indiana University Press, 1985: 274.

[71]   Gale A. Yee, "By the Hand of a Woman: The Metaphor of the Woman Warrior in Judges 4," *Semeia* 61 (1993): 112.

aside, my lord, turn aside to me; have no fear." So he turned aside to her into the tent, and she covered him with a rug. (19) Then he said to her, "Please give me a little water to drink; for I am thirsty." So she opened a skin of milk and gave him a drink and covered him. (20) He said to her, "Stand at the entrance of the tent, and if anybody comes and asks you, 'Is anyone here?' say, 'No.'" (21) But Jael wife of Heber took a tent peg, and took a hammer in her hand, and went softly to him and drove the peg into his temple, until it went down into the ground – he was lying fast asleep from weariness – and he died. (22) Then, as Barak came in pursuit of Sisera, Jael went out to meet him, and said to him, "Come, and I will show you the man whom you are seeking." So he went into her tent; and there was Sisera lying dead, with the tent peg in his temple. (23) So on that day God subdued King Jabin of Canaan before the Israelites. (24) Then the hand of the Israelite bore harder and harder on King Jabin of Canaan, until they destroyed King Jabin of Canaan.

Note that Heber's encampment would have been located in the southern portion of the territory of Naphtali (Josh 19:33) near Mt. Tabor (see the earlier discussion on the Kenites in Judg 1:16). Interestingly, the oak tree at this site most likely served as a landmark and possibly as a cultic center and thus parallels the palm of Deborah in Judg 4:5 and the "Diviner's Oak" in Judg 9:37.

Sisera as a non-Semitic name raises the possibility that he is a mercenary chief, affiliated with Jabin of Hazor, or is the local ruler of an area referred to here as Harosheth-hagoiim (translated "forests of the nations" in the Septuagint), probably located in the vicinity of Beth-shean in the Jezreel Valley. Eliezer Oren makes the case for a tie to an Egyptian presence in that area during the Iron I period and Sisera's role there,[72] but this cannot be proven.

Deborah's exhortation, with its attention to geographic detail and stereotypical description of a military victory, suggests that it is part of a source independent of the remainder of the chapter. This would mean that the story of Jael is a separate tradition, introduced by Deborah's warning to Barak that a woman would bring him his victory, independent of the battle narrative. Deborah uses a familiar phrase here, crying out that on this day (see Josh 3:7; 10:12) the enemy will be given into his hand (see Num 21:34; Josh 8:7; 10:19; Judg 3:28).

---

[72] Eliezer D. Oren, "'Governor's Residences' in Canaan under the New Kingdom: A Case Study in Egyptian Administration," *JSSEA* 14 (1984): 37–56.

The Israelite strategy appears to be to lure Sisera's chariotry into the vicinity of the Wadi Kishon. Halpern argues that there is collaboration between Deborah and Heber the Kenite, with a false version of the Israelite battle plan being leaked to the enemy forces by the Kenite in order to draw Sisera into the vicinity of Mount Tabor.[73] He would have welcomed the opportunity to deploy his forces in a flat plain, where they could do the most damage to massed Israelite troops. However, a freak storm causes a flash flood that overflowed the banks of the Wadi Kishon, covering the plain with enough water to bog down the chariot wheels and leaving Sisera's army vulnerable to the Israelite infantry, which quickly decimated them. Other examples where Yahweh's control over the forces of nature is the decisive element in a battle are in Josh 10:7–13 (sun stands still) and 1 Sam 7:7–11 (thundering voice).

Sisera's flight (v. 17) from the battle parallels Barak's reluctance to participate in a battle without Deborah's presence. In both instances the men abandon the stereotypical image of the strong and courageous leader and thereby make themselves vulnerable to be superseded or, as in Sisera's case, eliminated entirely.[74] The story of Sisera and Jael contains so many violations of the hospitality code that it can only be concluded that a conscious attempt was made by the writer to justify Sisera's murder by Jael.[75] It fits into the world-turned-upside-down theme found in many of the stories in Judges and provides the reader with a black comedy or even a farce in which the violations of custom are so exaggerated that they become both transparent and funny.

PROTOCOL OF HOSPITALITY

1. There is a sphere of hospitality that comprises a zone of obligation for both the individual and the village or town within which people have the responsibility to offer hospitality to strangers. The size of the zone is of course smaller for the individual than for the urban center.
2. The stranger must be transformed from potential threat to ally by the offer of hospitality.
3. The invitation of hospitality can be offered only by the male head of household or a male citizen of the town or village.

---

[73] Baruch Halpern, *The First Historians: The Hebrew Bible and History*. San Francisco: Harper & Row, 1988b: 85–86.
[74] J. C. Exum, "Feminist Criticism," in *Judges and Method* (1995): 72.
[75] Victor H. Matthews, "Hospitality and Hostility in Judges 4," *BTB* 21 (1991): 13–21.

4. The invitation may include a statement about the duration of hospitality, but this can then be extended, if agreeable to both parties, on the renewed invitation of the host.

5. The stranger has the right of refusal, but this could be considered an affront to the honor of the host and could be cause for immediate hostilities or conflict.

6. Once the invitation is accepted, the roles of the host and the guest are set by the rules of custom.

    a. The guest must not ask for anything.

    b. The host provides the best available in the household – despite what may be modestly offered in the initial invitation of hospitality.

    c. The guest is expected to reciprocate with news, predictions of good fortune, or gracious responses based on what the guest has been given.

    d. The host must not ask personal questions of the guest.

7. The guest remains under the protection of the host until he/she has left the zone of obligation of the host.

Having been shamed by his military defeat, Sisera would seek refuge in the encampment of a neutral party like Heber the Kenite.[76] The logic breaks down, however, when he approaches Jael's, not Heber's, tent. If he were seeking sanctuary or shelter, he should have approached the tent of the head of the household, not that of his wife. By doing so Sisera robs Heber of his rights as head of the household to offer hospitality and to represent his household and its authority before a stranger.[77] This clearly dishonors Heber, and, in addition, it brings even greater shame on Sisera since he has failed to follow proper social protocol.

An argument could be made that Sisera in fact did approach the tent of the head of the household, but the text clearly says that it is "Jael's tent." In Middle Eastern pastoral encampments today, a wife may share the tent of her husband, but a man with multiple wives is expected to provide each wife with her own tent.[78] Thus it is completely possible that Jael had a tent to herself. This may have even been part of a strategy created for Sisera by the

[76] B. Halpern, *The First Historians* (1988b): 85.

[77] C. A. O. Van Nieuwenhuijze, *Sociology of the Middle East: A Stocktaking and Interpretation.* Leiden, Neth.: Brill, 1971: 701.

[78] A. M. A. Ahmed, "Tribal and Sedentary Elites: A Bridge between Two Communities." Page 79 in *The Desert and the Sown: Nomads in a Wider Society.* Edited by Cynthia Nelson. Berkeley: University of California Press, 1973.

narrator. One can assume that Sisera did not want to be found by pursuers and thus would choose the tent least likely to be searched. Of course, Heber would have been obligated to protect him once he had come under his protection (see Gen 19:8 for Lot's extreme measures on behalf of his guests). However, Sisera may have faced pursuit after leaving Heber's hospitality zone, or he may have needed to escape more quickly and could not wait for Barak's men to give up the chase. Whatever his reasoning, Sisera dishonors his potential host (Heber) by not coming directly to him, and he dishonors Jael simply by approaching her tent. By law and custom, the one obligation a woman had to her husband, other than providing him with an heir, was remaining chaste to him, an essential for the lineage of the clan to remain pure.[79] Sisera's approach to Jael's tent put them both in danger of an adultery charge.

One final question to be asked here is whether Jael was alone. The text is silent on this point; no witnesses are mentioned who could have spied on their affair. Yet it is extremely unlikely that Jael would have been left totally alone. One modern study of pastoral nomads notes that men are "available at all times to protect the women and animals."[80] Thus whether Heber was present or not, someone would certainly have been within the precincts of the encampment. That no one else is mentioned speaks both to the stealth with which Sisera approached the tent and to the breach of custom of the entire scene.

Jael's actions can also be characterized as a violation of hospitality customs. Only the male head of household had the right to offer hospitality.[81] Yee, however, argues that Jael's actions are a form of "guerilla warfare" designed to protect her household and are justified based on previously arranged ties to Deborah and the Israelites.[82] To be sure, as a literary link to Deborah's prediction in 4:9a, Jael's appearance would jar the reader into a new track, set up the horrific events to come,[83] and unravel the riddle of

---

[79] A. M. Abou-Zeid, "Honour and Shame among the Bedouin of Egypt." Page 253 in *Honour and Shame: The Values of Mediterranean Society*. Edited by J. G. Peristiany. Chicago: University of Chicago Press, 1965.

[80] Robert N. Pehrson, *The Social Organization of the Marri Baluch*. Chicago: Aldine, 1966: 85.

[81] C. A. O. Van Nieuwenhuijze, *Sociology of the Middle East* (1971): 287.

[82] G. A. Yee, "By the Hand of a Woman," *Semeia* 61 (1993): 112–14.

[83] Donald F. Murray, "Narrative Structure and Technique in the Deborah-Barak Story, Judges iv 4–22." Page 182 in *Studies in the Historical Books of the Old Testament*. Edited by John A. Emerton. Leiden, Neth.: Brill, 1979.

who would become the hero of the tale.[84] Since Jael's improper invitation[85] is missing from the poetic version of the story in Judg 5, it is possible that the editor added it to the later prose as a logical necessity to the plot.[86] This step provides Sisera with a hiding place and also places him in the prone position in which he will later be slain by Jael.

Jael's assurance to Sisera that he should "have no fear" (v. 18) has no basis in fact or custom. It functions as part of the deception and as another piece of literary irony and perhaps plays on Sisera's vulnerability and need for a form of motherly support in this tense and frightening situation.[87] The phrase "fear not" appears elsewhere in the context of theophanies, a situation in which fear is justified, but it is set aside under the assurance of the divine being (Gen 15:1; Judg 6:23). By approaching Jael's tent, Sisera has violated custom, and Jael's invitation can then be seen as a subterfuge to lure him to his death, using the hospitality code as a framework. Both characters are thus in violation of custom. Therefore the question is whether the law allows a woman to deceive a man to preserve her life and her honor.

As a member of Heber's household, Jael is obligated to honor his alliances and to do what she can to strengthen them. This does not apply, however, when the ally proves to be a threat to the household. Sisera places himself at risk, not by trusting the political loyalty of Jael but by violating the hospitality code and bringing shame on both Jael and Heber. Jael, of course, also places herself at risk by leaving the protection of her tent and coming out to speak to Sisera (see Dinah's fate in Gen 34:1–2). Her courage is demonstrated here, and it can be argued that her intent to protect the household from the hostility of the Israelites by harboring Sisera also may have contributed to her actions and outweighed her own safety.[88] This shows her loyalty to her

---

[84]   Yairah Amit, "Judges 4: Its Contents and Form," *JSOT* 39 (1987): 89.

[85]   Examples of proper exercise of the invitation of hospitality are found in Gen 18:2–3 and 24:30–31, and other examples of improper invitation are found in Gen 19:2 and Judg 19:20 (see Victor H. Matthews, "Hospitality and Hostility in Genesis 19 and Judges 19," *BTB* 22 [1992]: 3–11). In the former the heads of households invite strangers to share the comforts of their homes and thereby to remove their status as potential enemies (Julian Pitt-Rivers, "The Stranger, the Guest, and the Hostile Host." Page 23 in *Contributions to Mediterranean Sociology*. Edited by J. G. Peristiany. Paris: Mouton, 1968), while in the latter two examples resident aliens improperly offer hospitality to a stranger.

[86]   B. Halpern, *The First Historians* (1988b): 83.

[87]   J. C. Exum, "Feminist Criticism," in *Judges and Method* (1995): 72.

[88]   J. A. Soggin, *Judges* (1987): 78.

group and is not a violation of her conscience or common decency. Jael operates within her rights against a violator of the customs of hospitality and a physical threat to her person.

When Sisera accepted Jael's improper invitation, he is removed from the protection afforded to a guest by hospitality customs, and from this point on he is in mortal danger. Jael's murder of Sisera is therefore to be understood not as a woman's free political act but rather as a proper reaction to the violation of the code of hospitality. Sisera's action, freely taken, marks him as a danger, which must be dealt with by any means at hand.[89]

The placing of the rug over Sisera may simply represent a comfort given to an exhausted man, who is probably wet from sweat and the muddy slime that had consumed his chariots. It is also possible that this rug is actually a curtain separating the public and private sections of her tent.[90] If Jael had drawn Sisera within this more private area, then it would further hide his presence and might give him a false sense of security, or even present an overt sexual invitation.

Sisera then compounds his flaunting of custom by requesting a drink of water. Ritual demands, however, that once hospitality has been accepted, it is improper for the guest to ask for anything from the host. It infringes on the honor of the host, implying through this request that all needs of the guest have not been met and reverses the roles of guest and host.[91] Jael's reaction of giving him milk (probably fermented goat's milk) may be part of the one-upmanship of the hospitality ritual, which requires the host to offer simple necessities but delivering much more (see Gen 18:4–8). In this case her providing him with a soothing drink, one that will promote drowsiness in an already exhausted man, can be construed as a further step in Jael's use of hospitality to trap and kill Sisera.[92]

The repetition of her covering him (v. 19) serves the same function as the milk and provides an enclosing framework to the narrative. Both of Jael's acts elicit images of maternal care, and the expansion upon his request beyond a simple drink of water restores her position as hostess, which had been threatened by Sisera's request. It may be compared to the title of "mother of Israel" given to Deborah in Judg 5:7 as well as to the concern of Sisera's mother

---

[89]   Mieke Bal, *Murder and Difference: Gender, Genre, and Scholarship on Sisera's Death.* Bloomington: Indiana University Press, 1988a: 60.

[90]   J. A. Soggin, *Judges* (1987): 67; M. Bal, *Murder and Difference* (1988a): 122.

[91]   J. Pitt-Rivers, "The Stranger, the Guest, and the Hostile Host," in *Contributions to Mediterranean Sociology* (1968): 27.

[92]   Arthur E. Cundall, *Judges: An Introduction and Commentary.* Leicester, Eng.: InterVarsity Press, 1968: 95.

in Judg 5:28–30.[93] These parallels may then function as an empowerment in the narrative of Jael as a surrogate for Deborah, fulfilling the prophecy that a woman would gain the victory (4:9).

Sisera's second improper request comes when he asks Jael to "stand at the entrance" and to say no man is with her. Once again he is questioning the intentions of the hostess to protect her guest.[94] Sisera's insistence is both an unnecessary statement and in fact an implied threat against his hostess. At that point, if previous blunders had not already released Jael from any obligation to him, she is free to take action against him. By pressing his point and asserting a status other than guest, Sisera falls back into the role of hostile stranger.[95] His underestimation of Jael as a woman and the Kenites as a vassal people could be another ironic factor utilized by the narrator. The irony is particularly acute given that he had fled the battle and abandoned his men, and was now relying on a woman to protect him, thereby emasculating himself.[96] Furthermore, when he tells her to say that no man is present he is describing his eventual fate since he will cease to exist.[97]

Having lulled Sisera into falling asleep,[98] Jael takes the common tools used by women to pitch their tents and uses the strength normally employed to drive them securely into the ground to pin Sisera's head to the floor. In this way she completes Deborah's call for Barak to defeat Jabin's army utterly (4:6–7). The last survivor of the battle, Sisera, is dispatched in much the same way that Samuel kills King Agag of the Amalekites in 1 Sam 15:32–33. In both cases the generals (Barak and Saul) have failed to complete the victory, and it is left to a noncombatant to complete the job.[99] Furthermore, there are clear sexual overtones in this narrative. Jael's act strikes an ironic note since it is the male who is penetrated and it is the female who asserts her power to control the situation.[100] This is reinforced in the poetic version of the story (Judg 5:27), which states that Sisera "fell between her legs."[101]

[93] James G. Williams, *Women Recounted: Narrative Thinking and the God of Israel.* Sheffield, Eng.: Almond Press, 1982: 73; M. Bal, *Murder and Difference* (1988a): 64.

[94] A. M. Abou-Zeid, "Honour and Shame," in *Honour and Shame* (1965): 252.

[95] J. Pitt-Rivers, "The Stranger, the Guest, and the Hostile Host," in *Contributions to Mediterranean Sociology* (1968): 21–22.

[96] J. A. Soggin, *Judges* 1987: 77; M. Bal, *Murder and Difference* (1988a): 92.

[97] B. G. Webb, *Book of Judges* (1987): 135.

[98] This scene could easily be compared to Samson falling asleep in Delilah's lap while she prepares to betray him to the Philistines (Judg 16:14, 19) and to Paghat's inducing her intended victim Yatpan to fall into a drunken stupor (*CTA* 19.213–24; *COS* 1.103: 355–56).

[99] Sam Dragga, "In the Shadow of the Judges: The Failure of Saul," *JSOT* 38 (1987): 42.

[100] Danna N. Fewell and David M. Gunn, "Controlling Perspectives: Women, Men, and the Authority of Violence in Judges 4 and 5," *JAAR* 58 (1990a): 393–94.

[101] M. Bal, *Murder and Difference* (1988a): 120.

V. 22 forms an inclusio (paralleled with 4:16) drawing Barak back into the story and completing his search for Sisera. Once again Jael goes out to speak with a man, fulfilling at last Deborah's prediction of a female victory. Of course, this time Jael is not offering hospitality, merely the evidence of Sisera's fate (4:9). There is no mention in the text of Barak's reaction, nor is there any statement explicitly condemning or glorifying Jael here. However, the poetry version (Judg 5:24) proclaims her the "most blessed of women," a person who has taken the proper, if bloody, steps to serving Israel and demonstrating that she is a "friend" of Yahweh (5:31).

Inserted at the end of this story is a phrase in v. 23 that intends to draw the reader back to the theological point that, while Jael, Barak, and Deborah have participated in this drama, it is the divine warrior, named Elohim in this verse, who has provided the victory. This conforms to the pattern established in the literary framework first spelled out in the Ehud episode (3:12–30), which also credits God with giving the enemy into the hands of Israel (vv. 28–30). Although the storyteller makes the point that, although these are very troubled times, the people of Israel can rely on God to give them a victory and to relieve them from oppression if they trust in the covenantal promise and recognize who is in fact their true deliverer.

CHAPTER 5

(1) Then Deborah and Barak son of Abinoam sang on that day, saying: (2) "When locks are long in Israel, when the people offer themselves willingly – bless the Lord! (3) Hear, O kings; give ear, O princes; to the Lord I will sing, I will make melody to the Lord, the God of Israel. (4) Lord, when you went out from Seir, when you marched from the region of Edom, the earth trembled, and the heavens poured, the clouds indeed poured water. (5) The mountains quaked before the Lord, the One of Sinai, before the Lord, the God of Israel. (6) In the days of Shamgar son of Anath, in the days of Jael, caravans ceased and travelers kept to the byways. (7) The peasantry prospered in Israel, they grew fat on plunder, because you arose, Deborah, arose as a mother in Israel. (8) When new gods were chosen, then war was in the gates. Was shield or spear to be seen among forty thousand in Israel? (9) My heart goes out to the commanders of Israel who offered themselves willingly among the people. Bless the Lord. (10) Tell of it, you who ride on white donkeys, you who sit on rich carpets and you who walk by the way. (11) To the sound of musicians at

the watering places, there they repeat the triumphs of the Lord, the triumphs of his peasantry in Israel. Then down to the gates marched the people of the Lord. (12) Awake, awake, Deborah! Awake, awake, utter a song! Arise, Barak, lead away your captives, O son of Abinoam. (13) Then down marched the remnant of the noble; the people of the Lord marched down for him against the mighty. (14) From Ephraim they set out into the valley, following you, Benjamin, with your kin; from Machir marched down the commanders, and from Zebulun those who bear the marshal's staff; (15) the chiefs of Issachar came with Deborah, and Issachar faithful to Barak; into the valley they rushed out at his heels. Among the clans of Reuben there were great searchings of heart. (16) Why did you tarry among the sheepfolds, to hear the piping for the flocks? Among the clans of Reuben there were great searchings of heart. (17) Gilead stayed beyond the Jordan; and Dan, why did he abide with the ships? Asher sat still at the coast of the sea, settling down by his landings. (18) Zebulun is a people that scorned death; Naphtali too, on the heights of the field. (19) The kings came, they fought; then fought the kings of Canaan, at Taanach, by the waters of Megiddo; they got no spoils of silver. (20) The stars fought from heaven, from their courses they fought against Sisera. (21) The torrent Kishon swept them away, the onrushing torrent, the torrent Kishon. March on, my soul, with might! (22) Then loud beat the horses' hoofs with the galloping, galloping of his steeds. (23) Curse Meroz, says the angel of the Lord, curse bitterly its inhabitants, because they did not come to the help of the Lord, to the help of the Lord against the mighty. (24) Most blessed of women be Jael, the wife of Heber the Kenite, of tent-dwelling women most blessed. (25) He asked water and she gave him milk, she brought him curds in a lordly bowl. (26) She put her hand to the tent peg and her right hand to the workmen's mallet; she struck Sisera a blow, she crushed his head, she shattered and pierced his temple. (27) He sank, he fell, he lay still at her feet; at her feet he sank, he fell; where he sank, there he fell dead. (28) Out of the window she peered, the mother of Sisera gazed through the lattice: 'Why is his chariot so long in coming? Why tarry the hoofbeats of his chariots?' (29) Her wisest ladies make answer, indeed, she answers the question herself: (30) 'Are they not finding and dividing the spoil? – A girl or two for each man; spoil of dyed stuffs for Sisera, spoil of dyed stuffs embroidered, two pieces of dyed work embroidered for my neck as spoil?' (31) So perish all your enemies, O Lord! But may your friends be like the sun as it rises in its might!" And the land had rest forty years.

Chapters 4 and 5 in Judges complement each other's treatment of the Deborah/Jael narrative. It is quite likely that they are based on a common source, although the poetic version of chapter 5 probably predates the prose version of chapter 4.[102] The Song of Deborah also places greater emphasis on Yahweh's role as divine warrior, the details of the battle, and the glorification of Jael as the most blessed of women. Plus, it presents the reader with an additional ironic twist at the end of the poem, drawing Sisera's mother into the circle of significant women in this story. The differences between the two versions are charted here.

JUDGES 4: NARRATIVE	JUDGES 5: SONG
Barak and Sisera are shamed by their failures and superseded by Deborah's and Jael's speech and actions.	Barak and Sisera are secondary characters, backgrounded amidst the larger events of the battle, while Deborah and Jael are praised for their actions.
The battle is only briefly mentioned while most time is given to the exchange between Sisera and Jael.	The failure of the tribes to aid Barak provides a backdrop to Yahweh's victory with little space given to Sisera and Jael.
The world-turned-upside-down theme is displayed by the violations of the hospitality code and the shaming of Sisera.	There is no explicit dialogue between Sisera and Jael. His "sinking" at her feet provides the image of role reversal.
Barak's final chagrin and shame comes when Jael displays Sisera's body. Yahweh gains the victory, not Barak.	Sisera's mother parallels Barak's failure. Both are deprived of the normal booty and glory associated with winning a battle.

With regard to the political implications of the song, the failure of the tribes of Reuben, Dan, and Asher, as well as the Israelite territory in Gilead, to respond to Deborah's call provides a realistic appraisal of the situation during the settlement period. The tribes in the northern areas of Canaan or on the borders with the Philistines or Transjordanian peoples would be less likely to send aid since they were concerned with maintaining their own

---

[102] Athalya Brenner, "A Triangle and a Rhombus in Narrative Structure: A Proposed Integrative Reading of Judges iv and v," *VT* 40 (1990): 129–38; K. Lawson Younger, "Heads! Tails! Or the Whole Coin?! Contextual Method and Intertextual Analysis: Judges 4 and 5." Page 135 in *Scripture in Context, IV: The Biblical Canon in Comparative Perspective.* Edited by K. Lawson Younger et al. Lewiston, N.Y.: Edwin Mellen Press, 1991.

borders or were economically allied with their more powerful neighbors.[103] That more attention is given in the song to the breakdown of which tribes chose to come fight and taunts those who did not is very suggestive of an active political agenda on the part of the storyteller.[104] What may be reflected here is the disdain of a self-reliant, agro-pastoral group, living in the difficult terrain of Ephraim's territorial allotment, for the peoples living along the coast or in richer agricultural areas.[105]

The epiphany of Yahweh in Judg 5:4–5 may be the oldest example of this genre in the Hebrew Bible.[106] In form, an epiphany consists of God triumphantly appearing from some distant locale (in this case the Seir desert region south of Canaan) and marching or striding through these territories while nature erupts in violent response (earthquake and storm). It is likely that the literary form has its origins in the ancient Near East, but in the Israelite version there is no hint of polytheism, and the event is squarely placed in history rather than in the world of myth.[107] The purpose of this divine appearance is to intervene in history to liberate or provide military victory to Israel (see 5:11, 31). As in the case of the statement in 4:23, the purpose of this epiphanic song is to demonstrate the source of Israel's victory over Jabin and Sisera as divine in origin. Its manifestations of God's power over nature also provide a theological foundation for the flooding torrents of the Wadi Kishon described in terms of a cosmic battle in vv. 19–21.[108]

The reference in v. 20 to cosmic participation in the battle is consistent with a similar expression of divine intervention in warfare found in the Gebel Barkal stele of Pharaoh Thutmoses III (1479–1425 BCE), which mentions a "flashing star" from the south that drove the enemy forces before it. This could also be compared to the destruction of the Egyptian chariotry in the

---

103 Lawrence E. Stager, "Archaeology, Ecology, and Social History: Background Themes to the Song of Deborah," VTSup 40 (1986): 228–32.

104 K. Lowson Younger, "Heads! Tails! Or the Whole Coin?!" in *Scripture in Context* (1991): 130.

105 Sandra Scham, "The Days of the Judges: When Men and Women Were Animals and Trees Were Kings," *JSOT* 97 (2002): 48–53. For information on the demographics and economics of the Ephraimite hill country settlements in the Iron Age, see Elizabeth Bloch-Smith and Beth Nakhai, "A Landscape Comes to Life: The Iron Age I," *NEA* 62 (1999): 62–92, 101–27; Israel Finkelstein, *The Archaeology of the Settlement of Israel*. Jerusalem: Israel Exploration Society, 1988: 65–80.

106 Dale A. Patrick, "Epiphanic Imagery in Second Isaiah's Portrayal of a New Exodus," *HAR* 8 (1984): 127.

107 Joseph Blenkinsopp, "Ballad Style and Psalm Style in the Song of Deborah: A Discussion," *Bib* 42 (1961): 68; Claus Westerman, *The Praise of God in the Psalms*. Richmond, Va.: John Knox, 1965: 97.

108 Alexander Globe, "The Text and Literary Structure of Judges 5, 4–5," *Bib* 55 (1974): 175.

Red Sea in Exod 14:24–25, when God's pillar of fire panicked them.[109] In fact, the celebratory nature of Deborah's victory song can be compared in several respects with the Song of Moses in Exod 15, in particular with the image of Yahweh as divine warrior and marshal of the elements of creation.[110]

The elements most often found in victory songs include:

1. Repetition of the Divine Name: Exod 15:1–3, 6; Judg 5:2–5
2. Stress of Yahweh's Role in Victory: Exod 15:2, 6, 11; Judg 5:3–5
3. Use of Water Motif as Motive Element: Exod 15:1–4, 10; Judg 5:4–5, 11
4. Mocking the Enemy's Failures: Exod 15:1–2, 9; Judg 5:3, 28–30
5. Use of "Fall" Motif for Enemy: Exod 15:1, 4–5, 7, 10; Judg 5:24–27.

The dominance of female characters in both the prose and poetic versions may be reflection of the underdog theme in typical portrayals of the Israelites throughout the Book of Judges. Having Deborah and Jael serve as heroic figures also provides the sense of role reversal common in these narratives. It both surprises and entertains the reader and even allows for a form of comedic satire in which male characters are superseded or humiliated, and power figures (kings, generals) can be laughed at for their greed and self-serving rationalization. Even Sisera's mother serves as a surrogate for her son's ambitions as she mentally counts the spoil,[111] leaving the reader free to see the irony of her situation while celebrating the unexpected success of Israelite forces and their allies. Her musings also are an indication that female characters are portrayed as acquiescing to the rape and capture of women who are not of their own group, perhaps putting aside in their minds that this violence might happen to them as well.[112]

OVERVIEW OF GIDEON/JERUBBAAL NARRATIVE

The story of Gideon/Jerubbaal is the first extended narrative in the Book of Judges. Since more than an isolated incident is described here, the character

---

[109] Moshe Weinfeld, "Divine Intervention in War in Ancient Israel and in the Ancient Near East." Pages 124–27 in *History, Historiography and Interpretation.* Edited by Hayim Tadmor and Moshe Weinfeld. Jerusalem: Magnes Press, 1983.

[110] Alan J. Hauser, "Two Songs of Victory: Exodus 15 and Judges 5." Pages 266–79 in *Directions in Biblical Hebrew Poetry.* Edited by Elaine R. Follis. JSOTSup 40. Sheffield, Eng.: JSOT Press, 1987.

[111] The rhetorical progression used by Sisera's mother, "a girl or two," is described by Werner Weinberg, "Language Consciousness in the Old Testament," *ZAW* 92 (1980): 199, as a means to "express the exuberance of victory," as in Gen 4:24 ("seventy-sevenfold") and Judg 15:16 ("heaps upon heaps").

[112] J. C. Exum, "Feminist Criticism," in *Judges and Method* (1995): 74–75; D. N. Fewell and D. M. Gunn, "Controlling Perspectives," *JAAR* 58 (1990a): 408.

will be more fully developed and more than one facet of his personality and career will be discussed. It is possible to identify with the story of his tricking the Ammonites by grinding his grain in a winepress, and readers can relate to Gideon's fear in the presence of God. They can cheer his destruction of the Baal altar and his unlikely military victories and wonder at his lapses in judgment. Perhaps because Gideon's cycle of tales stands at the midpoint of the book, his story contains both the heroic qualities found in the episodes about Othniel, Ehud, Shamgar, and Deborah as well as his successes and failures. There is also a dark side to his character that foreshadows the deterioration of leadership qualities of the judges and the increasing idolatry of the Israelite tribes. The scope of his tale extends from his call narrative in chapter 6 through the episodes involving his son Abimelech in chapter 9.

Abimelech is included in this section because he represents the abuse of power that quite naturally filled the vacuum of authority left by Gideon's death, despite his leaving a household of seventy sons. These events may have also been set in motion by Gideon's assumption of kingly powers (request for a portion of the spoils taken in battle and the installation of an ephod in his home city; Judg 8:22–27). From that point on, the progression of horrific deeds in the stories leads to the climax in the final five chapters (Judg 17–21), with rampant cultic violations and a civil war that nearly exterminates the tribe of Benjamin.

A CLOSER LOOK AT BAAL AND ASHERAH

The gods Baal, Anat, Asherah, El, and Yamm are best known from the Ugaritic texts (1600–1200 BCE). The epic literature from this prominent seaport city on the northern Syrian coast describes the adventures of gods and heroes, and gives us a sense of ancient understandings of cosmic struggle (Yamm the sea god vs. Baal the storm god) as well as the romantic exploits of these deities. Although El is technically the supreme god in the Ugaritic pantheon, Baal is most prominently mentioned, quite likely because he is the god of rain and storm and thus the one deity most responsible for bringing fertility to the land. Dwelling on Mt. Zaphon, he is often represented standing as if on a mountaintop with a menacing, military affect and holding both a club and a lance that is a representation of a thunderbolt.[113] The biblical text frequently mentions Baal or the Baals (Judg 2:11; 3:7) and local manifestations of the god, such as Baal-Hazor (2 Sam 13:23) or Baalzebub of Ekron (2 Kings

---

[113] Izak Cornelius, *The Iconography of the Canaanite Gods Reshef and Ba'al.* Fribourg, Switz.: Vandenhoeck & Ruprecht Göttingen, 1994: 134–61.

1:2).[114] Clearly, the prominent place that Baal has suggests how great a threat he represented to Yahweh worship, especially given that the new settlers in the time of the judges lived as neighbors with the Canaanites and were often witness to or present at their cultic activity. The presence of a high place and altar dedicated to Baal in Gideon's village (6:25) attests to the high degree of mixed worship practice among the Israelites, who were apparently willing to seek help from a variety of gods to increase their harvests.

While Anat is the female consort to Baal in the Ugaritic texts, Asherah is most often mentioned in conjunction with Baal in the biblical narratives. The plural form, Asheroth, found in Judg 3:7 simply matches the plural use of Baal and suggests that the goddess had a variety of local cult sites. These cultic installations are generally mentioned in reference to Asherah, but it is clear that the name refers to the goddess herself in several passages (1 Kings 15:13; 18:19; 2 Kings 21:7).[115] The "cultic poles," or stylized groves, erected in her honor (1 Kings 14:15; 16:33; 2 Kings 17:16) become physical symbols of her worship and objects of scorn for the Israelite prophets (Isa 27:9; Jer 17:2).

Because Asherah can be equated with the Ugaritic goddess Athirat, the consort of El, it is quite likely that the Israelites, who borrowed many of El's attributes and ascribed them to Yahweh, also saw Asherah as Yahweh's consort. The argument for this position has been strengthened or at least ignited by the discovery of the drawing and inscriptions at Kuntillet 'Ajrud, which contains the phrase *lyhwh . . . wl'šrth* (by Yahweh . . . and his *'ăšērâ*).[116] While it is not necessary to associate the pictographs of animals and human figures with the inscription, this has raised a great deal of speculation.[117] It is perhaps enough to say that the Israelites, in their need to obtain as much assistance as possible in their daily fight to survive in a marginal environment, found that calling on both Yahweh and a Canaanite goddess or her cult object was not incongruous.[118]

---

[114] See John Day, "Asherah" and "Baal (Deity)." Pages 485–86, 547–49 of vol. 1 in *The Anchor Bible Dictionary*. Edited by David N. Freedman. New York: Doubleday, 1992, for a more detailed discussion of the role of Baal and Asherah in both the Old Testament and extrabiblical texts.

[115] J. Day, *Yahweh and the Gods and Goddesses of Canaan*. JSOTSup 265. Sheffield, Eng.: Sheffield Academic Press, 2000: 43–45.

[116] John Emerton, " 'Yahweh and His Asherah': The Goddess or Her Symbol?" *VT* 49 (1999): 316–17.

[117] Judith Hadley, "Some Drawings and Inscriptions on Two Pithoi from Kuntillet 'Ajrud," *VT* 37 (1987): 180–213; Ziony Zevit, "The Khirbet el-Qôm Inscription Mentioning a Goddess," *BASOR* 255 (1984): 599–610.

[118] J. Emerton, " 'Yahweh and His Asherah,' " *VT* 49 (1999): 334; J. Day, *Yahweh and the Gods and Goddesses of Canaan* (2000): 47.

CHAPTER 6

(1) The Israelites did what was evil in the sight of the Lord, and the Lord gave them into the hand of Midian seven years. (2) The hand of Midian prevailed over Israel; and because of Midian the Israelites provided for themselves hiding places in the mountains, caves and strongholds. (3) For whenever the Israelites put in seed, the Midianites and the Amalekites and the people of the east would come up against them. (4) They would encamp against them and destroy the produce of the land, as far as the neighborhood of Gaza, and leave no sustenance in Israel and no sheep or box or donkey. (5) For they and their livestock would come up, and they would even bring their tents, as thick as locusts; neither they nor their camels could be counted; so they wasted the land as they came in. (6) Thus Israel was greatly impoverished because of Midian; and the Israelites cried out to the Lord for help. (7) When the Israelites cried to the Lord on account of the Midianites, (8) the Lord sent a prophet to the Israelites; and he said to them, "Thus says the Lord, the God of Israel: I led you up from Egypt, and brought you out of the house of slavery; (9) and I delivered you from the hand of the Egyptians, and from the hand of all who oppressed you, and drove them out before you, and gave you their land; (10) and I said to you, 'I am the Lord your God; you shall not pay reverence to the gods of the Amorites, in whose land you live.' But you have not given heed to my voice."

The first portion of this chapter provides a classic example of the Judges cycle as described earlier (see Judg 2:19; 3:7, 12; 4:1) and thus functions as a stock phrase introducing yet another story in the sequence, the Gideon narrative. What differs here is the degree to which the storyteller develops the theme of apostasy among the people and by the judge.[119] The failure of the Israelites to obey the covenant with Yahweh results in their oppression by the Midianites and other surrounding peoples. In fact, they are taxed beyond their ability to pay, despite the comparative richness of the territory of Manasseh, with its fertile valleys and proximity to the major trade route of the Jezreel Valley.[120] Thus the people face an economic nightmare. The incursions of hoards of pastoral nomadic peoples strips the grazing land, drains the water from the streams, and tramples and consumes cultivated fields and terraces. Faced with the consequences of their disobedience, the

[119] J. Marais, *Representation in Old Testament* (1998): 106.
[120] S. Scham, "Days of the Judges," *JSOT* 97 (2002): 53.

Israelites cry out to Yahweh, triggering first a prophetic message to provide a legal explanation (theodicy) for their suffering and then the raising of a judge, who with the assistance of the divine warrior will aid them in removing their oppressors.

The appearance of an unnamed prophet in this episode is unique to the Book of Judges. In no other case is a prophet mentioned, and in this instance the message is quite generic, based almost directly on the first of the Ten Commandments in Exod 20:2–3. The reference to "the gods of the Amorites" provides a link to Joshua's covenant renewal ceremony at Shechem (Josh 24:15), and, despite the mention of Amalekites and Midianites earlier in the passage, also supplies a collective ethnic designation for the physical and cultural enemies of the Israelites.[121] The speech of the prophet gives Yahweh an opportunity to engage in a soliloquy, criticizing Israel's history of disobedience, but without abandoning them.[122]

(11) Now the angel of the Lord came and sat under the oak at Ophrah, which belonged to Joash the Abiezrite, as his son Gideon was beating out wheat in the winepress, to hide it from the Midianites. (12) The angel of the Lord appeared to him and said to him, "The Lord is with you, you mighty warrior." (13) Gideon answered him, "But sir, if the Lord is with us, why then has all this happened to us? And where are all his wonderful deeds that our ancestors recounted to us, saying 'Did not the Lord bring us up from Egypt?' But now the Lord has cast us off, and given us into the hand of Midian." (14) Then the Lord turned to him and said, "Go in this might of yours and deliver Israel from the hand of Midian; I hereby commission you." (15) He responded, "But sir, how can I deliver Israel? My clan is the weakest in Manasseh, and I am the least in my family." (16) The Lord said to him, "But I will be with you, and you shall strike down the Midianites, every one of them." (17) Then he said to him, "If now I have found favor with you, then show me a sign that it is you who speak with me. (18) Do not depart from here until I come to you, and bring out my present, and set it before you." And he said, "I will stay until you return." (19) So Gideon went into his house and prepared a kid, and unleavened cakes from an

---

[121] The Amorites are most often mentioned as part of a standard list of enemy nations (i.e., "the Canaanites, the Hittites, the Amorites, the Perizzites, the Hivites, and the Jebusites" in Exod 3:8; 13:5; 33:2 and varied lists in Deut 7:1; 20:17 and Josh 3:10; 13:4). However, they also appear alone, especially in reference to the Amorite kingdoms of Sihon and Og (Num 21:21–34; Deut 1:4–7). See also Edwin Hostetter, *Nations Mightier and More Numerous*. Berkeley: Bibal, 1995.

[122] J. Marais, *Representation in Old Testament* (1998): 107–8.

ephah of flour; the meat he put in a basket, and the broth he put in a pot, and brought them to him under the oak and presented them. (20) The angel of God said to him, "Take the meat and the unleavened cakes, and put them on the rock, and pour out the broth." And he did so. (21) Then the angel of the Lord reached out the tip of the staff that was in his hand, and touched the meat and the unleavened cakes; and fire sprang up from the rock and consumed the meat and the unleavened cakes; and the angel of the Lord vanished from his sight. (22) Then Gideon perceived that it was the angel of the Lord; and Gideon said, "Help me, Lord God! For I have seen the angel of the Lord face to face." (23) But the Lord said to him, "Peace be to you; do not fear, you shall not die." (24) Then Gideon built an altar there to the Lord, and called it, The Lord is peace. To this day it still stands at Ophrah, which belongs to the Abiezrites. *military victory is so temporary!*

Yet another unique aspect of the episodes about Gideon is his call narrative. No other judge has a similar tale, and this further distinguishes these stories, strengthening the traditional importance attached to this figure. Gideon's call is surprisingly like that of Moses (Exod 3–4:17) and prophets like Isaiah (Isa 6) and Jeremiah (Jer 1). It contains many of the elements found in the commissioning of these spokespersons for Yahweh.[123] However, there is an additional element, emphasizing his "fearfulness and reluctance" at each stage of his career.[124] Here are the elements of his call:

(1) A theophany occurs in a significant place (compare Mt. Sinai for Moses and Mt. Horeb for Elijah). Gideon is on a threshing floor, an agricultural installation that is intimately tied to the economic prosperity of the community and a place where the distribution of grain occurs and legal decisions are made.[125] There are a number of other stories, including that of Ruth and Boaz (Ruth 3) as well as David's theophany on the threshing floor of Araunah (2 Sam 24:18–25), that are set on this important site.

(2) A declaration of divine purpose is made. This sometimes functions as recognition of the condition of the people's suffering (Exod 3:7–10) or as

---

123 Norman Habel, "The Form and Significance of the Call Narratives," *ZAW* 77 (1965): 297–323; Ellen Davis Lewin, "Arguing for Authority: A Rhetorical Study of Jeremiah 1.14–19 and 20.7–18," *JSOT* 32 (1985): 106–10.

124 A. Graeme Auld, "Gideon: Hacking at the Heart of the Old Testament," *VT* 39 (1989): 264.

125 D. C. Hopkins, *The Highlands of Canaan*. Sheffield, Eng.: Almond Press, 1985: 226; Oded Borowski, *Agriculture in Iron Age Israel*. Winona Lake, Ind.: Eisenbrauns, 1987: 62–63.

a declaration, as in Gideon's case, of the role to be played by the person called to serve. The term used by the angel in addressing Gideon, *gibbôr ḥayil* (valiant warrior) sets a tone of confidence in his ability to complete the assigned task. It also provides a sense of irony for the reader, who has just been shown that Gideon is a trickster, busily engaged in fooling the oppressing Midianites.

(3) The one who is addressed is quick to offer an excuse for why he should not be chosen for this mission. That the first pericope in this chapter is a generic statement that is not directly related to the story of Gideon is made clear by Gideon's accusation that God has abandoned the people and by his questioning the veracity of the old stories of the exodus from Egypt.[126] His attitude is very much like that of Job, who also questions God's motives in allowing his suffering to occur and the wicked to prosper (Job 19:6–22; 21:7–34). Another facet of Gideon's demur is his exclamation of alarm that he has seen the angel of the Lord "face to face." The obvious fear contained in this cry is evidence of Gideon's realization that he has in fact been in the presence of the divine (compare Jacob's similar response in Gen 28:16–17), something that he apparently had not previously believed possible. With this revelation comes the fear of the "glory" (*melammu*) of a divine being, which is considered deadly to mortals in ancient Near Eastern literature.[127] He would also now have to face up to the responsibilities of becoming a military leader during a time of crisis.

(4) The excuses of the person called to be God's representative are set aside with the assurance that God will be with him and therefore he cannot fail in his mission. This is often accompanied by a physical gesture empowering the mortal to speak or act. Thus Moses receives several signs that he can duplicate for the Egyptian court (Exod 4:1–9), and both Isaiah and Jeremiah are strengthened for their activities by a divine touching of their mouth (Isa 6:6–7; Jer 1:9). In Gideon's case he asks for a sign, and there is an almost comic nature to the patience that the angel shows in reassuring this reluctant

---

[126] Note, however, the attempt by Bernon Lee, "Fragmentation of Reader Focus in the Preamble to Battle in Judges 6.1–7.14," *JSOT* 97 (2002): 73–74, to posit a chiastic structure tying together each segment in what he terms "narrative strand B" (6:8b–9; 6:8b–10; 6:13b). In this way the reader is presented with the promise of deliverance as well as Gideon's matching skepticism, which plays on God's statement and references their current situation as the result of God's failure to keep this promise.

[127] Victor H. Matthews, "Theophanies Cultic and Cosmic: 'Prepare to Meet Thy God.'" Page 308 in *Israel's Apostasy and Restoration: Essays in Honor of R. K. Harrison*. Edited by Avraham Gileadi. Grand Rapids, Mich.: Baker Book House, 1988.

general. The cultic ritual described here of offering a sacrifice on a makeshift altar and its being consumed at the touch of the angel's staff is reminiscent of Moses' use of his staff to open the Red Sea (Exod 14:15–21) and bring forth water from a rock (Num 20:7–11). The use of a table-type object for the sacrifice also formalizes the act and draws it clearly into the standard procedures of cultic activity rather than of hospitality.[128]

(5) Once it is made clear that there is no escape from this call and that divine assistance will indeed be made available, the person chosen acquiesces either with a statement of submission (Isa 6:8b: "Here am I; send me!") or with an act of devotion (Ezek 3:22–23). In Gideon's case, like Jacob at Bethel (Gen 28:18–19), the newly appointed judge builds an altar and gives it a name to commemorate the event. This "sanctuary legend" also provides the basis for an inclusio (concluded at Judg 8:27), which invests the town of Ophrah as Gideon's seat of power.[129] Interestingly, like the hero stories of Judges and the story of Gideon itself, which are structured to demonstrate the progressive disobedience of the Israelites during the settlement period, the mention of Ophrah begins with an act of devotion to Yahweh and concludes with idolatry or corruption.[130]

(25) That night the Lord said to him, "Take your father's bull, the second bull seven years old, and pull down the altar of Baal that belongs to your father, and cut down the sacred pole that is beside it; (26) and build an altar to the Lord your God on the top of the stronghold here, in proper order; then take the second bull, and offer it as a burnt offering with the wood of the sacred pole that you shall cut down." (27) So Gideon took ten of his servants, and did as the Lord had told him; but because he was too afraid of his family and the townspeople to do it by day, he did it by night. (28) When the townspeople rose early in the morning, the altar of Baal was broken down, and the sacred pole beside it was cut down, and the second bull was offered on the altar that had been

---

[128] Paul Heger, *The Development of Incense Cult in Israel.* BZAW 245. Berlin: Walter de Gruyter, 1997: 154–55. That this is an offering and not just a meal offered by a host to a guest is made even clearer in Judg 13:15–20, where the angel refuses to eat but allows Manoah and his wife to present a burnt offering.

[129] See Benedikt Otzen, "Heavenly Visions in Early Judaism: Origin and Function." Pages 200–202 in *In the Shelter of Elyon.* Edited by William B. Barrick and John R. Spencer. JSOTSup 31. Sheffield, Eng.: JSOT Press, 1984, for a discussion of the literary genre of sanctuary legend or cult legend, which is also found in Gen 12:6–7 (Abraham at Shechem) and Gen 22 (sacrifice of Isaac at Moriah).

[130] See Daniel I. Block, "Will the Real Gideon Please Stand Up? Narrative Style and Intention in Judges 6–9," *JETS* 40 (1997a): 361–63.

built. (29) So they said to one another, "Who has done this?" After searching
and inquiring, they were told, "Gideon son of Joash did it." (30) Then the
townspeople said to Joash, "Bring out your son, so that he may die, for he has
pulled down the altar of Baal and cut down the sacred pole beside it." (31) But
Joash said to all who were arrayed against him, "Will you contend for Baal?
Or will you defend his cause? Whoever contends for him shall be put to death
by morning. If he is a god, let him contend for himself, because his altar has
been pulled down." (32) Therefore on that day Gideon was called Jerubbaal,
that is to say, "Let Baal contend against him," because he pulled down his
altar.

*I*n this continuation of Gideon's call narrative, the hero is called upon
to remove the symbols of idolatry in his village, objects that are said
to "belong to his father." Again, comparison can be made with the Moses
narrative, where the chosen representative of God cannot begin his mission
until he and his family are brought into compliance with the law (circumcision of Moses' son: Exod 4:24–26). The destruction of Baal's altar and the
cutting of Asherah's sacred pole[131] must be accomplished first or there will
be confusion over which divine warrior will provide the military victories to
come. It is also necessary, as in the case of Elijah's contest on Mt. Carmel
(1 Kings 18:20–40), to demonstrate the impotence of Baal to defend his sacred
installations and to replace them with an altar dedicated to Yahweh.[132]

The parallel between this story and that in Judg 17:1–13 should also be
noted. In Gideon's tale he removes a household shrine to Baal and performs
sacrificial acts according to the law (Deut 16:21; 27:5–7). In the story of
Micah's idol, an Ephraimite establishes a shrine in his home, which includes
an ephod and teraphim (17:3–5), thereby violating the law against graven
images (Exod 20:4–5). Curiously, Gideon also crafts an ephod later in his
career and it, like Micah's, becomes the basis for the idolatry of his people
(8:22–27).

The anger of the townspeople is understandable on two counts. First, they
have been deprived of a sacred installation, which to their minds is the basis
for the prosperity and fertility of their community.[133] Like their Canaanite
neighbors, these members of the tribe of Manasseh, living in a culturally

---

131 A. G. Auld, "Gideon: Hacking at the Heart," *VT* 39 (1989): 264–65, argues for the etiological
       character of this episode, tying the cutting down of sacred Asherah poles to the pun
       associated with Gideon's name, which means "hacker."

132 P. Heger, *Development of Incense Cult* (1997): 147, n. 8.

133 Ziony Zevit, *The Religions of Ancient Israel*. New York: Continuum, 2001: 644.

diverse area, would have depended upon the goodwill of a number of gods, including Baal and Asherah and Yahweh, to provide for their needs.[134] In that sense they seem to be totally unaware of their exclusive covenant with Yahweh and thus cannot be readily distinguished from the Canaanites.

Second, they have been faced with a clandestine event perpetrated in the dead of night. There was no argument made by Gideon for why this should have been done, and in fact he does not even come forward to admit to his action, even though there are ten witnesses from his own household to the destruction of the altar and sacred pole. His timidity, which simply follows the pattern demonstrated by his surreptitious grinding of his grain and his disclaimer that he is a very insignificant person, is proven by his fear and inability to justify his own actions. It is left to his father, the owner of the altar, to stand up for him, even threatening the crowd against taking mob action against his son (something that would be expected of a head of household in this situation).

Thus the new name given to Gideon may be considered somewhat ironic since Gideon publicly "contended" not with Baal but with Yahweh's angel.[135] However, by comparing the symbolic names found in the prophetic literature (Isa 7:14; 8:1–3; Hos 1:4–9), the use of such a name reinforces and calls to mind repeatedly that Baal could not defend himself against even such a timid contender as Gideon. Although there have been attempts to argue that the separate names, Gideon and Jerubbaal, actually represent the result of edited, divergent narrative lines describing two different heroes,[136] the elements of the narrative are sufficiently cohesive and the later tradition about this character is consistent enough to allow it to stand as is.[137]

(33) Then all the Midianites and the Amalekites and the people of the east came together, and crossing the Jordan they encamped in the Valley of Jezreel. (34) But the spirit of the Lord took possession of Gideon; and he sounded the trumpet, and the Abiezrites were called out to follow him. (35) He sent

---

[134] George Mendenhall, "The Worship of Baal and Asherah: A Study in the Social Bonding Functions of Religious Systems." Pages 153–56 in *Biblical and Related Studies Presented to Samual Iwry*. Edited by Ann Kort and Scott Morschauser. Winona Lake, Ind.: Eisenbrauns, 1985; S. Scham, "Days of the Judges," *JSOT* 97 (2002): 55.

[135] L. R. Klein, *The Triumph of Irony* (1989): 54–55.

[136] A. G. Auld, "Gideon: Hacking at the Heart," *VT* 39 (1989): 264; Uwe Becker, *Richterzeit und Königtum: Redaktionsgeschichtliche Studien zum Richterbuch*. BZAW 192. Berlin and New York: Walter de Gruyter, 1990: 152.

[137] John Emerton, "Gideon and Jerubbaal," *JTS* 27 (1976): 289–312; D. I. Block, "Will the Real Gideon Please Stand Up?" *JETS* 40 (1997a): 355–56.

messengers throughout all Manasseh, and they too were called out to follow him. He also sent messengers to Asher, Zebulun, and Naphtali, and they went up to meet them. (36) Then Gideon said to God, "In order to see whether you will deliver Israel by my hand, as you have said, (37) I am going to lay a fleece of wool on the threshing floor; if there is dew on the fleece alone, and it is dry on all the ground, then I shall know that you will deliver Israel by my hand, as you have said." (38) And it was so. When he rose early next morning and squeezed the fleece, he wrung enough dew from the fleece to fill a bowl with water. (39) Then Gideon said to God, "Do not let your anger burn against me, let me speak one more time; let me, please, make trial with the fleece just once more; let it be dry only on the fleece, and on all the ground let there be dew." (40) And God did so that night. It was dry on the fleece only, and on all the ground there was dew.

The enemies of the Israelites take the path that runs east from the Jordan Valley – west through the Jezreel Valley between Beth-shean and Megiddo, a strategic place with a long history of military activity (see 1 Sam 29:1–11; Hos 1:5).[138] Taking on the mantle of leadership promised him in his call narrative and now filled with the "spirit of the Lord," Gideon begins to build his coalition to meet this threat. Other judges who have an experience of divinely inspired power include Othniel (3:10), Jephthah (11:29), and Samson (14:6, 19; 15:14). In each of those cases, however, a different terminology is used. For Othniel and Jephthah a simple prepositional phrase describes how the spirit of Yahweh "came upon" them, and they were empowered to direct military action by the Israelites. In Samson's case a more evocative phrase is used, the "spirit of the Lord came mightily upon him," but it was to engage in individual exploits of strength rather than to lead the people in battle. Only in Gideon's narrative is the phrase "the spirit of the Lord took possession" or more accurately "clothed" (*lābᵉšā*) the judge with divine power and summoned him to battle as the Israelite commander.[139]

There is an interesting similarity between Gideon's experience and that described in the Babylonian account of creation, the *Enuma Elish*. In that epic story, the god Marduk is recruited by the other gods to be their champion in a cosmic struggle against the Tiamat, the watery goddess of chaos.

---

[138] See the description of Pharaoh Thutmose III's (1479–1425 BCE) campaign in *COS* 2.2A: 7–13, in which he captures Megiddo and thereby gains control of the strategic trade route through the Jezreel Valley.

[139] B. G. Webb, *Book of Judges* (1987): 222, n. 13.

In preparation for his battle against her and her monstrous hordes, Marduk is given divine weapons and then covers his body "with raging fire," symbolic of his enhanced powers (*COS* 1.111: 397). Investiture ceremonies depicted in Egyptian art also evoke an aspect of Gideon's receipt of divine power. For example, the scenes in the El Amarna tomb paintings of Meryra portray the divine pharaoh placing the robes and insignia of office upon his favored official.[140] This bears a striking resemblance to the investiture scenes described in the Joseph narrative (Gen 41:42–43) and in the Assyrian Annals of Sargon II and Ashurbanipal.[141]

Having received this divine impetus and been clothed with God's spirit, Gideon begins to marshal the tribal forces, and his efforts are similar to those described in the Deborah story. However, the list of participating tribes is different, and there is no mention of any tribe refusing to come at Gideon's call:

DEBORAH'S FORCES	GIDEON'S FORCES
Ephraim and Benjamin (5:14)	Manasseh/Abiezrites (6:34; 7:23)
Zebulun and Naphtali (5:18)	Asher, Zebulun, Naphtali (6:35; 7:23)
Issachar (5:15a)	Ephraim is called later (7:24)
Did not come: Reuben, Gilead, Dan, Asher (5:15b–17)	*No other tribes mentioned*

Curiously, at the point when the reader could expect a battle scene (vv. 36–40), Gideon once again stops the action and demonstrates his timidity or lack of faith, even though he received God's spirit in the previous section. The scene in which a mortal bargains with God is first found in the story of Abraham in Gen 18:22–33, where the patriarch repeatedly negotiates for a smaller number of "righteous" persons necessary to save Sodom from destruction. That Gideon's "test" occurs on a threshing floor fits well into the village culture's use of this facility as a place for agricultural activities, distribution of grain (and presumably business), and legal matters (compare Ruth's petitioning of Boaz in Ruth 3). The double test might be explained by the fact that in the first case it would not be difficult for the absorbent fleece to retain moisture from the dew while the ground remained dry; the reverse would constitute a real test of divine control over the elements.[142]

---

[140] N. de G. Davies, *The Rock Tombs of El Amarna. I. The Tomb of Meryra.* London: Gilbert & Rivington, 1903: 35–36.

[141] Victor H. Matthews, "The Anthropology of Clothing in the Joseph Narrative," *JSOT* 65 (1995): 33–34.

[142] R. G. Boling, *Judges* (1975): 141; L. R. Klein, *The Triumph of Irony* (1989): 55.

The episode in which Gideon tests God's willingness to aid him is closely
paralleled in the story of Jephthah's vow (Judg 11:29–33). In both cases the
chosen leader already has been invested with the spirit of the Lord (6:34;
11:29a), and he has begun to raise an army (6:35; 11:29b). At that point both
leaders seem to falter in their resolve and attempt to obtain reassurances or
even a form of victory insurance from God. The somewhat disjointed feel of
this element in the overall narrative may be the result of a blending of various
sources. However, the principle of "resumptive repetition," which allows
the storyteller temporarily to end a story line, shift to a complementary or
entirely different scene, and then resume the main narrative theme, provides
another interpretive option.[143] Of the two stories, Gideon's seems much
more light-hearted and provides another example, more commonly found
in the Exodus and Joshua material, in which God demonstrates the ability
to manipulate all aspects of creation (compare Exod 14:21–31; Josh 3:14–17;
10:12–13).

CHAPTER 7

(1) Then Jerubbaal (that is, Gideon) and all the troops that were with him
rose early and encamped beside the spring of Harod; and the camp of Midian
was north of them, below the hill of Moreh, in the valley. (2) The Lord said to
Gideon, "The troops with you are too many for me to give the Midianites into
their hand. Israel would only take the credit away from me, saying 'My own
hand has delivered me.' (3) Now therefore proclaim this in the hearing of the
troops, 'Whoever is fearful and trembling, let him return home.' " Thus Gideon
sifted them out; twenty-two thousand returned, and ten thousand remained.
(4) Then the Lord said to Gideon, "The troops are still too many; take them
down to the water and I will sift them out for you there. When I say, 'This one
shall go with you,' he shall go." (5) So he brought the troops down to the water;
and the Lord said to Gideon, "All those who lap the water with their tongues, as
a dog laps, you shall put to one side; all those who kneel down to drink, putting
their hands to their mouths, you shall put to the other side." (6) The number of
those that lapped was three hundred; but all the rest of the troops knelt down
to drink water. (7) Then the Lord said to Gideon, "With the three hundred

---

[143] B. Lee, "Fragmentation of Reader Focus," *JSOT* 97 (2002): 66–68.

that lapped I will deliver you, and give the Midianites into your hand. Let all the others go to their homes." (8) So he took the jars of the troops from their hands, and their trumpets; and he sent all the rest of Israel back to their own tents, but retained the three hundred. The camp of Midian was below him in the valley. (9) That same night the Lord said to him, "Get up, attack the camp; for I have given it into your hand. (10) But if you fear to attack, go down to the camp with your servant Purah; (11) and you shall hear what they say, and afterward your hands shall be strengthened to attack the camp." Then he went down with his servant Purah to the outposts of the armed men that were in the camp. (12) The Midianites and the Amalekites and all the people of the east lay along the valley as thick as locusts; and their camels were without number, countless as the sand of the seashore. (13) When Gideon arrived, there was a man telling a dream to his comrade; and he said, "I had a dream, and in it a cake of barley bread tumbled into the camp of Midian, and came to the tent, and struck it so that it fell; it turned upside down, and the tent collapsed." (14) And his comrade answered, "This is no other than the sword of Gideon son of Joash, a man of Israel; into his hand God has given Midian and all the army." (15) When Gideon heard the telling of the dream and its interpretation, he worshiped; and he returned to the camp of Israel, and said, "Get up; for the Lord has given the army of Midian into your hand." (16) After he divided the three hundred men into three companies, and put trumpets into the hands of all of them, and empty jars; with torches inside the jars, (17) he said to them, "Look at me, and do the same; when I come to the outskirts of the camp, do as I do. (18) When I blow the trumpet, I and all who are with me, then you also blow the trumpets around the whole camp, and shout, 'For the Lord and for Gideon!'" (19) So Gideon and the hundred who were with him came to the outskirts of the camp at the beginning of the middle watch, when they had just set the watch; and they blew the trumpets and smashed the jars that were in their hands. (20) So the three companies blew the trumpets and broke the jars, holding in their left hands the torches, and in their right hands the trumpets to blow; and they cried, "A sword for the Lord and for Gideon!" (21) Every man stood in his place all around the camp, and all the men in camp ran; they cried out and fled. (22) When they blew the three hundred trumpets, the Lord set every man's sword against his fellow and against all the army; and the army fled as far as Beth-shittah toward Zererah, as far as the border of Abel-meholah, by Tabbath. (23) And the men of Israel were called out from Naphtali and from Asher and from all Manasseh, and they pursued after the Midianites.

*I*t is quite clear that this story follows the pattern set in Exod 17:8–16 (vs. Amalekites) and in Josh 6:1–21 (vs. Jericho) in which the divine warrior instructs the Israelite leader to employ a very unorthodox military strategy. In this way it is made clear that it is God who gives them a victory that would otherwise be impossible given the military odds.[144] The single variation is the explanation given by God for these instructions (v. 2). It is assumed that Moses and Joshua will follow orders and that it will be evident to the people that God is responsible for the victory. However, in the uncertainty that always seems to surround the actions in the Gideon narrative, an explanation is provided for the systematic reduction of the Israelite forces to a ridiculously low number, and these the most inattentive, least vigilant of his assembled forces (vv. 5–7).

The pattern of drawing Gideon into action continues at v. 10. Here, as in the case of his call (Judg 6:36–40) and the reduction of his troops (7:2), God provides evidence or explanation for why Gideon should obey the commands given to him. Rather than the dialogue over obedience found in Moses' call narrative (Exod 3:7–4:17), in which Moses repeatedly makes excuses for why he cannot obey God's command, in the Gideon account God anticipates that the hero will be reluctant and provides proof without being asked. This also stands in sharp contrast to the pattern found in the Joshua narrative, where the Israelite hero is given a command and he immediately, without negotiation or question, carries it out (Josh 4:15–16; 5:2–3; 6:2–7).

One explanation for this may be the unsettled, near-anarchic character of the society and its leaders in the Book of Judges. Gideon is reluctant from the very beginning, and no matter how many proofs he is given there seems to be an assumption that he must be convinced each time he is called to lead the people. What we may also have here, however, is an editorial ploy that draws the reader, like this hesitant hero, into the story where God is able to demonstrate the ability to overcome any obstacles in liberating the Israelites from their oppressors. There is also the opportunity to use non-Israelites as the voice of assurance in Yahweh's control over events, an example of the universalism theme that has been embedded into the narrative by the editor.[145] Thus when Gideon descends into the Midianite camp he hears the soldier's dream and its interpretation (7:13–14), which portrays a faith in God's power that seems to be sorely lacking among the Israelites (compare

---

[144] Ibid., 77.
[145] Victor H. Matthews, *Old Testament Themes*. St. Louis, Mo.: Chalice Press, 2000: 75–79.

Rahab's statement in Josh 2:8–11). The tension is broken at this point, with the apprehension that had been building with every mention of the size of the Midianite host canceled out by this new evidence of insecurity among the enemy soldiers. Lee terms this a "bi-polar perspective," with Gideon's fears juxtaposed by Yahweh's assurances of victory.[146]

The subsequent battle is almost an afterthought in the narrative. The nocturnal attack on the Midianite encampment takes advantage of surprise attack and the confusion caused by the lighted torches, trumpets blaring, and smashing of the pots (compare Jonathan's ploy to confuse the Philistines in 1 Sam 14:6–15). Note that Gideon's battle cry (7:18) allows him to share billing with Yahweh, exhorting the soldiers to fight for their God and their general. The additional mention of Gideon's sword (7:20) parallels its mention in the interpretation of the Midianite's dream (7:14) and may represent a belief in a magical or heroic character ascribed to the blade (compare Goliath's *+ Ehud's sword.* sword in 1 Sam 21:9).[147] Amidst the mass hysteria caused by the three small groups accompanying Gideon, the Israelite leader can count on the enemy's striking out blindly, without clear leadership. He can then drive them to flee and thus be cut down by the waiting tribal armies of Manasseh, Asher, and Naphtali (compare other routed armies in Josh 10:9–11; 1 Sam 7:10–11; 11:11).

(24) Then Gideon sent messengers throughout all the hill country of Ephraim, saying, "Come down against the Midianites and seize the waters against them, as far as Beth-barah, and also the Jordan." So all the men of Ephraim were called out, and they seized the waters as far as Beth-barah, and also the Jordan. (25) They captured the two captains of Midian, Oreb and Zeeb; they killed Oreb at the rock of Oreb, and Zeeb they killed at the winepress of Zeeb, as they pursued the Midianites. They brought the heads of Oreb and Zeeb to Gideon beyond the Jordan.

CHAPTER 8

(1) Then the Ephraimites said to him, "What have you done to us, not to call us when you went to fight the Midianites?" And they upbraided him

---

[146] B. Lee, "Fragmentation of Reader Focus," *JSOT* 97 (2002): 80–81.

[147] One indication of the importance of the leader's weapon is found in the pseudepigraphal story of Kenaz and his magical sword in LAB 27:9–12 (J. M. Charlesworth, *The Old Testament Pseudepigrapha*, vol. 2. New York: Doubleday, 1985: 339–40).

violently. (2) So he said to them, "What have I done now in comparison with you? Is not the gleaning of the grapes of Ephraim better than the vintage of Abiezer? (3) God has given into your hands the captains of Midian, Oreb and Zeeb; what have I been able to do in comparison with you?" When he said this, their anger against him subsided.

*I*n the aftermath of the battle, a mopping-up campaign is waged to complete the routing of the Midianites and to capture their leaders. The Ephraimites, who had not previously been summoned, are prominent in this later stage, using their control of the fords of the Jordan River to trap the fleeing enemy (compare the strategic control of the fords in Judg 3:28; 12:5–6). It is interesting to see the entrance of the Ephraimites so late into the story considering their control of the fords of the Jordan and their integral role in the Israelite victory (Ehud's story in Judg 3:27–29). While the list of tribes that did not heed Deborah's call to battle signals the disunity of the Israelites during this period, here, for the first time, real enmity is shown between specific Israelite tribes. The anger of the Ephraimites is based on their failure to benefit from the loot garnered from the fallen Midianites and perhaps on the loss of honor in not being called to join what was in essence an army made up of Gideon's closest allies. Unlike Jephthah in Judg 12:1–6, Gideon skillfully deflects their hostility by once again displaying his humility (cf. Judg 6:15), comparing the wealth of the Ephraimite territories and fields to the meager stores of his own Manassite clan. Reminded that they have captured the Midianite chiefs, and presumably their entourage and baggage, the Ephraimites are mollified by this diplomatic response and withdraw from further argument. The progression from full participation to a lesser role and, finally, in the Jephthah narrative to full enmity follows the pattern of going from good to bad throughout the Book of Judges.[148]

(4) Then Gideon came to the Jordan and crossed over, he and the three hundred who were with him, exhausted and famished. (5) So he said to the people of Succoth, "Please give some loaves of bread to my followers, for they are exhausted, and I am pursuing Zebah and Zalmunna, the kings of Midian." (6) But the officials of Succoth said, "Do you already have in your possession the hands of Zebah and Zalmunna, that we should give bread to your army?" (7) Gideon replied, "When then, when the Lord has given Zebah and Zalmunna into my hand, I will trample your flesh on the thorns of the wilderness and on briers."

[148] D. Jobling, "Structuralist Criticism," in *Judges and Method* (1995): 110–14.

(8) From there he went up to Penuel, and made the same request of them; and the people of Penuel answered him as the people of Succoth had answered. (9) So he said to the people of Penuel, "When I come back victorious, I will break down this tower." (10) Now Zebah and Zalmunna were in Karkor with their army, about fifteen thousand men, all who were left of all the army of the people of the east; for one hundred twenty thousand men bearing arms had fallen. (11) So Gideon went up by the caravan route east of Nobah and Jogbehah, and attacked the army; for the army was off its guard. (12) Zebah and Zalmunna fled; and he pursued them and took the two kings of Midian, Zebah and Zalmunna, and threw all the army into a panic. (13) When Gideon son of Joash returned from the battle by the ascent of Heres, (14) he caught a young man, one of the people of Succoth, and questioned him; and he listed for him the officials and elders of Succoth, seventy-seven people. (15) Then he came to the people of Succoth, and said, "Here are Zebah and Zalmunna, about whom you taunted me, saying 'Do you already have in your possession the hands of Zebah and Zalmunna, that we should give bread to your troops who are exhausted?'" (16) So he took the elders of the city and he took thorns of the wilderness and briers and with them he trampled the people of Succoth. (17) He also broke down the tower of Penuel, and killed the men of the city. (18) Then he said to Zebah and Zalmunna, "What about the men whom you killed at Tabor?" They answered, "As you are, so were they, every one of them; they resembled the sons of a king." (19) And he replied, "They were my brothers, the sons of my mother; as the Lord lives, if you had saved them alive, I would not kill you." (20) So he said to Jether his first-born, "Go kill them!" But the boy did not draw his sword, for he was afraid, because he was still a boy. (21) Then Zebah and Zalmunna said, "You come and kill us; for as the man is, so is his strength." So Gideon proceeded to kill Zebah and Zalmunna; and he took the crescents that were on the necks of their camels. *Kings of Midian.*

*I*n every war the people are called upon to choose sides. Gideon's petition on behalf of his men once again displays his humility as a leader willing to ask rather than take what he needs by force. As such, his request for food (like that of David at Nob in 1 Sam 21:2–6) functions as a means of obtaining not only nourishment but also political support.[149] In this case the people of Succoth and Penuel, who had presumably sworn allegiance or at least

[149] Compare the gift of loaves to Saul from a group of three men going to worship God at Bethel in 1 Sam 10:3–4. Samuel has just anointed the young man as ruler of the Israelites, and this is one of a series of events on his homeward path that collectively serve as acknowledgment by the people of Saul's new political role.

neutrality to the Midianite kings, now are being asked by Gideon to supply his troops with food. If they do so, then they will be subject to the wrath of the Midianites, who they quite obviously believe are stronger than Gideon's small army. Instead of extending hospitality to Gideon's forces, the leaders of Succoth, like the wealthy landowner Nabal in the David narrative (1 Sam 25:2–11), mock the Israelite leader, who may or may not come to power. And like Nabal, they will come to a bad end. Gideon's predictive threats therefore provide a narrative path that will close with the promised destruction in Judg 8:13–17.

This portion of the narrative is filled with hostile retorts and acts of retribution, little of which has anything to do with serving as Yahweh's representative or as the champion of the covenant.[150] Gideon is set on destroying the Midianite army and on capturing Midian's kings. However, he has also sworn to provide full recompense to the cities that had taunted him and refused to aid his famished army (compare David's order in 2 Sam 5:6–8 vs. the taunting Jebusites). In addition, the blood guilt incurred by Zebah and Zalmunna for slaying members of Gideon's household must be addressed (compare Joab's slaying of Abner in 2 Sam 3:27–30). Gideon's order to his young son to execute these two kings is also an example of requiting a debt based on blood guilt. His order may be a sign that this young man is Gideon's heir, but it also dishonors the kings. They at least expect to die at the hands of a peer capable of delivering a swift, killing blow, not a boy who would lack the strength for an efficient execution. Gideon, once again facing a public challenge, even if from two condemned men, must then take action and execute them himself (compare Samuel's humiliation of Saul when he executes the Amalekite king Agag in 1 Sam 15:32–33).

(22) Then the Israelites said to Gideon, "Rule over us, you and your son and your grandson also; for you have delivered us out of the hand of Midian." (23) Gideon said to them, "I will not rule over you, and my son will not rule over you; the Lord will rule over you." (24) Then Gideon said to them, "Let me make a request of you; each of you give me an earring he has taken as booty." (For the enemy had golden earrings, because they were Ishmaelites.) (25) "We will willingly give them," they answered. So they spread a garment, and each threw into it an earring he had taken as booty. (26) The weight of the golden earrings that he requested was one thousand seven hundred shekels

---

[150] Robert H. O'Connell, *The Rhetoric of the Book of Judges*. VTSup 3. Leiden, Neth.: Brill, 1996: 157.

of gold (apart from the crescents and the pendants and the purple garments worn by the kings of Midian, and the collars that were on the necks of their camels). (27) Gideon made an ephod of it and put it in his town in Ophrah; and all Israel prostituted themselves to it there, and it became a snare to Gideon and to his family. (28) So Midian was subdued before the Israelites, and they lifted up their heads no more. So the land had rest forty years in the days of Gideon.

The offer of kingship to Gideon serves as a precursor to the Saul narrative in 1 Samuel 9–11. Given the relative prosperity and more unified character of the territory of Manasseh, it would appear that they were ripe for the establishment of a chiefdom, which would be a step toward a monarchy.[151] Gideon's refusal of this position is in character, based on previous examples, of both his humility as well as his stated reluctance to accept responsibility. However, he is quick to assume the rights and privileges of a monarch and demonstrate that he is no longer the same meek young man grinding his grain in a winepress.[152] He shows his new desire for power by (1) requesting a portion of the spoil from his army, (2) keeping for himself the symbols of wealth and authority held by the Midianite kings (camel crescents, purple robes, and pendants of office), and (3) serving as the sponsor of cultic activity by authorizing the creation of an "ephod" (possibly a richly decorated garment meant to adorn the statue of a god).[153]

The division of spoils after a battle was considered a sacred act by ancient Near Eastern armies. Mari documents (ARM 2 13:25–36; 5 72:5–24′) record the indignation caused when an officer took more than he was entitled to from the store of booty, and his punishment was based on his having violated their rights.[154] Thus Gideon's request for a portion of the loot (golden earrings weighing 43 pounds) must be couched in such a way that it does not appear that he is infringing on their rightful share. They had freely offered him the kingship, and in refusing them he seems to be asking that they sacrifice a portion of the spoil as an offering to Yahweh, the divine warrior who had brought them the victory.

what happened to "the Lord will rule over you"?!

---

[151] S. Scham, "Days of the Judges," *JSOT* 97 (2002): 56; Victor H. Matthews and Don C. Benjamin, *The Social World of Ancient Israel*. Peabody, Mass.: Hendrickson, 1993: 96–101.

[152] J. Marais, *Representation in Old Testament* (1998): 113–14.

[153] D. I. Block, "Will the Real Gideon Please Stand Up?" *JETS* 40 (1997a): 361, n. 35, suggests this explanation based on the Akkadian word *epattu*, a garment "worn by high officials and/or draped over images of gods."

[154] Victor H. Matthews, "The Role of the *RABI AMURRIM* in the Mari Kingdom," *JNES* 38 (1979): 131.

It is the erection of an ephod as an object of worship in Gideon's home city of Ophrah that ultimately will replace the altar to Baal as a religious "trap" for the people of Israel. By doing this, Gideon encourages the same idolatrous pattern that he had worked to destroy. This feature of the story provides an inclusio to the narrative: beginning and ending with activity at a cultic installation. It also begs the question of the effects on a judge of the infusion of God's spirit. Why would someone who had been personally chosen and strengthened by Yahweh choose to set up an object that could cause the people to "prostitute themselves" and become a "snare" to his own family (v. 27)? It may be that the failure of the judges to retain their loyalties to God or to focus their energies entirely to serving God's plan for the people is simply a reflection of the covenantal failures of the people as a whole during this period.[155]

While Gideon's narrative continues in chapter 9 with the tale of Abimelech's aborted attempt to claim the kingship that his father had, at least officially, rejected, in many ways it is the prostituting of the people that ties the entire piece together.[156] Joash had challenged Baal to contend with Gideon/Jerubbaal, and apparently Baal wins.[157]

(29) Jerubbaal son of Joash went to live in his own house. (30) Now Gideon had seventy sons, his own offspring, for he had many wives. (31) His concubine who was in Shechem also bore him a son, and he named him Abimelech. (32) Then Gideon son of Joash died at a good old age, and was buried in the tomb of his father Joash at Ophrah of the Abiezrites. (33) As soon as Gideon died, the Israelites relapsed and prostituted themselves with the Baals, making Baal-berith their god. (34) The Israelites did not remember the Lord their God, who had rescued them from the hand of all their enemies on every side; (35) and they did not exhibit loyalty to the house of Jerubbaal (that is, Gideon) in return for all the good that he had done to Israel.

the Israelites relapsed. 8:3↑3

This segment of text forms an unusual postscript to the Gideon account. Up to this point in the Judges account, the editor employs a formula statement (Judg 8:28b) that "the land had rest _____ years in the days of _____" (compare 3:11; 3:30). The parallel here, however, is to Joshua at the end of his career (Judg 2:6–10). Like Joshua (Josh 19:49–50), Gideon

---

155 See D. I. Block, "Empowered by the Spirit of God," *SBJT* 1 (1997b): 42–61, for a more complete examination of this concept of the empowering of an individual by the spirit of God.

156 R. H. O'Connell, *Rhetoric of the Book of Judges* (1996): 139–71.

157 D. I. Block, "Will the Real Gideon Please Stand Up?" *JETS* 40 (1997a): 365.

retires to his family estates and seemingly disappears from both the public eye and memory. This form of selective memory also applies to the people's appreciation of Yahweh's actions as the divine warrior and their covenant partner. Thus the emotional call of Jotham (Judg 9:16–20) for the people to remember how Gideon/Jerubbaal had fought for them is also a call to remember their covenant obligations to Yahweh. Joshua is portrayed late in life exhorting the people to remain true to the covenant and conducting a covenant renewal ceremony at Shechem (Josh 23–24:28), but like Gideon (Judg 8:33), the memory of Joshua's endeavors die with him (Judg 2:10).

It is interesting to note that Jacob had seventy descendants (Exod 1:5) and that King Ahab is also said to have had "seventy sons" (2 Kings 10:1). Quite likely this is simply a number signifying "many" (as in Judg 1:7; 1 Sam 6:19) or is tied to a sort of sabbatical structure as seems to be the case for the seventy elders of Israel (Exod 24:1; Num 11:16). Its relation to an idealized number for a royal household or even the pantheon of gods has been suggested as well.[158] It also stands in contrast to the one son who will destroy the seventy and whose deeds may be foreshadowed by his name, meaning "my father is king." Perhaps this is Gideon's way of signaling that he accepted his leadership role and expected it to be passed on to his heir. To be more consistent with regard to his character, however, Gideon more likely chose this name as an indicator that Yahweh, "the God–father," is the patron of this child.[159] Abimelech's actions indicate that he preferred to rely on Jerubbaal's reputation rather than Yahweh's and that choice signals the irony and inevitability of his ultimate fall.[160]

CHAPTER 9

(1) Now Abimelech son of Jerubbaal went to Shechem to his mother's kinsfolk and said to them and to the whole clan of his mother's family, (2) "Say in the hearing of all the lords of Shechem, 'Which is better for you, that all seventy of the sons of Jerubbaal rule over you, or that one rule over you?' Remember also that I am your bone and your flesh." (3) So his mother's kinsfolk spoke all these words on his behalf in the hearing of all the lords of Shechem; and their hearts inclined to follow Abimelech, for they said, "He is our brother."

[158] Ibid., 362; F. C. Fensham, "Numeral Seventy in the Old Testament and the Family of Jerubbaal, Ahab, Panammuwa and Athirat," *PEQ* 109 (1977): 113–15.

[159] R. G. Boling, *Judges* (1975): 163.

[160] L. R. Klein, *The Triumph of Irony* (1989): 71.

(4) They gave him seventy pieces of silver out of the temple of Baal-berith with which Abimelech hired worthless and reckless fellows, who followed him. (5) He went to his father's house at Ophrah, and killed his brothers the sons of Jerubbaal, seventy men, on one stone; but Jotham, the youngest son of Jerubbaal, survived, for he hid himself. (6) Then all the lords of Shechem and all Beth-millo came together, and they went and made Abimelech king, by the oak of the pillar at Shechem. (7) When it was told to Jotham, he went and stood on the top of Mt. Gerizim, and cried aloud and said to them, "Listen to me, you lords of Shechem, so that God may listen to you. (8) The trees once went out to anoint a king over themselves. So they said to the olive tree, 'Reign over us.' (9) The olive tree answered them, 'Shall I stop producing my rich oil by which gods and mortals are honored, and go to sway over the trees?' (10) Then the trees said to the fig tree, 'You come and reign over us.' (11) But the fig tree answered them, 'Shall I stop producing my sweetness and my delicious fruit, and go to sway over the trees?' (12) Then the trees said to the vine, 'You come and reign over us.' (13) But the vine said to them, 'Shall I stop producing my wine that cheers gods and mortals, and go to sway over the trees?' (14) So all the trees said to the bramble, 'You come and reign over us.' (15) And the bramble said to the trees, 'If in good faith you are anointing me king over you, then come and take refuge in my shade; but if not, let fire come out of the bramble and devour the cedars of Lebanon.' (16) Now therefore, if you acted in good faith and honor when you made Abimelech king, and if you have dealt well with Jerubbaal and his house, and have done to him as his actions deserved – (17) for my father fought for you, and risked his life, and rescued you from the hand of Midian; (18) but you have risen up against my father's house this day, and have killed his sons, seventy men on one stone, and have made Abimelech, the son of his slave woman, king over the lords of Shechem, because he is your kinsman – (19) if, I say, you have acted in good faith and honor with Jerubbaal and with his house this day, then rejoice in Abimelech, and let him also rejoice in you; (20) but if not, let fire come out from Abimelech, and devour the lords of Shechem, and Beth-millo; and let fire come out from the lords of Shechem, and from Beth-millo, and devour Abimelech." (21) Then Jotham ran away and fled, going to Beer, where he remained for fear of his brother Abimelech.

The Abimelech narrative is a continuation of the tale of Gideon and should not be seen as a separate story.[161] While Gideon is drawn, reluctantly, into the role of judge by Yahweh, he ultimately takes up the task and derives great benefit from it in terms of political power and wealth. One sign

---

[161] B. G. Webb, *Book of Judges* (1987): 154–59.

of this is in the sheer number of sons that he has. However, the storyteller is always quick to turn what seems to be a tale of prosperity and personal success into one filled with irony and spiraling fortunes. Thus the seventy sons become one and the notoriety becomes ignominy.

Boogaart, using the model first advanced by Koch,[162] identifies a "retribution theme" in these events that is designed to ensure that the reader understands that those leaders who take advantage of their position to oppress the people and become tyrants ultimately must, as a consequence of their own actions, face the retribution of God. In fact, this is perhaps better termed reciprocity based on the concept that "the doer of mischief suffers in return the same evil he has inflicted on another."[163]

Karma

Given this overriding theme of retributive reciprocity, one way to interpret the story of Abimelech's rise to power is to examine the repeated use of specific numbers in each episode.[164] In his speech to the elders of Shechem, Abimelech makes the persuasive case that it is better to be ruled by one rather than by seventy. Acknowledging the logic of this argument and Abimelech's claim of clan ties through his mother, the elders of Shechem give him "seventy" coins, with which he hires a small army. This in turn allows him to round up his "seventy" brothers. He kills them all on "one" stone, but "one" survives, setting up a later challenge and Abimelech's death at the hands of a single woman wielding a single stone. The interchange of the numbers one and seventy and the repeated mention of a stone thereby carry the narrative along and signal its ironic nature.[165]

An unusual aspect of Abimelech's speech is his invocation of maternal kin ties as the basis for his request for support. Ancient Israelite society was dominated by adherence to patrilineal descent, and one would expect him first to make reference to his father.[166] In Abimelech's case, of course, he is the least of Gideon/Jerubbaal's sons as the child of a secondary, and quite possibly non-Israelite, wife (*pîlegeš*: traditionally translated as "concubine"). His claim to his father's estate or leadership is so tenuous that he must resort to a quite remarkable and unconventional strategy. It can be posited that the elders of Shechem choose to accept his kinship claim primarily because they

[162] Thomas A. Boogaart, "Stone for Stone: Retribution in the Story of Abimelech and Shechem," *JSOT* 32 (1985): 47–48; Klaus Koch, "Gibt es ein Vergeltungsdogma im Alten Testament?" *ZTK* 52 (1955): 1–42.

[163] K. Koch, "Gibt es ein Vergeltungsdogma?" *ZTK* 52 (1955): 32.

[164] J. G. Janzen, "A Certain Woman in the Rhetoric of Judges 9," *JSOT* 38 (1987): 35.

[165] Graham S. Ogden, "Jotham's Fable: Its Structure and Function in Judges 9," *Bible Translator* 46 (1995): 302.

[166] Naomi Steinberg, "Social Scientific Criticism: Judges 9 and Issues of Kinship." Pages 57–60 in *Judges and Method.* Edited by Gale A. Yee. Minneapolis: Fortress Press, 1995.

see this as their opportunity to gain greater economic and political power within the central hill country of Manasseh and Ephraim now that the Midianites have been driven out by Gideon.[167] Perhaps they thought their seventy pieces of silver bought both loyalty and control over Abimelech, but they were quick to learn, as Jerubbaal's sons did, that there was to be only one power broker and that was Abimelech.

A CLOSER LOOK AT MARRIAGE CUSTOMS

Marriage is often thought of as an orchestrated event, with certain protocols being followed that were designed to establish the alliance between families and to spell out the contract in exact terms. Within the structure of a patriarchal household, it would be expected that the father or the eldest brother would negotiate the arrangement of marriage with the bride's parents or "guardians" (Gen 24:52–54).[168] The various factors weighed in the negotiations of a marriage involved social parity, economic advantage, and expansion of the kinship network.

Social parity was always a minimum goal. No family wanted to marry down socially, at least when arranging the contract for the first wife. Thus the participants had to be at least of the same social class and have approximately the same economic standing. In this way marriages served not only to produce children and a new generation to inherit property but also to establish social ties, economic connections, and a network of association that benefited both parties. Other considerations included kinship obligations (Gen 24:3–4), political advancement (see David's marriages to Michal in 1 Sam 18:17–28 and to Ahinoam in 1 Sam 25:43), and, occasionally, personal desire (Exod 22:16; Judg 14:3; 2 Sam 11:27). The contractual arrangement consisted of several parts in addition to the mutual agreement for the couple to wed. These included the giving of a bride-price (*terḫatum* in Akkadian texts) and prenuptial agreements regarding potential divorce by either party. There may also have been stipulations on obligations regarding debts and, depending on the social status of the bride, the exact inheritance rights of their children.

The concluding of a marriage contract between families was a sacred compact, comparable to the covenant agreement made with Yahweh (see

---

167 Ibid., 60.
168 Samuel Greengus, "Old Babylonian Marriage Ceremonies and Rites," *JCS* 20 (1966): 59.

Ezek 16:8). The "pledge" agreement set a bride-price as well as the amount of the dowry (Exod 22:16–17), guaranteed that the bride would be a virgin at the time of marriage (Deut 22:13–21), and required complete fidelity of the parties. Marriage was such an important economic and social factor in the ancient Near East that it was the basis of a huge amount of legislation. For instance, the Laws of Eshnunna 28–29 and CH 128 explain the importance of having an official marriage contract for both parties. The latter simply states, "If a man marries a wife but does not draw up a formal contract for her, she is not a wife."[169]

By consummating the marriage, both parties fulfill the oral arrangements and legal technicalities that had been decided by their representatives. They had therefore changed their legal status and their social standing within the community. In addition, the wife now lived under her husband's name and benefited from his protection and social standing.[170]

For purposes of legal identification, however, the Old Testament has no specific term for wife, other than 'iššâ (woman). Still, since not all marriages were based on economic and social parity, some women came to their husband's household without a dowry[171] and were therefore considered to be a secondary wife or "concubine" (pîlegeš). To be sure, the husband of a wife or concubine was still obligated to provide her with "food, clothing, and oil" (Exod 21:10).[172] Where the legal difference arose was in the sense of unquestioned membership in a specific household and in the inheritance rights of the children of a concubine.[173] They were not recognized as their father's heir nor could they share in his estate without being specifically named by him (see Gen 35:22).[174] Thus Abimelech was forced to seek aid from his

---

[169] Martha T. Roth, *Law Collections from Mesopotamia and Asia Minor.* Atlanta: Scholars Press, 1995: 105.

[170] Karel van der Toorn, *Family Religion in Babylonia, Syria and Israel.* Leiden, Neth.: Brill, 1996: 47.

[171] A full discussion of the biblical and cuneiform legal materials centering on the giving of a dowry and its implications for inheritance is found in Raymond Westbrook, *Property and the Family in Biblical Laws.* JSOTSup 113. Sheffield, Eng.: Sheffield Academic Press, 1991: 142–64.

[172] Shalom Paul, "Exod 21:10: A Three-fold Maintenance Clause," *JNES* 28 (1969): 48–51.

[173] Karla G. Bohmbach, "Conventions/Contraventions: The Meanings of Public and Private for the Judges 19 Concubine," *JSOT* 83 (1999): 97.

[174] Samuel Greengus, "Sisterhood Adoption at Nuzi and the 'Wife-Sister' in Genesis," *HUCA* 46 (1975): 15–16, finds precedent for this secondary status for women who either lack a dowry or bring very little into the marriage in the Nuzi documents. In several of these cases involving an *ahatūtu* (adopted sister), the women were originally manumitted slaves.

mother's kinship group rather than his father's (Judg 9:1–4), and the concubine in Judg 19 seems to have had few personal rights and was "sacrificed" with apparently little regret by her Levite husband (19:24–29).[175]

The prominence of trees as reference points in biblical stories suggests that they served cultic as well as benchmark purposes.[176] Thus "the oak of the pillar" at Shechem is reminiscent of Abraham's oak of Mamre (Gen 18:1),[177] Gideon's "oak at Ophrah" (6:11), and Deborah's palm tree (4:5). Comparison can also be drawn with the oak at Shechem where Joshua conducted his covenant renewal ceremony and the stone that he placed beneath the tree near the sanctuary on that site (Josh 24:25–26). The ethnic makeup of the people of Shechem in the Joshua account is unknown, although it is likely that the editor of this material would not have placed such an important cultic event in the midst of a Canaanite settlement. The political events surrounding the Abimelech episode, however, do not have these constraints, and it is quite possible that the people of Shechem at that time were predominantly Canaanite, which lowers Abimelech's status as an ethnically mixed member of Jerubbaal's household.[178] It may also indicate that the pillar and oak were associated with Baal/Asherah worship (see 2 Kings 3:2; 10:27).

Parables are a fairly rare occurrence in the Hebrew Bible (e.g., Nathan's parable of the ewe lamb in 1 Sam 12), but they are found more often in the wisdom literature of the ancient Near East, for example, the story of the "Heron and the Turtle" (*COS* 1.178: 571) and two segments of the "Sayings of Ahiqar." These entertaining sayings provide the storyteller the opportunity to make a subtle point while allowing readers to draw their own conclusions about the staged situation.

SAYINGS OF AHIQAR (SEVENTH-CENTURY BCE ASSYRIAN)

> Once there was a leopard, who was hungry. Once there was a goat, who was cold. The leopard asked, "Would you like my coat, would you like me to cover you?" The goat answered, "What comfort is your coat? You only want my hide."[179]

---

[175] Phyllis Trible, *Texts of Terror: Literary-Feminist Readings of Biblical Narratives.* Philadelphia: Fortress Press, 1984: 66–79.

[176] Kirsten Nielsen, *There Is Hope for a Tree: The Tree as Metaphor in Isaiah.* JSOTSup 65. Sheffield, Eng.: JSOT Press, 1989: 74–85.

[177] F. Nigel Hepper and Shimon Gibson, "Abraham's Oak of Mamre: The Story of a Venerable Tree," *PEQ* 126 (1994): 94–105.

[178] T. J. Schneider, *Judges* (2000): 134–36.

[179] viii:118; Victor H. Matthews and Don C. Benjamin, *Old Testament Parallels: Laws and Stories from the Ancient Near East.* Mahwah, N.J.: Paulist Press, 1997: 285–86.

A thorn bush asked a pomegranate tree, "Why so many thorns to protect so little fruit?" The pomegranate tree said, "Why so many thorns to protect no fruit at all?"[180]

In the case of Jotham's parable, the sole surviving son of Jerubbaal uses apolitical creatures to make political predictions about the disastrous choice of the elders of Shechem. While there is no direct condemnation of the choice of the bramble as king, it is left to the reader to decide based upon Abimelech's subsequent actions.[181] It is possible that this parable is a late addition to the story of Abimelech, but it serves as an artful device foreshadowing Abimelech's and Shechem's eventual ruin.[182]

One curiosity is Jotham's use of Shechem and specifically Mt. Gerizim as the stage for his public complaint against Abimelech. Shechem's place in Israelite history goes back to Abram's first entrance into the Promised Land and his construction of an altar there. Subsequently, its cultic associations continue with Moses and Joshua (see Deut 11:29; Josh 8:33), and its political nature is found in the story of the "rape of Dinah" and Rehoboam's confrontation with the elders of the northern tribes (see table). The account in Deut 27:11–28 identifies Mt. Gerizim and Mt. Ebal as cultic centers from which the Levites pronounce blessings and curses based on obedience or disobedience to the covenant.[183] Jotham's parable and curse therefore occur on a significant site and thereby obtain greater authority in their condemnation of Abimelech and the lords of Shechem.

TRACING EVENTS AT SHECHEM

Initial Event	Subsequent Event #1	Subsequent Event #2	Subsequent Event #3
Abram first arrives in Canaan and builds an altar to God (Gen 12:6–7)	Rape of Dinah; massacre of men of Shechem by Jacob's sons (Gen 34:2–26)	Joshua stages covenant renewal ceremony after the conquest (Josh 24:1–32)	Rehoboam meets with tribal elders; kingdom divides (1 Kings 12:1–17)

---

[180] xi:165; V. H. Matthews and D. C. Benjamin, *Old Testament Parallels* (1997): 287.

[181] J. Marais, *Representation in Old Testament* (1998): 116.

[182] Volkmar Fritz, "Abimelech und Sichem in Jdc. IX," *VT* 32 (1982): 129–44, identifies the fable as originally unrelated to the Abimelech narrative strand. According to this interpretation Jotham's fable is plugged into this episode to reinforce the idea that Shechem has made a bad decision by raising Abimelech to power.

[183] Richard D. Nelson, *Deuteronomy: A Commentary*. OTL. Louisville, Ky.: Westminster/John Knox, 2002: 315–16.

The repetitive, rhetorical structure of the parable indicates the importance of the fruit trees and vineyards in ancient Israel. In Syria-Palestine, the favorable climate and topography allowed for the maintenance of vineyards and their attendant installations (such as winepresses) in nearly every village in the hill country. Ugaritic sources contain more mentions of wine than oil, thereby indicating how extensive the vineyards were in that area of northern Syria and how valuable a commodity wine was.[184] Another sign of just how pervasive viticulture was in the Israelite village culture can be found in Ahlstrom's survey of the Megiddo area.[185] He discovered 117 winepresses of various types at small sites radiating from Megiddo's urban center. Some of the installations discovered contained two pressing floors, indicating both the size of the harvest and a dual process in extracting the juice.[186] It took four or five years for vineyards to mature, and the law prohibited the consumption of the grapes until the fifth year (Lev 19:24–25). It is therefore understandable that there would be great joy when they are finally harvested and processed in the winepress.

The large number of instances in which the Hebrew prophets mention the vineyard or use it as a metaphor for the Israelites points up the high value of viticulture in the ancient Near East (e.g., Jer 2:21; Ezek 17:5–6; Hos 10:1). As Sasson notes, its economic importance made it a natural metaphor for stability and prosperity (2 Kings 4:25; Isa 36:16).[187] And, the loss of the vineyard easily served to demonstrate the height of religious and economic disorder (Jer 8:13; Joel 1:11–12). Thus the refusal of the vine, as well as the fruit-bearing trees in this parable, makes good economic sense. They should be allowed to continue to serve the needs of the people and thereby maintain their prosperity.

The break in the thrice-repeated rhetorical structure, when the kingship is offered to the bramble, jars the reader but also focuses attention on this most important element in the now-dislocated sequence.[188] The transparent metaphor of the bramble equated with Abimelech then stands out as the blatant risk taken by the elders of Shechem. The bramble grows where no

---

[184] Michael Heltzer, "Vineyards and Wine in Ugarit," *UF* 22 (1991): 119.

[185] Gosta W. Ahlstrom, "Wine Presses and Cup-Marks of the Jenin-Megiddo Survey," *BASOR* 231 (1978): 20.

[186] LaMoine F. DeVries, "Ancient Winepresses," *Biblical Illustrator* 8 (1982): 68.

[187] Jack M. Sasson, "The Blood of Grapes: Viticulture and Intoxication in the Hebrew Bible." Page 401 in *Drinking in Ancient Societies: History and Culture of Drinks in the Ancient Near East*. Edited by Lucio Milano. HANE Studies, 6. Padua, Italy: Sargon, 1994.

[188] G. S. Ogden, "Jotham's Fable," *Bible Translator* 46 (1995): 303.

other vegetation can, and thus it becomes an apt symbol of wilderness, and as such the equation can be made between Abimelech and the chaos associated with the untamed and dangerous wilderness areas (see Exod 14:11; 16:3; Deut 8:11–16). For instance, his use of trees to stoke the fires he uses to destroy the tower at Shechem (Judg 9:46–49) provides a graphic example of the type of human and ecological disaster he could cause.[189] Although the text is not explicit about whether he cuts down valuable, fruit-bearing trees (a violation of Deut 20:19–20), his rage is such that any thing that came to hand would probably be thrown on the blaze. His demise will restore order to the area and drive back the wilderness/chaos from the "civilized" areas of Manasseh and Ephraim.

(22) Abimelech ruled over Israel three years. (23) But God sent an evil spirit between Abimelech and the lords of Shechem; and the lords of Shechem dealt treacherously with Abimelech. (24) This happened so that the violence done to the seventy sons of Jerubbaal might be avenged and their blood be laid on their brother Abimelech, who killed them, and on the lords of Shechem, who strengthened his hands to kill his brothers. (25) So, out of hostility to him, the lords of Shechem set ambushes on the mountain tops. They robbed all who passed by them along that way; and it was reported to Abimelech. (26) When Gaal son of Ebed moved into Shechem with his kinsfolk, the lords of Shechem put confidence in him. (27) They went out into the field and gathered the grapes from their vineyards, trod them, and celebrated. Then they went into the temple of their god, ate and drank, and ridiculed Abimelech. (28) Gaal son of Ebed said, "Who is Abimelech and who are we of Shechem, that we should serve him? Did not the son of Jerubbaal and Zebul his officer serve the men of Hamor father of Shechem? Why then should we serve him? (29) If only this people were under my command? Then I would remove Abimelech; I would say to him, 'Increase your army, and come out.'" (30) When Zebul the ruler of the city heard the words of Gaal son of Ebed, his anger was kindled. (31) He sent messengers to Abimelech at Arumah saying, "Look, Gaal son of Ebed and his kinsfolk have come to Shechem, and they are stirring up the city against you. (32) Now therefore, go by night, you and the troops that are with you, and lie in wait in the fields. (33) Then early in the morning, as soon as the sun rises, get up and rush on the city; and when he and the troops that are with him come out against you, you may deal with them as best you can." (34) So Abimelech and all the troops with him got up by night and lay in wait

---

[189] S. Scham, "Days of the Judges," *JSOT* 97 (2002): 57.

against Shechem in four companies. (35) When Gaal son of Ebed went out and stood in the entrance of the gate of the city, Abimelech and the troops with him rose from the ambush. (36) And when Gaal saw them, he said to Zebul, "Look, people are coming down from the mountaintops!" And Zebul said to him, "The shadows on the mountains look like people to you." (37) Gaal spoke again and said, "Look, people are coming down from Tabbur-erez, and one company is coming from the direction of Elon-meonenim." (38) Then Zebul said to him, "Where is your boast now, you who said, 'Who is Abimelech, that we should serve him?' Are not these the troops you made light of? Go out now and fight with them." (39) So Gaal went out at the head of the lords of Shechem, and fought with Abimelech. (40) Abimelech chased him, and he fled before him. Many fell wounded, up to the entrance to the gate. (41) So Abimelech resided at Arumah; and Zebul drove out Gaal and his kinsfolk, so that they could not live on at Shechem. (42) On the following day the people went out into the fields. When Abimelech was told, (43) he took his troops and divided them into three companies, and lay in wait in the fields. When he looked and saw the people coming out of the city, he rose against them and killed them. (44) Abimelech and the company that was with him rushed forward and stood at the entrance of the gate of the city, while the two companies rushed on all who were in the fields and killed them. (45) Abimelech fought against the city all that day; he took the city, and killed the people that were in it; and he razed the city and sowed it with salt. (46) When all the lords of the Tower of Shechem heard of it, they entered the stronghold of the temple of El-berith. (47) Abimelech was told that all the lords of the Tower of Shechem were gathered together. (48) So Abimelech went up to Mount Zalmon, he and all the troops that were with him. Abimelech took an ax in his hand, cut down a bundle of brushwood, and took it up and laid it on his shoulder. Then he said to the troops with him, "What you have seen me do, do quickly, as I have done." (49) So every one of the troops cut down a bundle and following Abimelech put it against the stronghold, and they set the stronghold on fire over them, so that all the people of the Tower of Shechem also died, about a thousand men and women. (50) Then Abimelech went to Thebez, and encamped against Thebez, and took it. (51) But there was a strong tower within the city, and all the men and women and all the lords of the city fled to it and shut themselves in; and they went to the roof of the tower. (52) Abimelech came to the tower, and fought against it, and came near to the entrance of the tower to burn it with fire. (53) But a certain woman threw an upper millstone on Abimelech's head, and crushed his skull. (54) Immediately he called to the young man who carried his armor and said to him, "Draw your sword and kill me, so people will not say about me, 'A woman killed him.'" So the young man thrust him through, and he died. (55) **When the Israelites saw that Abimelech was dead, they all went home.** (56) Thus God repaid Abimelech for the crime he committed against his father in killing his seventy brothers; (57) and God also made all the wickedness of the people of Shechem fall back on their heads, and on them came the curse of Jotham son of Jerubbaal.

*T*he apparent use of an "evil spirit" as Yahweh's operative device for creating a split between Abimelech and his allies may be a literary vehicle that allows the editor to make clear that there is a divine touch involved in these events (compare the "lying spirit" sent to Ahab in 1 Kings 22:19–23 and the "evil spirit from the Lord" sent to torment Saul in 1 Sam 16:14).[190] On a more fundamental level, however, it may be that the growing disaffection (i.e., "evil intentions") between the leaders of Shechem and Abimelech is based on the Shechemites feeling that they were not receiving adequate value for their support of the warlord. In both cases the sphere of evil that encompasses both parties is based on their greed and that neither truly trusts the other.[191]

Possibly the elders thought that they could control Abimelech or that he would remove their rivals (compare the deal struck by Jephthah with the leaders of Gilead in Judg 11:5–11). Certainly, they hoped this gambit would allow them to take economic advantage of the situation now that the Midianite raiders had been driven from their lands. Their "ambushes" were probably similar to the kind of preying on caravans and farmsteads that the Midianites had done (Judg 6:2–6). Abimelech, of course, expected to control all of the economic resources of the region and was not going to be pleased when the men of Shechem began operating on their own. They were driving off the merchants whom he expected to charge for safe passage through that area.

The appearance of a potential rival to Abimelech, in the person of Gaal, must have heartened the leaders of Shechem since it would keep Abimelech occupied and out of their business. That Gaal brings "kinsfolk" with him also means that they will not have to pay out any additional monies to hire mercenaries, as they did for Abimelech, and it strengthens their defenses against Abimelech's forces. Their drunken celebration in the temple of their god shows not only their foolhardy bravado but also their

---

[190] The editorial aside in v. 24, like that in Judg 14:4, may have functioned as a quick reminder to the reader of why events took a particular turn. Or, it may be a sign of the redactor providing a theological explanation for what may originally have been a secular tale.

[191] T. A. Boogaart, "Stone for Stone," *JSOT* 32 (1985): 56, n. 12.

nonworship of Yahweh. This adds to the case being made by the storyteller that Shechem will be destroyed once again for its violations of custom and its greed.[192]

Gaal's rhetorical challenge to Abimelech has affinities to the speech of Absalom when he challenged his father David's authority to rule Israel (2 Sam 15:1–6). In both cases these men raise their arms to heaven and wistfully proclaim, "If only I were a judge in the land" (2 Sam 15:4). Both play upon discontent and the desire for change that is ever a part of the political climate in ancient and modern times. Gaal also insults Abimelech in absentia reminding his audience of Abimelech's low birth (compare Nabal's insult to David in 1 Sam 25:10) and calling on him, as if he were a coward, to come out and fight. Ironically, Gaal labels Abimelech and Zebul as "servants." However, Gaal is always referred to in the narrative as the son of Ebed, which means servant.[193]

Zebul, Abimelech's appointed governor (*pāqîd*) in Shechem, secretly calls on his master to attack Shechem and to destroy Gaal's forces.[194] The strategy of attack is similar to the one employed against Ai in Josh 8:10–17, in which the Israelites divide their own forces into companies and make an early morning ambush. They use the rising sun as a way of distorting the size of the Israelite forces in front of the city, draw the enemy to fight in the open rather than remain within the walls of the city, and then send groups of soldiers into the enemy from the rear (in Abimelech's case from Mt. Gerizim to the south of the city). Throughout the episode, Zebul functions as an agent provocateur. In an almost comic exchange, he first reassures Gaal and then taunts him into precipitous action that makes his forces easy prey for Abimelech's army.[195]

Abimelech's unreasoned excesses in destroying the city[196] and its people harkens back to Shechem's destruction at the hands of Jacob's sons in Gen 34:25–30. Certainly, the treachery of the elders of Shechem justifies a measure of punishment, but Abimelech is vindictive in his trapping ordinary citizens in the fields and cutting them off from escape through the city

---

[192] In the story of the "rape of Dinah" the son of the king violates Jacob's daughter and then he and his father justify his action as one that will, after they submit to circumcision, bring great economic prosperity to their city (Gen 34:20–24).

[193] R. G. Boling, *Judges* (1975): 176.

[194] M. Reviv, "The Government of Sichem in the Amarna Period and in the Days of Abimelek," *IEJ* 16 (1966): 255.

[195] J. A. Soggin, *Judges* (1987): 188.

[196] It is unclear what the significance of sowing the remains of the city with salt entails. While it could be symbolic of sterility, as in Deut 29:23 in reference to Sodom, salt is also used to purify, as in Elisha's cleansing of the polluted water in 2 Kings 2:20–21.

gates. Furthermore, his fiery destruction of the tower along with a thousand people is matched in its callous disregard for life only in his father Gideon's destruction of the Tower of Penuel (Judg 8:17) and in Samson's pulling down the temple of Dagon in Judg 16:29–30.[197]

The fire and destruction predicted in Jotham's parable (Judg 9:15, 20) takes tangible and graphic form in these events.[198] Fire represents the devastation promised by the bramble if its "conditions" are not met.[199] In an editorial aside, the storyteller draws the tale full circle by placing the doom of Abimelech and Shechem squarely on their own heads.[200]

The obvious convergences between the conclusions of the Jael/Sisera story and the Abimelech/"certain woman" account suggest both an evident editorial hand as well as a common thread in which villains are destroyed by an unlikely hero, a woman.[201] If Yee is correct, then the woman at Thebez contributes to the war effort by casting her stone onto Abimelech's head just as Jael did her part by dispatching Sisera when she had the chance.[202]

Note that a clear contrast can be made between Abimelech's final request and King Saul's. When asked to dispatch his master, Abimelech's armorbearer immediately obeys. However, when Saul makes a similar request, his armor-bearer is "terrified," perhaps because of the claim made by David in 1 Sam 24:6, 10 and 26:9–11 that Saul is the "Lord's anointed" and thus cannot be slain except by God's instrument (1 Sam 31:4). The Deuteronomistic editor thereby differentiates between Saul, the legitimate king, and Abimelech, the self-proclaimed king over Israel.[203] Abimelech, like Saul, falls victim to the chaotic military and political situation of the time. Even if he had been successful once again at Thebez, there is little prospect that Abimelech or the land would "rest" during his reign.[204]

---

[197] If a cultic interpretation could be drawn from Abimelech's actions, the "stronghold of the temple of El-Berith" serves as an altar to a false god, destroyed in much the same way that Josiah later destroys the altar and high place of Jeroboam at Bethel (2 Kings 23:15). In the same way, the burning bundles of wood, which weakened the walls of the tower and caused it to fall, might be compared to the wood cut for Abraham's sacrifice of his son Isaac in Gen 22:3–6.

[198] B. G. Webb, *Book of Judges* (1987): 155–56.

[199] G. S. Ogden, "Jotham's Fable," *Bible Translator* 46 (1995): 304–5.

[200] Similar examples of divine punishment of evil doers is found in the flood narrative (Gen 6:5), the destruction of Sodom (Gen 19:13), and the Deuteronomistic Historian's justification of Israel's taking the Promised Land from its Canaanite inhabitants based on the judgment of the "wickedness of these nations" (Deut 9:4–5).

[201] R. H. O'Connell, *Rhetoric of the Book of Judges* (1996): 162.

[202] G. A. Yee, "By the Hand of a Woman," *Semeia* 61 (1993): 112–14.

[203] S. Dragga, "In the Shadow of the Judges," *JSOT* 38 (1987): 43.

[204] N. Steinberg, "Social Scientific Criticism," in *Judges and Method* (1995): 61.

CHAPTER 10

MINOR JUDGES

(1) After Abimelech, Tola son of Puah son of Dodo, a man of Issachar, who lived at Shamir in the hill country of Ephraim, rose to deliver Israel. (2) He judged Israel twenty-three years. Then he died, and was buried at Shamir. (3) After him came Jair the Gileadite, who judged Israel twenty-two years. (4) He had thirty sons who rode on thirty donkeys; and they had thirty towns, which are in the land of Gilead, and are called Havvoth-jair to this day. (5) Jair died, and was buried in Kamon.

*T*he rather enigmatic listing of these two minor judges seems to serve little purpose other than to separate the Gideon and Jephthah narratives. The Judges cycle, as it appears in the accounts of Ehud, Deborah, and Gideon, is not mentioned here. Instead there is what might be termed a genealogical note (compare Gen 5) or an index listing like those that appear at the end of the reign of many of the kings of Israel (1 Kings 14:29; 15:7–8, 23–24; 16:27–28). However, there is a definite structure to these brief notices on the minor judges, indicating an editor at work who chooses to minimize the role of these leaders.[205] For instance, the emphasis on genealogy, tribal affiliation, and the place of burial for each of these figures provides a measure of legitimacy as well as location within the land. The less stylized number of years that each serves also indicates a more realistic accounting. In addition, the repeated phrase "after him" (v. 3), which appears for each minor judge after Tola (12:8, 11, 13), suggests smooth transition, although the actual details of their calling and the events of their period of leadership are missing.[206]

STRUCTURAL ELEMENTS FOR MINOR JUDGES
Name
Tribe, clan, or region
Years as judge

[205] Beverly Beem, "The Minor Judges: A Literary Reading of Some Very Short Stories." Pages 147–51 in *The Biblical Canon in Comparative Perspective: Scripture in Context IV*. Edited by K. Lawson Younger et al. Lewiston, N.Y.: Edwin Mellen Press, 1991.

[206] E. T. Mullen, "The 'Minor Judges,'" *CBQ* 44 (1982): 194; Alan J. Hauser, "The 'Minor Judges' – A Re-evaluation," *JBL* 94 (1975): 193–95.

Death notice

Burial place

A personal detail (i.e., number of children)

It is possible that Tola's twenty-three-year period of stability as judge serves as an editorial contretemps to Abimelech's three years of chaotic frenzy. After Abimelech's violent death at Thebez, "they [the Israelites] all went home" (Judg 9:55). He had not brought them any rest from their oppressors, but Gideon had seen to that by defeating the Midianites and providing forty years of "rest" (Judg 8:28). Thus, with the exception of Abimelech's brief disruption of public tranquility, Tola "rose" not to meet a new outside threat but to serve as the arbiter who restores the equilibrium of Gideon's time and extends it for an additional score of years.[207] The lack of detail about his exploits and the absence of God from his brief account may signal the continuing spiral downward, away from the divine direction of the judges and toward personal caprice.[208]

The rather curious details that the editor chooses to include about Jair the Gileadite provide a clue to a time when the Transjordanian territory was at peace and enjoyed prosperity. It also serves as a contrast to the turbulent story of Jephthah the Gileadite, which follows immediately within the text. In that sense the transition provided by the inclusion of these minor judges provides a bad/good – good/bad structure for Abimelech/Tola – Jair/Jephthah.

A man with thirty sons, like Gideon who had seventy sons, is one who has been able to acquire many wives and the political and economic alliances that accompany them. That each son in turn has his own donkey to ride shows that the father is both wealthy and evenhanded with his sons (compare the many sons and donkeys of Abdon in Judg 12:13–14). Social distinction and perhaps the justification for his position as judge[209] seem to be based on wealth, influence, and the differentiation between those who ride and those who must walk (see Judg 5:10).[210] Yet, the next judge, Jephthah, has none of these benefits. In what can only be described as an ironic counterpoint, he must rely on the desperation of a leaderless people and the

---

[207] B. Beem, "The Minor Judges," in *The Biblical Canon* (1991): 149.

[208] T. J. Schneider, *Judges* (2000): 155.

[209] B. Beem, "The Minor Judges," in *The Biblical Canon* (1991): 152; J. A. Soggin, *Judges* (1987): 196.

[210] Abraham Malamat, "Mari," *BA* 34 (1971b): 18, cites ARM 6 76:20–25, in which the king of Mari is advised to "drive in a wagon and mules" rather than to ride a horse, which was considered to be undignified. Thus royalty and leadership are associated with the ass and its genetic counterparts.

spirit of Yahweh to succeed and, in the end, is forced to sacrifice his only child.[211]

JEPHTHAH

(6) The Israelites again did what was evil in the sight of the Lord, worshiping the Baals and the Astartes, the gods of Aram, the gods of Sidon, the gods of Moab, the gods of the Ammonites, and the gods of the Philistines. Thus they abandoned the Lord, and did not worship him. (7) So the anger of the Lord was kindled against Israel, and he sold them into the hand of the Philistines and into the hand of the Ammonites, (8) and they crushed and oppressed the Israelites that year. For eighteen years they oppressed all the Israelites that were beyond the Jordan in the land of the Amorites, which is in Gilead. (9) The Ammonites also crossed the Jordan to fight against Judah and against Benjamin and against the house of Ephraim; so that Israel was greatly distressed. (10) So the Israelites cried to the Lord, saying, "We have sinned against you, because we have abandoned our God and have worshiped the Baals." (11) And the Lord said to the Israelites, "Did I not deliver you from the Egyptians and from the Amorites, from the Ammonites and from the Philistines? (12) The Sidonians also, and the Amalekites, and the Maonites, oppressed you; and you cried to me, and I delivered you out of their hand. (13) Yet you have abandoned me and worshiped other gods; therefore I will deliver you no more. (14) Go and cry to the gods whom you have chosen; let them deliver you in the time of your distress." (15) And the Israelites said to the Lord, "We have sinned; do to us whatever seems good to you; but deliver us this day!" (16) So they put away the foreign gods from among them and worshiped the Lord; and he could no longer bear to see Israel suffer. (17) Then the Ammonites were called to arms, and they encamped in Gilead; and the Israelites came together, and they encamped at Mizpah. (18) The commanders of the people of Gilead said to one another, "Who will begin the fight against the Ammonites? He shall be head over all the inhabitants of Gilead."

*I*n what appears to be a resumption of the Judges cycle, the apostasy of the people is recounted followed by oppression and then a crying to the Lord for deliverance. Where the cycle now breaks down, however, is in God's extremely frustrated and ultimately negative response. The taunting answer that they should "go and cry to the gods whom you have chosen" plays on

---

[211] J. Cheryl Exum, "The Centre Cannot Hold: Thematic and Textual Instabilities in Judges," *CBQ* 52 (1990): 421.

the same theme introduced by Joash's call for Baal to defend, if he can, the altar that Gideon had just destroyed (Judg 6:31). It is also a sufficient surprise response to signal to the reader that such a possibility is yet likely to come and will in fact occur in the Samson account, the first in the collection of stories "to lack a statement of Israel's deliverance from their oppressors."[212]

The recitation of God's saving acts forms a geographical and historical pattern in much the same way as the geographic circle drawn in Amos's Bethel sermon, which also includes seven names other than Israel (Amos 1:3–2:5).[213] In God's set of place names each period from the exodus through the prior history of the settlement is chronicled.[214] Thus Egypt and the Amorite kings (Sihon and Og; Num 21:21–31) represent the exodus and the postwilderness trek victories prior to the entrance into the land of Canaan. The Ammonites, who function as both a past (Judg 3:13) and present enemy, represent the continuing struggle for existence as well as for potential cultural absorption. The Philistines and Sidonians may be paired as successor states founded by groups of the Sea Peoples after 1200 BCE along the Syro-Palestinian coast, and they are listed among the enemy peoples "left to test" the newly arrived Israelites (Judg 3:1–3). Finally, the traditional enemy among the pastoral nomadic peoples of the wilderness of Midian and the Negeb, the Amalekites (Exod 17:8–16; Num 13:29), are paired with another herding group, the Maonites.[215] The seriousness of this situation is found in a wider area of conflict than was found in the past. Both sides of the Jordan are affected by these incursions by neighboring peoples.

Eventually the Israelites do more than just call out for help. They physically "put away" their foreign gods, a charge that Joshua had given them (Josh 24:14, 23) and a command that Samuel will repeat in the next generation (1 Sam 7:3). Apparently unable to withhold support in the face of their misery, Yahweh relents, but no specific divine action is taken or promised.[216] God's willingness to show compassion for the Israelites was first spelled out in Judg 2:18 in the description of the raising of a judge because God was "moved to pity by their groaning." This sense of a God who hears heartfelt prayer and

---

212 R. H. O'Connell, *Rhetoric of the Book of Judges* (1996): 179, n. 232.

213 The prophet rhetorically proceeds in his condemnation of Israel's neighbors, in the following order: Damascus (Aram/Syria), Gaza (Philistines), Tyre (Phoenicians), Edom, Ammon, Moab, Judah.

214 R. G. Boling, *Judges* (1975): 192.

215 The LXX emends Maonite to Midianite, assuming correctly the previous oppression of these people who were defeated by Gideon. This is probably based on the pairing of Midianites and Amalekites in Judg 6:3.

216 Barry G. Webb, "The Theme of the Jephthah Story (Judges 10:6–12:7)," *RTR* 45 (1986): 37.

recognizes the acts of repentance continues in later traditions (see Solomon's prayer in 1 Kings 8:46–53 and the hymn of praise in Isa 25:1–10).

The narrative then resumes with an imminent invasion of Gilead by the Ammonites, and the Israelites make yet another tactical mistake in their dealings with Yahweh. Instead of leaving the choice of judge or military leader to God, they asked among themselves who would lead them. Their question "who will begin" is hauntingly reminiscent of Judg 1:1, in which the Israelites inquired of God "who shall go up first" since they no longer had Joshua to lead them. At least in that instance they sought divine direction, but in this preface to the story of Jephthah the Israelites seek their own counsel, not God's.[217] They offer the one who will lead them in this struggle the right to rule over them, an offer similar, if on a higher scale, to Caleb's offer of a wife to the man who captures Kiriath-sepher (Judg 1:12).[218]

CHAPTER 11

(1) Now Jephthah the Gileadite, the son of a prostitute, was a mighty warrior. Gilead was the father of Jephthah. (2) Gilead's wife also bore him sons; and when his wife's sons grew up, they drove Jephthah away, saying to him, "You shall not inherit anything in our father's house; for you are the son of another woman." (3) Then Jephthah fled from his brothers and lived in the land of Tob. Outlaws collected around Jephthah and went raiding with him. (4) After a time the Ammonites made war against Israel. (5) And when the Ammonites made war against Israel, the elders of Gilead went to bring Jephthah from the land of Tob. (6) They said to Jephthah, "Come and be our commander, so that we may fight with the Ammonites." (7) But Jephthah said to the elders of Gilead, "Are you not the very ones who rejected me and drove me out of my father's house? So why do you come to me now when you are in trouble?" (8) The elders of Gilead said to Jephthah, "Nevertheless, we have now turned back to you, so that you may go with us and fight with the Ammonites, and become head over us, over all the inhabitants of Gilead." (9) Jephthah said to the elders of Gilead, "If you bring me home again to fight with the Ammonites, and the Lord gives them over to me, I will be your head." (10) And the elders of Gilead said to

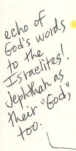

cf Abimelech!

echo of God's words to the Israelites! Jephthah as their "God" too.

---

217 J. Marais, *Representation in Old Testament* (1998): 118.
218 T. J. Schneider, *Judges* (2000): 161, also notes the similarity to Saul's offer of a royal bride to the man who defeats the Philistine giant Goliath (1 Sam 17:25).

Jephthah, "The Lord will be witness between us; we will surely do as you say." (11) So Jephthah went with the elders of Gilead, and the people made him head and commander over them; and Jephthah spoke all his words before the Lord at Mizpah.

*F*irst, Jephthah is referred to as the son of a prostitute. This may be a repetition of the foreign or dangerous woman theme that also appears in the story of Abimelech and his mother (Judg 8:31). By indicating that the principal character in the episode is born to a woman outside the community and therefore is a son outside the normal inheritance pattern, the story presents the reader from the start with one reason for his potential failure or fall.[219] This also prefaces the traditional story found elsewhere in ancient Near Eastern literature of a hero who is driven from his home by his brothers and ultimately triumphs over them.[220]

The laws of inheritance in the ancient Near East are quite explicit about whether a child is born to a wife "of the first rank" or a concubine or a slave woman, or is adopted. In CH 170–71, a male child of a slave must receive a formal declaration from his father acknowledging him as "my child" in order to share in the father's estate.[221] In any case the child of the slave is to be freed, along with his mother, on the death of the father, but a share proportionate to the other heirs depends on the father's legal disposition. Judg 11:1 makes it quite clear that Gilead is Jephthah's father, suggesting that a formal declaration has been made in his favor. However, his half-brothers have no intention of allowing him to share in the estate, and apparently he has no legal recourse and is forced to flee.

The second quality assigned to Jephthah in Judg 11:1 is that he is a "mighty warrior." Thus the reader is immediately faced with a contrasting character since he is first labeled as an outsider without inheritance rights and in the next breath he is extolled as a hero. This dual characterization is a perfect backdrop, however, to the world of the Israelites during the Judges period.[222] They are prostituting themselves in their worship of other gods

well, Gideon was given that name, too! (by God)

---

219 Pauline D. Guest, "Dangerous Liaisons in the Book of Judges," *SJOT* 11 (1997): 251.
220 Edward L. Greenstein and David Marcus, "The Akkadian Inscription of Idrimi," *JANESCU* 8 (1976): 76–77, provides comparisons between the mid-second millennium BCE King Idrimi of Alalakh, Jephthah, and David. The basic elements of this literary structure are (1) flight, (2) recognition by kin, (3) formation of exiled band of men, and (4) rise from fugitive to leadership position.
221 M. T. Roth, *Law Collections* (1995): 113–14.
222 J. Cheryl Exum, *Tragedy and Biblical Narrative: Arrows of the Almighty.* Cambridge: Cambridge University Press, 1992: 47.

and acceptance of foreign cultural ideas, but they have within them, with the help of the divine warrior, the potential for military and social victories.

Thus, in the face of a mounting Ammonite threat, the position initially offered to Jephthah by the elders is that of *qāsîn* (military commander or war chief), which is generally a temporary position and one that would have to submit to the authority of the elders (see Josh 10:24; Isa 22:3; Dan 11:18).[223] Their offer of limited authority appears to be based on Jephthah's military experience as a leader of a bandit gang, and their level of desperation suggests that he and his men are expendable mercenaries, to be bought but only tolerated for a short time.[224] He would not ordinarily be their first choice for any position of leadership within the clan.

Sensing the hypocrisy of the elders, Jephthah's incredulous response to them includes the rhetorical statement, "Are you not the very ones who rejected me and drove me out of my father's house?" He is basically saying that no one in their right minds should expect that such an offer would be accepted given the circumstances.[225] Since they previously rejected and expelled him, he now flatly rejects them.

Given the severity of the crisis, the elders press on with their negotiations since any response from Jephthah, even if initially negative, is a starting point.[226] They have little choice but to opt for experience over the normal channels of authority, and they now move to increase their offer, extending the promise that he will become their "head," or *rō'š*.[227] To be sure, Jephthah recognizes his position of strength with regard to the elders, and he negotiates for a restoration of his inheritance rights and of his legitimate membership in the clan.[228] This clearly means more to him at this point than titles that are meaningless if God does not give him the victory (Judg 11:9). Still it should be noted that *rō'š* is a more encompassing title, and used quite widely,[229] but in this situation it most likely gives Jephthah the position of clan chief

---

[223] Abraham Malamat, "The Period of the Judges." Page 158 in *The World History of the Jewish People, Vol. 3: Judges*. Edited by Benjamin Mazar. New Brunswick, N.J.: Rutgers University Press, 1971a.

[224] Kenneth M. Craig, "Bargaining in Tov (Judges 11, 4–11): The Many Directions of So-called Direct Speech," *Bib* 79 (1998): 19.

[225] David Marcus, "The Bargaining between Jephthah and the Elders (Judges 11:4–11)," *JANES* 19 (1989): 97–98.

[226] K. M. Craig, "Bargaining in Tov," *Bib* 79 (1998): 80–81.

[227] Alan J. Hauser, "Unity and Diversity in Early Israel before Samuel," *JETS* 22 (1979): 298.

[228] D. Marcus, "Bargaining between Jephthah and the Elders," *JANES* 19 (1989): 99.

[229] J. R. Bartlett, "The Use of the Word *rō'š* as a Title in the Old Testament," *VT* 19 (1969): 1–10.

and links him into the traditional, hereditary leadership of Gilead. In other words, this exiled, disinherited son of a prostitute is to have his clan rights restored and is to become the highest-ranking leader over all of the clans of Gilead.[230]

One additional factor distinguishing Jephthah as an independent spirit and clever negotiator is his willingness to stipulate that he will only acquire the title of clan chief if God provides him the victory. In this way he adds, as in ancient Near Eastern treaty language, the inclusion of the deity as witness to these terms. Any victory he gains will then be seen as divine affirmation of his position of leadership.[231] The bottom line, however, is that the elders have made this offer of both war chief and clan chief, and they are responsible for his rise to power, even if God grants him a victory. These stipulations between Jephthah and the elders of Gilead can be compared with a similar scene in the Babylonian creation epic *Enuma Elish*. In that instance Marduk negotiates with the other gods, saying, "If indeed I am to champion you, subdue Tiamat and save your lives, convene the assembly, nominate me for supreme destiny!" (*COS* 1.111: 395). Thus, even prior to the mortal combat between Marduk and Tiamat, the gods are quick to affirm his position as head of the divine assembly. Like the elders of Gilead, they are willing to give up a large measure of their authority in exchange for security, and if their champion falls, they are in no more danger than they had been from the first.

A CLOSER LOOK AT ELDERS

One of the most prominently mentioned groups in both Judges and Ruth are the village and tribal elders. These individuals were heads of prominent households in the villages and towns, and they derived their authority from the confidence placed in them by the members of their community who recognized the wealth of experience they held and its value to the tribe or kinship group.[232] Since ancient Israel was a kinship-based society, everyone in the community knew their place in terms of kin ties, clan obligations, and

---

230 Timothy M. Willis, "The Nature of Jephthah's Authority," *CBQ* 59 (1997): 41; R. G. Boling, *Judges* (1975): 195.

231 J. Cheryl Exum, "The Tragic Vision and Biblical Narrative: The Case of Jephthah." Pages 73–74, 78 in *Signs and Wonders: Biblical Texts in Literary Focus*. Edited by J. Cheryl Exum. Atlanta: Scholars Press, 1989a.

232 Hanoch Reviv, *The Elders in Ancient Israel*. Jerusalem: Magnes Press, 1989: 11.

relative economic level.[233] In the course of everyday life, the elders served as an assembly upholding the honor of the clan and the civil rights of the inhabitants of the village. Their function also included protecting the rights of those dwelling there without a household, such as the widow, the orphan, and the alien (Ruth 4:2; Prov 31:23).[234]

Plaintiffs initiated proceedings by going to the gate and impaneling a jury of elders to review their course of action (1 Sam 16:4; Zech 3:5; Ps 121:8; Ruth 4:1–2). Although plaintiffs could convene an assembly at any time, the standard time for a meeting was at daybreak. As a practical matter the greatest number of citizens came and went on their way to work at dawn (Ps 104:22–23). Standing at the gate when people were streaming out on their way to work in the fields, the plaintiff called for justice, and it would be the responsibility of the city elders to hear the case. When ten citizens had been impaneled, they adjourned to one of the bays in the gate to deliberate and to reach a consensus based on the statements made to them.

The honor and integrity of the village or city rested on the willingness of its citizens to support the legal system and to settle disputes through arbitration rather than by force or violence (Deut 5:17–20). They were obliged to do this without payment or prejudice (Exod 23:8; Deut 27:25; Ps 15:5). By acknowledging their need for one another in this style of legal justice, they guaranteed the solidarity of the community.[235]

Tribal elders continued to function even after more centralized political systems replaced the village in ancient Israel (see 1 Kings 8:1; Jer 26:17–18). Their influence, while weakened somewhat by the centralization of authority and the role of the state bureaucracy, persisted due to the power of kin-based relationships in the tribal territories and had to be reckoned with by the kings.[236]

(12) Then Jephthah sent messengers to the king of the Ammonites and said, "What is there between you and me, that you have come to me to fight against my

---

[233] Timothy M. Willis, *The Elders of the City: A Study of the Elders-Laws in Deuteronomy.* Atlanta: SBL, 2001: 21.

[234] Moshe Weinfeld, "Judge and Officer in the Ancient Near East," *IOS* 7 (1977): 81; Elizabeth Bellefontaine, "Customary Law and Chieftainship: Judicial Aspects of 2 Samuel 14.4–21," *JSOT* 38 (1987): 53.

[235] V. H. Matthews and D. C. Benjamin, *Social World of Ancient Israel* (1993): 126–27.

[236] T. M. Willis, *Elders of the City* (2001): 8–9.

land?" (13) The king of the Ammonites answered the messengers of Jephthah, "Because Israel, on coming from Egypt, took away my land from the Arnon to the Jabbok and to the Jordan; now therefore restore it peaceably." (14) Once again Jephthah sent messengers to the king of the Ammonites (15) and said to him: "Thus says Jephthah: Israel did not take the land of Moab or the land of the Ammonites, (16) but when they came up from Egypt, Israel went through the wilderness to the Red Sea and came to Kadesh. (17) Israel then sent messengers to the king of Edom, saying, 'Let us pass through your land'; but he would not consent. So Israel remained at Kadesh. (18) Then they journeyed through the wilderness, went around the land of Edom and the land of Moab, arrived on the east side of the land of Moab, and camped on the other side of the Arnon. They did not enter the territory of Moab, for the Arnon was the boundary of Moab. (19) Israel then sent messengers to King Sihon of the Amorites, king of Heshbon; and Israel said to him, 'Let us pass through your land to our country.' (20) But Sihon did not trust Israel to pass through his territory; so Sihon gathered all his people together, and encamped at Jahaz, and fought with Israel. (21) Then the Lord, the God of Israel, gave Sihon and all his people into the hand of Israel, and they defeated them; so Israel occupied all the land of the Amorites, who inhabited that country. (22) They occupied all the territory of the Amorites from the Arnon to the Jabbok and from the wilderness to the Jordan. (23) So now the Lord, the God of Israel, has conquered the Amorites for the benefit of his people Israel. Do you intend to take their place? (24) Should you not possess what your god Chemosh gives you to possess? And should we not be the ones to possess everything that the Lord our God has conquered for our benefit? (25) Now are you any better than King Balak son of Zippor of Moab? Did he ever enter into conflict with Israel, or did he ever go to war with them? (26) While Israel lived in Heshbon and its villages, and in Aroer and its villages, and in all the towns that are along the Arnon, three hundred years, why did you not recover them within that time? (27) It is not I who have sinned against you, but you are the one who does me wrong by making war on me. Let the Lord, who is judge, decide today for the Israelites or for the Ammonites." (28) But the king of the Ammonites did not heed the message that Jephthah sent him.

A t this point, the editor of this material injects an account of the exchange of communiqués between Jephthah and the Ammonite king. It is possible that he is employing an identifiable, scribal battle report form, which is used in this case to provide a shorthand account of past events justifying

Israelite title to defined territorial holdings.[237] To be sure, the exchange of views continues to demonstrate Jephthah's negotiating skills and could be described as a classic piece of diplomatic rhetoric designed to provide the legal underpinning for a "just war."[238]

With an interesting rhetorical facility for an exiled bandit chief, Jephthah is able to legitimize himself as the Israelite leader by systematically drawing on the traditional Israelite understanding of their origins in the land.[239] Throughout his rendition, Jephthah portrays himself and the Israelites as the injured parties in this land dispute between peoples in Transjordan. He plays the role of a prosecuting attorney, with Yahweh as judge, and recites a version (compare the other accounts in Num 21:22–35; Deut 1:4) of the events of the preconquest period when the Israelites intentionally skirt the Edomite and Moabite lands and then are forced to fight when Sihon marshals his Amorite army against them. They then defeat this aggressive Amorite king and are able by right of conquest to claim title to the land north of the Arnon River.[240]

In addition, Jephthah cites that the Israelites had received divine aid in their conquests, a fact that may be addressed as much to bolster his own forces as it is to intimidate the Ammonites.[241] Thus their claim to the land is based not on having first entered that territory but on a divine land grant. Furthermore, that they had then held onto this land for a long period (300 years is an inflated figure) signifies continued divine support. To conclude his argument, Jephthah invokes a challenge between Yahweh and the Ammonite god Chemosh to see who will remain in control of this territory. His challenge resembles that of Joash, Gideon's father, who also called on a foreign god to defend his rights and power over the people, if he can (Judg 6:31). It also invokes real irony when compared to Yahweh's rebuttal to the Israelites in Judg 10:14, daring them to call on the

---

237 John Van Seters, "The Conquest of Sihon's Kingdom: A Literary Examination," *JBL* 91 (1972): 186–89. Van Seters's argument and his use of Assyrian Annalistic battle accounts are based in part on the work of Wolfgang Richter, *Traditionsgeschichtliche Untersuchungen zum Richterbuch*, 2nd ed. BBB 18. Bonn, Ger.: Peter Hanstein, 1966. David M. Gunn, "The 'Battle Report': Oral or Scribal Convention?" *JBL* 93 (1974): 513–18, disputes this identification of a scribal "form" based on insufficient evidence.

238 Robert M. Good, "The Just War in Ancient Israel," *JBL* 104 (1985): 395.

239 T. J. Schneider, *Judges* (2000): 172–73.

240 Dennis T. Olson, "Dialogues of Life and Monologues of Death: Jephthah and Jephthah's Daughter in Judges 10:6–12:7." Page 47 in *Postmodern Interpretations of the Bible – A Reader*. Edited by A. K. M. Adam. St. Louis, Mo.: Chalice Press, 2001.

241 Pamela T. Reis, "Spoiled Child: A Fresh Look at Jephthah's Daughter," *Proof* 17 (1997): 280.

foreign gods that they have served rather than disturb God with their cries for assistance.

the Historian gives him authority

(29) Then the spirit of the Lord came upon Jephthah, and he passed through Gilead and Manasseh. He passed on to Mizpah of Gilead, and from Mizpah of Gilead he passed on to the Ammonites. (30) And Jephthah made a vow to the Lord, and said, "If you will give the Ammonites into my hand, (31) then (whoever) comes out of the doors of my house to meet me, when I return victorious from the Ammonites, shall be the Lord's, to be offered up by me as a burnt offering." (32) So Jephthah crossed over to the Ammonites to fight against them; and the Lord gave them into his hand. (33) He inflicted a massive defeat on them from Aroer to the neighborhood of Minnith, twenty towns, and as far as Abel-keramim. So the Ammonites were subdued before the people of Israel.

There are two seemingly incongruous aspects to this episode. Jephthah is said to be empowered when the "spirit of the Lord came upon" him. This is a singularly important moment for him, one shared only by Othniel (Judg 3:10), Gideon (Judg 6:34), and Samson (Judg 14:6, 19; 15:14) among the judges. The prepositional phrase translated "came upon" in 10:29 is exactly the same as that in 3:10 and signals a divine sanction or legitimating of his role as leader of his people. The Gideon account (see the comment on 6:46) uses different language and is more evocative of an investiture ceremony, although it also is the initial basis for his rise to tribal leadership. In the Samson narrative, the NRSV translates his moments of empowerment as a physical possession, describing how the "spirit of God rushed on him," but in his case this does not represent a formal leadership role. This variant use of language will be discussed in more detail in the section on Samson.

Jephthah's empowerment is a mark of divine presence and purpose and provides him with true legitimacy for his role as Gileadite leader and as charismatic marshal of a larger body of the Israelite tribes. With this divine credential and his recognized skills as a military leader, he now is able to draw support from the tribe of Manasseh as he prepares to meet the Ammonite forces.[242]

Given this situation, the question can be asked why he would feel it necessary to proclaim a vow, which in essence promised to give God an unasked-for gift in exchange for a military victory (compare Gideon's request for an

---

[242] T. M. Willis, "Nature of Jephthah's Authority," *CBQ* 59 (1997): 42.

additional sign in 6:36–40 after receiving God's spirit). Since he has already
been invested with the "spirit of the Lord," he should have been confident
of his coming victory. The reality of the situation, however, may hinge on
the fact that some gift-givers simply wish to bribe the powerful (Sir 20:29)
or curry favor with those in leadership positions (Prov 18:16). In some cases
there may be an effort by the donor to test the intent of the recipient and
thereby determine whether a balanced exchange can or will occur.[243] Since
balanced gift-giving is more socially acceptable and well received, any attempt to coax or coerce another person, or in this case a deity, into an
exchange, especially to increase the donor's own power or social status, may
well prove damaging to the gift-giver.[244]

perhaps he doesn't trust God?

Perhaps Jephthah has become a victim of his own negotiating skills, assuming that he must make an offer, as he did with the elders of Gilead, in
order to get what he desires. There may also be an element of uncertainty
even for a seasoned military campaigner,[245] who knows his future in Gilead
is dependent upon this victory.[246] Whether it is his desperation, like Saul's
in a later generation (1 Sam 14:24–46), that drives him to undertake this vow
or his own calculating style at work, Jephthah will discover that, like Saul, it
will cost him his future prospects.[247]

There is no response from God to Jephthah's vow. While this divine silence
could be interpreted as divine culpability,[248] it is more likely a signal that
Jephthah should not be ad-libbing and instead should rely on the instruction
provided by the investment of God's spirit. The victory over the Ammonites
was ensured by the placement of God's spirit within Jephthah, and it follows the same pattern as many other Israelite battle accounts, centered on
the phrase "gave them into the hand of Israel" (Josh 10:32; Judg 7:15; 11:21;
1 Sam 14:12, 23). The towns mentioned in the chronicle provide or strengthen

---

[243] J. F. Sherry Jr., "Gift Giving in Anthropological Perspective," *Journal of Consumer Research* 10 (1983): 159.

[244] Victor H. Matthews, "The Unwanted Gift: Implications of Obligatory Gift Giving in Ancient Israel," *Semeia* 87 (1999): 91–92.

[245] P. Trible, *Texts of Terror* (1984): 97, calls it an "act of unfaithfulness" in which he attempts to control God's actions rather than flow with the power given to him freely by God's spirit.

[246] Simon B. Parker, "The Vow in Ugaritic and Israelite Narrative Literature," *UF* 11 (1979): 699, points out that it is typical of the vow genre for it to be made in a situation of anxiety (compare the Ugaritic king Keret's vow [*CTA* 14.4.201–206] and Hannah's vow [1 Sam 1:11]).

[247] R. H. O'Connell, *Rhetoric of the Book of Judges* (1996): 180–83.

[248] See J. C. Exum, "Tragic Vision and Biblical Narrative," in *Signs and Wonders* (1989a): 66–67; idem, *Tragedy and Biblical Narrative* (1992): 60.

territorial claims of the Israelites between Rabbah, the Ammonite capital, and Heshbon.

A similar battle account and list of conquered territories and towns is found in the ninth-century BCE Stele of Mesha. This Moabite king describes, in terms very similar to the rhetoric of the Judges cycle, how his god Chemosh had been angry with them and had allowed the Israelites under King Omri to oppress them for thirty years. In his own day, however, the god had chosen to assist them in overcoming their Israelite enemies. After retaking this territory, Mesha settled his own people there, having "sacrificed 7000 men, women, and children from Nebo to Chemosh as I had vowed I would do."[249] This final detail suggests that Mesha had made a vow similar to that of Jephthah, offering to make a massive human sacrifice in exchange for a victory.

the relativity of the Hebrew Bible.

(34) Then Jephthah came to his home at Mizpah; and there was his daughter coming out to meet him with timbrels and with dancing. She was his only child; he had no son or daughter except her. (35) When he saw her, he tore his clothes, and said, "Alas, my daughter! You have brought me very low; you have become the cause of great trouble to me. For I have opened my mouth to the Lord, and I cannot take back my vow." (36) She said to him, "My father, if you have opened your mouth to the Lord, do to me according to what has gone out of your mouth, now that the Lord has given you vengeance against your enemies, the Ammonites." (37) And she said to her father, "Let this thing be done for me; Grant me two months, so that I may go and wander on the mountains, and bewail my virginity, my companions and I." (38) "Go," he said and sent her away for two months. So she departed, she and her companions, and bewailed her virginity on the mountains. (39) At the end of two months, she returned to her father, who did with her according to the vow he had made. She had never slept with a man. So there arose an Israelite custom that (40) for four days every year the daughters of Israel would go out to lament the daughter of Jephthah the Gileadite.

Jephthah's vow stands at the heart of this entire passage. It seems quite clear from the text that his intent was to make a human not an animal sacrifice,[250] and this would place him squarely within Canaanite religious

---

[249] V. H. Matthews and D. C. Benjamin, *Old Testament Parallels* (1997): 158.

[250] See David Marcus, *Jephthah and His Vow.* Lubbock: Texas Tech Press, 1986: 13–32, which discusses the arguments for and against whether Jephthah's daughter is actually to be sacrificed or whether she simply surrenders her right to marriage and children.

tradition and, based on Gen 22:9–18, in contradiction to Israelite tradition.[251] However, that human sacrifice did occur among the Israelites can be demonstrated by the actions of King Ahaz in 2 Kings 16:3 and the legislation in Lev 27:1–8, which provides monetary compensation for the life of a person offered in a vow.[252] Furthermore, it is likely that Jephthah was offering more than the life of a slave or even one of his men to obtain God's attention. He must have known that members of his household would lead the celebratory procession and would therefore be the subject of his vow.[253]

As is so often the case, this scene is not sufficiently peopled to reflect basic social reality. Just as Jael is seemingly the only person in her encampment in Judg 4:17–18, Jephthah's daughter is shown as the only person to greet him with a musical celebration of his victory over the Ammonites. Other examples of women greeting their victorious leaders are found in Exod 15:20–21 and 1 Sam 18:6–7, and in each case it is a body of dancing, timbrel-playing females, not just a lone individual, that comes out to meet them.[254] In fact, in a form of literary tunnel-vision the writer makes it clear that Jephthah has only this one child (compare the many sons of the minor judges Jair [Judg 10:4], Ibzan [Judg 12:9], and Abdon [Judg 12:14]). She represents the future that he had planned for when he bargained with the Gileadite elders, and now, as a result of his rash oath, he will lose her and his hopes for maintaining his name as a member of the clan.

Jephthah's realization of the scope of the tragedy that he has brought upon himself echoes the grief found in Greek drama.[255] His reaction to the appearance of his daughter is apparently one of shock and includes a quite self-serving wail of lamentation. Instead of blaming himself, he blames her for forcing him into a situation that he would have otherwise avoided at all costs. When he made his vow, he knew he would have to make the promised

[margin note: he blames her]

---

[251] P. T. Reis, "Spoiled Child," *Proof* 17 (1997): 281–82, argues that Jephthah had no intention of violating Israelite law. Instead he planned "to dedicate and redeem a slave" based on the redemptive value set in Lev 27:1–8. This slave, like an animal that had been designated for sacrifice and then redeemed, would become holy and therefore no longer required to work.

[252] S. B. Parker, "Vow in Ugaritic and Israelite Narrative Literature," *UF* 11 (1979): 700.

[253] J. Cheryl Exum, "Murder They Wrote: Ideology and the Manipulation of Female Presence in Biblical Narrative," *USQR* 43 (1989b): 22.

[254] Yochanan Muffs, "Abraham the Noble Warrior: Patriarchal Politics and Laws of War in Ancient Israel," *JSS* 33 (1982): 81, n. 1, in exploring another anomalous passage (Gen 14:17–18), points out that the normal elements of a triumphal return story can be reshaped to fit a new context by the storyteller.

[255] Gila Ramras-Rauch, "Fathers and Daughters: Two Biblical Narratives." Page 166 in *Mappings of the Biblical Terrain*. Edited by Vincent Tollers and Johann Maier. Lewisburg, Pa.: Bucknell University Press, 1990.

sacrifice. As in so many epic or folk tales, however, heroes who attempt to force the god/gods to their will are charged a high price for their hubris.[256]

Of course, Jephthah is not alone in trying to bargain with God. Jacob makes a conditional vow in Gen 28:20, calling on God to fulfill his covenantal promises in exchange for his worship and a tithe. What both characters discover eventually is that God is not malleable. No human can direct or force the deity into action by a promise. However, it is human nature to try, and Jephthah has already proven repeatedly how he relies upon hard bargaining to get what he wants.

Ironically, Jephthah's nameless daughter will be the stronger character in this situation. Such a role reversal is not unusual in the biblical text and is particularly apt in the topsy-turvy world of the Judges.[257] While her father wails, tears his clothing, and beats his breast over being tricked,[258] she is the one who insists on his keeping his vow. This is a curiously legalistic stance given the otherwise lawless character of much of the Judges narrative.[259]

What is particularly ironic is her bargaining with her father in much the same way that he had dealt with the elders of Gilead, and without the normal expressions of respect one would expect from a daughter when speaking to her father.[260] She proves herself to be his daughter by taking up his rhetorical bargaining style, insisting on a two-month reprieve so that she becomes more than a victim of this situation. While there is no clear explanation for this particular amount of time, it does set the daughter apart from her father, identifying her instead with her "companions" or female peers.[261] Since she is unmarried and probably quite young,[262] the emphasis she places on mourning her "virginity" most likely is tied to a lack of sexual experience

she goes to the world beneath

---

256 Compare the story of Agamemnon's sacrifice of his daughter Iphigenia to appease the angry god Poseidon (Euripides, *Iphigenia in Aulis*). Other examples of the gods taking vengeance on humans who either refuse them or attempt to set themselves up as their equal include the Sumerian king Gilgamesh's rebuff of the romantic advances of the goddess Ishtar, which results in the death of his companion Enkidu, and Aqhat, who is murdered by Anat's henchman Yatpan when the Ugaritic hero refuses to give his bow to the goddess.

257 Victor H. Matthews, "Female Voices: Upholding the Honor of the Household," *BTB* 24 (1994a): 8–11; G. Ramras-Rauch, "Fathers and Daughters," in *Mappings of the Biblical Terrain* (1990): 166.

258 J. C. Exum, "Murder They Wrote," *USQR* 43 (1989b): 21, makes the comparison with Oedipus, who unknowingly commits patricide and incest, and then must face the wrath of the gods for these crimes.

259 See Num 30:2–5 and Deut 23:22–25 for the inviolability of an oath.

260 P. T. Reis, "Spoiled Child," *Proof* 17 (1997): 285–86.

261 D. Marcus, *Jephthah and His Vow* (1986): 31–32, 36.

262 Mieke Bal, *Death and Dissymmetry: The Politics of Coherence in the Book of Judges.* Bloomington: Indiana University Press, 1988b: 46–49.

rather than to a hope of eventually having children. As Schneider notes, the power of female sexuality and sensuality is in evidence once again here as it is throughout the Book of Judges.[263] Motherhood as a physical, female identifier appears as a significant factor only in the stories of Sisera (Judg 5:28–30), Samson (Judg 13:2–7), and Micah (Judg 17:2–4).[264]

Thus the eloquent daughter chooses her own way of expressing her individuality. Her sacrifice is named as separate and distinct from that of her father and is commemorated in an etiological notice embedded into the text, which becomes the basis of a women's holiday that is attested nowhere else in Scripture.[265] By taking control of events, even though she will ultimately pay with her life, Jephthah's unnamed daughter acquires a name for herself, something that Jephthah will lose as his family line dies with her.

CHAPTER 12

(1) The men of Ephraim were called to arms, and they crossed to Zaphon and said to Jephthah, "Why did you cross over to fight against the Ammonites, and did not call us to go with you? We will burn your house down over you!" (2) Jephthah said to them, "My people and I were engaged in conflict with the Ammonites who oppressed us severely. But when I called you, you did not deliver me from their hand. (3) When I saw that you would not deliver me, I took my life in my hand, and crossed over against the Ammonites, and the Lord gave them into my hand. Why then fight against me?" (4) Then Jephthah gathered all the men of Gilead and fought with Ephraim; and the men of Gilead defeated Ephraim, because they said, "You are fugitives from Ephraim, you Gileadites – in the heart of Ephraim and Manasseh." (5) Then the Gileadites took the fords of the Jordan against the Ephraimites. Whenever one of the fugitives of Ephraim said, "Let me go over," the men of Gilead would say to him, "Are you an Ephraimite?" When he said, "No," (6) they said to him, "Then say Shibboleth," and he said, "Sibboleth," for he could not pronounce it

---

[263] T. J. Schneider, *Judges* (2000): 181.

[264] Deborah is referred to as a "mother in Israel" in Judg 5:7, but this is an honorific similar to "elder" or "protector" of the tribe or nation, not a reference to her biological function as a mother.

[265] R. T. Reis, "Spoiled Child," *Proof* 17 (1997): 287, suggests that Jephthah's daughter and her companions actually sought the aid of other gods in an attempt to spare her. According to her argument, their "holiday" was later "sanctified" by the Jews into Rosh Hodesh, the celebration of the new moon.

right. Then they seized him and killed him at the fords of the Jordan. Forty-two thousand of the Ephraimites fell at that time. (7) Jephthah judged Israel six years. Then Jephthah the Gileadite died, and was buried in his town in Gilead.

The military sequence resumes with civil unrest between the Israelites of Gilead and Ephraim. In this hostile exchange between Jephthah and the Ephraimites, this preeminent northern tribal group is portrayed negatively, based on both their military stance and their incompetence in following simple instructions. In fact, the degree to which the Ephraimites are presented as positive or negative in Judges serves as a sort of literary-social barometer of the fortunes of the Israelites in this period.[266] Early in the book the Ephraimites are quick to answer the call to battle (Ehud in Judg 3:27; Deborah in Judg 4:5; 5:14). They are not as helpful in the Gideon narrative (Judg 7:24–25; 8:1–3), and in their encounter with Jephthah they are seen as a greedy and contentious people.

In Jephthah's dealings with the Ephraimites, no mention is made of his vow or the death of his daughter. As wrenching as that experience must have been, one would think he would have mentioned it in his bitter response to the Ephraimites who are threatening him, now that the war is over, with having left them out of the taking of the spoil from the Ammonites (see Judg 14:15 for a similar fiery threat). There is some irony here in the sense that they threaten to burn down Jephthah's "house," but he has already effectively done that by sacrificing his only child.

Ever the master of words, Jephthah resorts to an interesting stratagem to test the fleeing Ephraimite soldiers as they attempted to cross the Jordan River. He asks each man to pronounce a common word, *shibbōleth* (ear of corn or stream), but the dialectic variations between the Israelites is demonstrated by the apparent inability of the enemy soldiers to provide the "correct" inflection.[267] It is possible that the regional differences in pronunciation and perhaps the tension of the moment prevented the Ephraimites from making the *sh* sound, and they pronounced it *sibbōleth*.[268] However,

---

[266] D. T. Olson, "Dialogues of Life and Monologues of Death," in *Postmodern Interpretations* (2001): 52.

[267] John Emerton, "Some Comments on the Shibboleth Incident (Judges XII 6)." Pages 154–55 in *Mélanges bibliques et orientaux en l'honneur de M. Mathias Delcor*. Edited by Andre Caquot, S. Légasse, and M. Tardieu. Neukirchen-Vluyn, Ger.: Verlag-Butzon & Bercker Kevelaer, 1985.

[268] See David Marcus, "Ridiculing the Ephraimites: The Shibboleth Incident (Judg 12:6)," *MAARAV* 8 (1992): 96, for a discussion of the linguistic arguments explaining why these dialectical differences occurred and why *šin* may be pronounced by using a samekh as *śin*.

it is also possible that this is another example of a parody or spoof in the text, which tries to show that the Ephraimites are so incompetent, foolish, or inattentive that they cannot mimic the pronunciation of a word that they just heard spoken.[269] The ruthlessness of Jephthah's forces in executing thousands of Ephraimites is perhaps simply an extension of their leader's determination to win at all costs, a fatal flaw both for him and for his people.[270] While both hope for stability, they instead are faced with short-term gains and the reality of civil dispute and familial tragedy.

MINOR JUDGES REPRISE

(8) After him Ibzan of Bethlehem judges Israel. (9) He had thirty sons. He gave his thirty daughters in marriage outside his clan and brought in thirty young women from outside for his sons. He judged Israel seven years. (10) Then Ibzan died, and was buried at Bethlehem. (11) After him Elon the Zebulunite judged Israel ten years. (12) Then Elon the Zebulunite died, and was buried at Aijalon in the land of Zebulun. (13) After him Abdon son of Hillel the Pirathonite judged Israel. (14) He had forty sons and thirty grandsons, who rode on seventy donkeys; he judged Israel eight years. (15) Then Abdon son of Hillel the Pirathonite died, and was buried at Pirathon in the land of Ephraim, in the hill country of the Amalekites.

A listing of three more minor judges now concludes the Jephthah narrative, possibly indicating a continuation of the military emergency that had brought Jephthah to leadership of Gilead.[271] While one could argue, based on the very few years that Jephthah served as judge, that he is to be numbered among these minor figures, there is a real difference between them and him. His tumultuous six years stand in stark contrast to the apparently quite prosperous and placid administrations of the minor judges. For instance, Jephthah has only a single child, who he loses due to his own, uncharacteristic misuse of words, while most of the minor judges have many children, representing their wealth and potential power. Ibzan has sixty children, all of whom have contracted marriages. The notice that these marriages were made outside the clan simply indicates how successful Ibzan was in acquiring a network of support through marriage alliances and how he added to his own territorial holdings through these extrafamilial

---

[269] Ibid., 100–101.
[270] Robert Alter, "Introduction." Page 21 in *The Literary Guide to the Bible.* Edited by Robert Alter and Frank Kermode. Cambridge, Mass.: Harvard University Press, 1987.
[271] E. T. Mullen, "The 'Minor Judges,'" *CBQ* 44 (1982): 200.

links. It is also possible that not all of these children are his. Some may be clients or political allies over whom he has the power to choose marriage partners and thereby magnify his own authority within the region.[272]

The little that can be learned from the brief notice of Elon's ten years as judge over the tribe of Zebulon is centered on his name and the name of the city where he operated and was buried. While Boling may be correct in tying Elon's name, meaning "oak," to an Israelite takeover of an old Canaanite shrine built on the site of an ancient oak tree, this cannot be proven.[273] Certainly, if this is the case, it could be compared to Gideon's theophany at the oak of Ophrah (Judg 6:11–24) and his destruction of the Baal altar in his village (Judg 6:28–32).

Abdon's only accomplishment seems to be in the large number of sons and grandsons that he has. That each rides on a donkey is a display of wealth (compare Judg 5:10), and since more than one generation is mentioned it is possible to point to a long period of prosperity and apparent stability. However, Abdon serves as a judge only for eight years. Either the number is incorrect or in his case, and perhaps in those of the other minor judges, it represents a period of time he served as first among the elders of his clan or as a civil administrator as is described in the Mari texts.[274] This seems possible since none of these final three minor judges is said to have been "raised" to his position by God. In fact, there is no mention of a crisis that, under the normal turn of the Judges cycle, would require a judge to emerge to lead the people out of oppression. Instead these figures, including Tola and Jair in 10:1–5, function as literary bookends demarking Jephthah's account and speeding the reader toward the growing apostasy and failure of the Israelites throughout the remainder of the book.

BRIDGING THE HORIZONS

The stories in which the judges served as leaders of their tribes come to an end with Jephthah. Samson operates as an individual and never leads his people in battle or judges their civil disputes. Thus this is an appropriate point to stop and consider some of the issues raised by the Judges cycle and the characters who were raised to the position of judge.

[272] B. Beem, "The Minor Judges," in *The Biblical Canon* (1991): 155.
[273] R. G. Boling, *Judges* (1975): 216.
[274] Abraham Malamat, *Mari and the Early Israelite Experience.* Oxford: Oxford University Press, 1989: 34; Angel Marzal, "The Provincial Governor at Mari: His Title and Appointment," *JNES* 30 (1971): 190.

(1) One of the most popular themes in literature is the hero. Every society has its list of persons who qualify for this distinction, and in fact the hero is considered a universal archetype by folklorists and psychologists. Some of the characters in Judges clearly fit this category (Othniel, Shamgar, Deborah), while others do not and must be spoken of in qualified tones (Ehud, Jael, Gideon, and Jephthah). A reexamination of those qualities associated with the hero might be productive and startling when taken in context of events and national interests.

(2) The trickster is another archetypal character common to cultures throughout the world. This person is often considered amusing (e.g., Ulysses' outwitting the cyclops Polyphemus in Homer's *Odyssey*) or sly (Jacob's methods for overcoming Laban's plan to cheat him out of his wages in Gen 20:25–43). In Judges the trickster takes on a more sinister or even murderous quality. Ehud tricks Eglon into meeting with him alone behind closed doors and thus facilitates the assassination. Sisera falls into a trap based on his inability to think of a woman as a threat and ends up with a tent peg driven through his temple. Is it the underdog mentality of the ancient Israelites that caused them to glorify these violent acts against the enemy, or is it simply entertainment that leads to the composition of stories of the secret agent or femme fatale?

(3) Despite the common conception that ancient Israelite society was strictly patriarchal in orientation, there are a number of strong or prominent female figures in the Judges accounts in chapters 3–15. Achsah will not allow her father to shortchange her on her dowry, and Deborah is clearly in control of the situation involving Barak and the war with Jabin. Jael and Jephthah's daughter take matters into their own hands when the male characters are, or are in danger of, violating custom. Only in the final portions of the book, chapters 16–21, are women portrayed more often as victims who have little control over their fate or are dominated by male characters. Realizing that the portrayal of women in ancient Israel is more complex may help to eliminate stereotypes or naïve conclusions.

(4) Given the very direct intervention of God in the events in Joshua and Judges, it would be wise to evaluate more closely the role God plays in these stories. In many cases this involves warfare, and God is portrayed as the divine warrior. While individuals are raised to leadership positions, the text makes a point of saying that God has given the enemy "into the hand" of the Israelites or of the judge (Josh 8:7, 18; 10:19; Judg 3:28; 4:7). In these instances

some discussion or analysis of the ethics of a just war or a divinely ordained conflict might prove useful.

(5) Gideon's questioning of God's messenger (6:11–24) and testing of God's intent (6:36–40) raise interesting questions about individual calls to leadership or ministry as well as about the doubts everyone faces in a difficult or life-threatening situation. For example, Gideon's remark in 6:13 seems quite valid. In the midst of suffering it is only normal to ask why God has allowed the people to fall into such a situation and to refer to the "old stories" of the exodus as tales of "wonderful deeds" that have little to do with the reality in his own time.

(6) There are a number of acts of individual courage and daring in these tales: Ehud's single-handed mission (3:16–23), Jael's defense of her honor (4:17–22), the unnamed woman who strikes down Abimelech with her millstone (9:50–54), Jephthah's daughter's insistence that her father keep his vow and sacrifice her (11:34–40), and Jephthah's defiant stand against the bullying Ephraimites (12:1–6). While the Israelites as a whole are punished for their disobedience to the covenant, these stories of individuals who met the challenge of their times with resourcefulness and direct action make an otherwise bleak picture come alive for readers.

THEMATIC OVERVIEW OF THE SAMSON NARRATIVE

Much of the scholarship on the Samson narrative has centered on his Nazirite vows, his riddle, his amazing acts of strength, and his women. Some commentators have described each chapter in Judges 13–16 as representing separate traditions, tied together theologically and by reference to a common hero.[275] Others consider these chapters to be a coherent, consistent, unified story whose central themes are (1) filial devotion versus sexual desire,[276] (2) violation of the Nazirite vows, in whole or in part,[277] and (3) Samson as a symbol of the nation and a figure illustrating the Deuteronomistic

[275] Otto Eissfeldt, *Die Quellen des Richterbuches*. Leipzig, Ger.: Hinrichs, 1925: 81–87; James A. Wharton, "The Secret of Yahweh: Story and Affirmation in Judges 13–16," *Int* 27 (1973): 48–66.

[276] James L. Crenshaw, "The Samson Saga: Filial Devotion or Erotic Attachment?" *ZAW* 86 (1974): 471; Mark Greene, "Enigma Variations: Aspects of the Samson Story Judges 13–16," *Vox Evangelica* 21 (1991): 54–55.

[277] Joseph Blenkinsopp, "Structure and Styles in Judges 13–16," *JBL* 82 (1963): 65–76; Edward L. Greenstein, "The Riddle of Samson," *Proof* 1 (1981): 237–60.

theology.[278] To justify these thematic claims, the episodes are shown to emphasize the importance of (1) Samson's personal conflict over loyalty to family and the desire to experience and receive love,[279] (2) the consequences of his eventual failure to keep his Nazirite vows,[280] and (3) his dependence on Yahweh's spirit for his strength and his deliverance.[281] Plus a literary unity is achieved in what may have originally been disparate episodes by continual reference to the condition of being either powerful or powerless in given situations.[282]

A CLOSER LOOK AT THE NAZIRITE

Based on the biblical narrative, the Nazirite initially was a title or designation given to a person who took lifelong vows to maintain ritual purity beyond the norm for Israelites (see 1 Sam 1:22). Thus the law concerning the Nazirite in Num 6:1–21, which describes specific time limits (*kol yemê nizrô*) to the period of dedication (*yaplî*), may be a later manifestation of the tradition or a means for someone either to settle an obligation God or to purify self.[283] The Nazirites, whether lifelong or temporary, can be described as persons who have "separated" themselves by means of self-denial (*nāzîr*) and performed elaborate sacrifices once the period of the vow was over. The vows taken by these individuals, both male and female, include:

(1) **Abstinence from strong drinks and wine.** Like priests who are forbidden to drink wine while serving in the tabernacle (Lev 10:9), the Nazirite also must abstain throughout the period of the vow from drinking wine. The words used to describe fermented drinks are likely those only made from grapes (*yayîn wešēkār*). While intoxicants were made from other ingredients (e.g., grain), they were more common to daily consumption and in any case were restricted from use in sacrifice based on the priestly restrictions against the use of leavened dough in offerings (Lev 2:11).[284]

278 John Vickery, "In Strange Ways: The Story of Samson." Pages 58–73 in *Images of Man and God: Old Testament Stories in Literary Focus*. Edited by B. O. Long. Sheffield, Eng.: Almond Press, 1981; J. Cheryl Exum, "Aspects of Symmetry and Balance in the Samson Saga," *JSOT* 19 (1981): 9; idem, "The Theological Dimension of the Samson Saga," *VT* 33 (1983): 30–45.

279 J. L. Crenshaw, "Samson Saga," *ZAW* 86 (1974): 503.

280 D. I. Block, "Empowered by the Spirit of God," *SBJT* 1 (1997b): 51.

281 J. C. Exum, "Aspects of Symmetry and Balance," *JSOT* 19 (1981): 8, 24.

282 Carol Smith, "Samson and Delilah: A Parable of Power?" *JSOT* 76 (1997): 49–51.

283 Tony W. Cartledge, "Were Nazirite Vows Unconditional?" *CBQ* 51 (1989): 411–15.

284 Baruch Levine, *Numbers 1–20: A New Translation with Introduction and Commentary*. New York: Doubleday, 1993: 220.

(2) **Abstinence from grape products.** The prohibition against the consumption of all grape products might be interpreted as a glorification of the nomadic lifestyle prior to the settlement in Canaan, but that would have been of less concern to the priestly community of the monarchy and post-exilic periods.[285] The grape is one of the economic and dietary mainstays of Canaanite cultures, but it also has that same value for the Israelites (Deut 23:24; Judg 9:27). Thus giving up grape products would be a true dietary restriction that would have separated the Nazirite from his or her neighbors and would have been considered a personal sacrifice made for God.

(3) **Unshorn Hair.** The hair has symbolic value as a sign of social distinction, whether it is allowed to grow or to be cut, colored, or styled.[286] In the case of the Nazirite, the hair must be "untouched" by a razor for a specific period and then shorn, at which point it is consumed in the fire of the sacrifice (Num 6:18). Certainly, long strands of hair would have been an immediate physical indicator of someone who is a Nazirite, marking them as set aside in the community. When the vow is completed and the hair shaved, it is a ritual step toward moving that person back into the normal flow of everyday life with families and neighbors.[287]

(4) **Corpse Prohibition.** The normal regulations for Israelites with respect to contact with the dead (*nepeš mēt*) are in Num 19. Only the high priest had as high a level of corpse prohibition as the Nazirite (Lev 21:11). Such a magnified level of ritual purity for the Nazirite dramatizes the separation from normal practice and draws a contrast between the luxuriant growth of hair (symbolizing life and fertility) and the lifelessness of a corpse.[288] In circumstances such as the unexpected death of a person near or touching the Nazirite, a ritual purification is prescribed, including both animal sacrifice as a sin offering and the shaving of the now-contaminated hair, which completed the process by giving back to God the substance that originally had been dedicated as part of the vow.

The final section of the chapter (vv. 13–21) details the process of "desacralization" by which the Nazirite is returned to the community and

---

[285] Timothy R. Ashley, *The Book of Numbers*. Grand Rapids, Mich.: Eerdmans, 1993: 142; Israel Knohl, *The Sanctuary of Silence: The Priestly Torah and the Holiness School*. Minneapolis: Fortress Press, 1995: 105

[286] C. R. Hallpike, "Social Hair," *Man* 4 (1969): 257.

[287] Saul M. Olyan, "What Do Shaving Rites Accomplish and What Do They Signal in Biblical Ritual Contexts?" *JBL* 117 (1998): 615.

[288] B. Levine, *Numbers 1–20* (1993): 221–22.

resumes consumption of wine. It involves expensive offerings of animals (two lambs and a ram), grain, oil, and wine. Finally, the hair is shaved and placed on the altar to be consumed in the holy fire. The lack of any prayer or dedicatory statement in these regulations suggests that the purpose of Naziritism, at least in this form, is to fulfill an obligation rather than simply to offer oneself in a deeper sense to God.[289]

Given these expressed themes, one additional factor to consider that may assist the analysis of the stories is the centrality of freedom in the narrative. What other Israelite hero is described as having more freedom than Samson? Who else is so immune to law, morality, and dangerous situations? And yet, who is more tightly fettered "from the womb" than he is by vows, by the decisions and claims made upon him by women, and by the decisions of his God, who is "seeking a pretext to act against the Philistines" (Judg 14:4)? The escalation of violence on the part of both Samson and the Philistines is, as Vickery has noted, part of a "calculated program of harassment, incitement, and confrontation" designed to entrap both the hero and his enemies into a final catastrophic event that will liberate Israel and, in death, Samson.[290] Thus, if there is a central theme within the Samson narrative, it is whether the hero will ever actually be free of these snares; that is, whether his apparent physical power can be overcome and, ironically, how he will be trapped and overpowered by those characters who ordinarily lack power.

The traps that ensnare Samson begin at his birth and run through a series of encounters with Philistine women. The setting for the narrative places the Israelites in subjection to the "uncircumcised" Philistines. It is this very precarious power situation that predicates Samson's responses (aided directly at times by Yahweh's spirit) to the oppressors of his people. While Samson is at times in command of the situation, there is a clear sense that he is not always aware of the consequences of his actions, any more than are his parents, the Philistines, or the women in his life.

Running throughout the narrative and providing a measure of literary glue to hold together otherwise possibly separate and unconnected episodes

---

[289] T. W. Cartledge, "Were Nazirite Vows Unconditional?" *CBQ* 51 (1989): 415. B. Levine, *Numbers 1–20* (1993): 224–25, provides a linguistic comparison of the term *šelāmîm* (sacred gifts of greeting) with an example from the Ugaritic epic of Keret in which the king offered gifts (*šlmm*) to an attacker to end a siege. This further suggests how the Nazirite offers the gifts to God as a means of obtaining "peace" or perhaps restitution of order in his or her life.

[290] J. Vickery, "In Strange Ways," in *Images of Man and God* (1981): 66.

is a knowledge theme. Lack of knowledge often generates a degree of uncertainty, which provides an ironic touch to the stories. It gives the readers, who are often clued in by the narrator (as in Judg 14:4, 9) or by the use of paronomasia, a chance to anticipate events and be amused when they see characters falling into traps or taking paths that will lead them astray. As will be demonstrated, it is the act of deception and the condition of being deceived that marks the basic interaction of characters in these stories.[291]

It is not surprising therefore that upon reaching manhood Samson demonstrates actions of a "wild man" and of a trickster figure. Samson can be identified as a wild man by his hairiness, his use of physical force to deal with his problems or dangerous situations, and his fatal attraction to the wrong sort of women. In this sense he parallels the ancient Sumerian hero Enkidu. Both of these animal-like males can be civilized only when they are "handled" effectively by a female character.[292]

Like all tricksters, Samson functions as hero, underdog, and dupe.[293] Mischievous and skillful, he deceives his enemies and falls victim to them.[294] The following trickster scale illustrates the range of possible roles for these mischievous characters and provides a key to many of Samson's actions.[295] Tricksters (like Jacob and Laban in Gen 29:15–31:55) move from one stage to another, sometimes playing the hero, sometimes the gambler, and sometimes the one tricked and thus the fool.

FOOL	GAMBLER	EVIL TRICKSTER	FELLOW TRICKSTER	EXEMPLARY TRICKSTER	HERO

├─────────┼─────────┼─────────┼─────────┼─────────┤

In the course of this commentary the patterns contained in the narrative that deal with Samson's role as trickster will be traced. At the same time, the question of freedom and the trap motif, within which the protagonist finds himself in thrall to the desires and plans of the deity, will be explored. While a more natural division of the narrative may be into four episodes,[296] I have

---

[291] J. C. Exum, "Aspects of Symmetry and Balance," *JSOT* 19 (1981): 4–5.

[292] Gregory Mobley, "The Wild Man in the Bible and the Ancient Near East," *JBL* 116 (1997): 228–29.

[293] S. Niditch, *Underdogs and Tricksters* (1987): xi.

[294] S. Niditch, "Samson as Culture Hero," *CBQ* 52 (1990): 620.

[295] This trickster scale is based on a similar scale found in an introductory essay by Karl Luckert in Berard Haile, *Navajo Coyote Tales*. Lincoln: University of Nebraska Press, 1984: 7.

[296] J. Marais, *Representation in Old Testament* (1998): 123.

chosen to divide it into five, allowing chapter 15 its own place even though it is a natural consequence of the events in chapter 14.

CHAPTER 13

(1) The Israelites again did what was evil in the sight of the Lord, and the Lord gave them into the hand of the Philistines forty years. (2) There was a certain man of Zorah, of the tribe of the Danites, whose name was Manoah. His wife was barren, having borne no children. (3) And the angel of the Lord appeared to the woman and said to her, "Although you are barren, having borne no children, you shall conceive and bear a son. (4) Now be careful not to drink wine or strong drink, or to eat anything unclean, (5) for you shall conceive and bear a son. No razor is to come on his head, for the boy shall be a Nazirite to God from birth. It is he who shall begin to deliver Israel from the hand of the Philistines." (6) Then the woman came and told her husband, "A man of God came to me, and his appearance was like that of an angel of God, most awe-inspiring; I did not ask him where he came from, and he did not tell me his name; (7) but he said to me, 'You shall conceive and bear a son. So then drink no wine or strong drink, and eat nothing unclean, for the boy shall be a Nazirite to God from birth to the day of his death.'" (8) Then Manoah entreated the Lord, and said, "O, Lord, I pray, let the man of God whom you sent come to us again and teach us what we are to do concerning the boy who will be born." (9) God listened to Manoah, and the angel of God came again to the woman as she sat in the field; but her husband Manoah was not with her. (10) So the woman ran quickly and told her husband, "The man who came to me the other day has appeared to me." (11) Manoah got up and followed his wife, and came to the man and said to him, "Are you the man who spoke to this woman?" And he said, "I am." (12) Then Manoah said, "Now when your words come true, what is to be the boy's rule of life; what is he to do?" (13) The angel of the Lord said to Manoah, "Let the woman give heed to all that I said to her. (14) She may not eat of anything that comes from the vine. She is not to drink wine or strong drink, or eat any unclean thing. She is to observe everything that I commanded her." (15) Manoah said to the angel of the Lord, "Allow us to detain you, and prepare a kid for you." (16) The angel of the Lord said to Manoah, "If you detain me, I will not eat your food; but if you want to prepare a burnt offering, then offer it to the Lord." (For Manoah did not know that he was an angel of the Lord.) (17) Then Manoah said to the angel of the Lord, "What is your name, so that we may honor you when your words come true?"

(18) But the angel of the Lord said to him, "Why do you ask my name? It is too wonderful." (19) So Manoah took the kid with the grain offering, and offered it on the rock to the Lord, to him who works wonders. (20) When the flame went up toward heaven from the altar, the angel of the Lord ascended in the flame of the altar while Manoah and his wife looked on; and they fell on their faces to the ground. (21) The angel of the Lord did not appear again to Manoah and his wife. Then Manoah realized that it was the angel of the Lord. (22) And Manoah said to his wife, "We shall surely die, for we have seen God." (23) But his wife said to him, "If the Lord had meant to kill us, he would not have accepted a burnt offering and a grain offering at our hands, or shown us all these things, or now announced to us such things as these." (24) The woman bore a son, and named him Samson. The boy grew, and the Lord blessed him. (25) The spirit of the Lord began to stir him in Mahanehdan, between Zorah and Eshtaol.

*F*ew men in the Bible are singled out as chosen from their mother's womb to become a pivotal character in the life of a people. Only Ishmael (Gen 16:7–16), Isaac (Gen. 17:16–21; 18:10–15), John the Baptist (Luke 1:5–25, 57–66), and Jesus (Luke 1:26–45; 2:1–7) are announced to their mothers and fathers in quite the same way that Samson is to Manoah and his wife (Judg 13:3–14).[297] Each of these annunciations, except for that of Isaac,[298] involves an angel speaking to the mother first and then to the father, and each signifies the beginning of a special relationship between Yahweh and the child. The only major departure in the pattern between the Samson narrative and these other theophanies is that the angel does not name the child of Manoah and his wife. These variations may simply reflect poetic license on the part of the storyteller since the annunciation type-scene often allows for flexibility of detail.[299]

The relationship invariably involves direction by the deity of the activities and life of the "called" mortal.[300] That Samson had no say in the matter of

---

[297] Similar annunciations, but without an angel present, are found in Isa 7:14–15; 8:3–4; Jer 1:5; and Gal 1:15. On this latter reference, see Charles W. Hedrick, "Paul's Conversion/Call: A Comparative Analysis of the Three Reports in Acts," *JBL* 100 (1981): 415–32.

[298] The anomaly in Isaac's case is difficult to explain. However, the argument could be made that the angel knew Sarah was hiding and listening to the men's conversation at the tent flap. See Robert Alter, "Biblical Type-Scenes and the Uses of Convention," *Critical Inquiry* 5 (2, 1978): 359, for discussion of this type-scene and its comparison with other barren wife and birth announcement stories.

[299] James G. Williams, "The Beautiful and the Barren: Conventions in Biblical Type-Scenes," *JSOT* 17 (1980): 110; Robert Alter, "How Convention Helps Us Read: The Case of the Bible's Annunciation Type-Scene," *Proof* 3 (1983): 115–30.

[300] N. Habel, "Form and Significance of the Call Narratives," *ZAW* 77 (1965): 298–99.

becoming a Nazirite is central to the overall theme of lack of freedom. It creates a sense of anticipation that, because it was not voluntary, will never be fulfilled and will serve as both the bane of Samson's life and the catalyst for many of his activities.[301] The decision has been made for him by the deity and perpetuated by the acceptance of the vow by his mother while he is still in the womb. Particularly significant is his mother's adherence to the requirements of the Nazirite vow (not drinking wine or eating unclean food) until his birth since it will be women who will subsequently trigger other signs of his lack of free action. The sign that he is to become a driven figure is found in the benediction at the end of chapter 13: "the spirit of the Lord began to stir in him" (v. 24).

The distinctive character of Manoah's wife, initially, is centered on her lack of a name and her barrenness. Under ordinary circumstances these factors would indicate that she is powerless and despised within her household and among her people. Yet it is to her that the angel appears twice. In both cases she is alone, a rather unusual circumstance for any woman in this period, unless she is so despised that her fate is of little concern to anyone (compare Hagar's flight into the desert in Gen 16:6).

Furthermore, Samson's mother, unlike the other women in his life, lacks any hint of overt sexuality. She is barren, alone, and quite unremarkable until the annunciation takes place. At that point she is transformed, if not named. Her pregnancy is announced by a similarly unnamed, male (the masculine pronoun is used in the text) divine messenger, but she neither asks the angel's name nor questions him about the event. In addition, there is no euphemistic (i.e., "he went in") or overt mention of Manoah having relations with his wife to demonstrate his paternity of the child (compare Gen 16:4 [Abram and Hagar]; 29:23 [Jacob and Leah]; 29:30 [Jacob and Rachel]). While displaying all of the stereotypical traits of the good wife (humble, deferential to her husband, sensible), Manoah's wife cannot be considered comparable to the Timnite woman, the prostitute of Gath, or Delilah, all of whom are actively and seductively sexual.[302]

When she refers to the angel as a "man of God," she also notes that he is like an angel, "awe-inspiring,"[303] and she does not, unlike her husband, ask her

---

[301] Adele Reinhartz, "Samson's Mother: An Unnamed Protagonist," *JSOT* 55 (1992): 25–26; J. C. Exum, "Theological Dimension," *VT* 33 (1983): 35.

[302] J. C. Exum, "Feminist Criticism," in *Judges and Method* (1995): 80–81.

[303] The *melammu* (shining countenance of the gods) in ancient Mesopotamia was part of their armament and was one physical measure distinguishing them from mortals. For example, in the "Hymnal Prayer of Enheduanna: The Adoration of Inanna in Ur," the goddess is described as having a "fierce countenance" (*ANET*, 581, ll. 128–30).

visitor his name or his place of origin. In that sense she shows greater abilities of perception than her husband.[304] She also exercises proper protocol in dealing with a divine being (see foiled attempt to learn God's name in Gen 32:27–29). While the annunciation of the angel follows established patterns, the charge that the mother must maintain Nazirite obligations prior to birth and that the child be a lifelong Nazirite adds an extra dimension to annunciation stories in the Hebrew Bible. It should be noted at this point, however, that the only Nazirite obligation imposed on Samson is not to cut his hair. As it becomes clear, the only time that God's spirit will not aid him and that his strength is lost is when his hair is shorn (16:19–22).[305]

The one story that is comparable to this annunciation episode is that involving Hannah's vow and sacrifice at Shiloh. Having also faced the ignominy of barrenness, she makes the wrenching decision that if she is granted a son he will be a Nazirite "until the day of his death" (1 Sam 1:11). Although the only obligation laid on her is to "lend" him to the Lord's service at Shiloh and thus deprive herself of his presence once he is weaned (1 Sam 1:22–28), she chooses to make that choice for her son, gaining the status of motherhood for herself and setting his life within a context he might not have otherwise chosen.[306]

Manoah may be concerned about unauthorized fraternization between his wife and an unknown man. It is also possible that he is feeling slighted by not being addressed by the "man of God" himself. Therefore he prays to God, presumably the one who has dispatched this messenger, to send him again so that he, Manoah, can learn more firsthand. Curiously, the angel appears to the wife again instead but does remain afterward and thereby allows Manoah to interview him. Unlike his wife, Manoah does not recognize the angel as a divine being. He deals with him as one would a "man of God"/prophet, offering him hospitality and asking for his name so that he could be honored at the time of the child's birth.

Instead the angel gives precedence to Manoah's wife as the one who had originally received his instructions and repeats that the instructions given to her must be obeyed. He provides a broad hint that he is not mortal by refusing to eat but allows for the offered animal to serve as a sacrifice to God. In this way the angel designates the sacrifice as a sign of Manoah's

---

[304] J. Cheryl Exum, "Promise and Fulfillment: Narrative Art in Judges 13," *JBL* 99 (1980): 45; M. Greene, "Enigma Variations," *Vox Evangelica* 21 (1991): 58.

[305] T. W. Cartledge, "Were Nazirite Vows Unconditional?" *CBQ* 51 (1989): 411.

[306] Carol L. Meyers, "The Hannah Narrative in Feminist Perspective." Pages 125–26 in *Go to the Land I Will Show You: Studies in Honor of Dwight W. Young.* Edited by Joseph Coleson and Victor H. Matthews. Winona Lake, Ind.: Eisenbrauns, 1996.

*"and His name
shall be
called -
Wonderful"*

acceptance of the message and indicates that he is no mortal guest who will be open to table fellowship.[307] The angel's response when asked his name is that "it is wonderful" (*pelî*), a term that also appears in the Song of Miriam in Exod 15:11 as an indicator of God's wonder-working abilities.[308]

The theophany and sacrifice can easily be compared to Gideon's divine encounter and call narrative, in which that hero also is not certain of the divine being's identity and also provides a meal/sacrifice (Judg 6:17–24). In both narratives it is only when the angel vanishes amidst the smoke of the sacrifice that they both realize they have experienced a theophany (Judg 6:21–22; 13:20–23). Both Gideon and Manoah are duly frightened by the implications of having seen God face to face,[309] but it is Manoah's wife who provides a practical evaluation of the event.[310] Unlike her frantic husband, who seems certain that he is now to be struck dead, she quite calmly explains, much like a mother would to a small child, that God would not have gone to the trouble of promising them a son if the intention was to kill them on the spot. Her commonsense analysis takes the place of the divine assurance not to fear that appears in other theophanies (Gen 32:31; Exod 3:6; Judg 6: 22).[311]

At the conclusion of the annunciation story a brief statement is appended in vv. 24–25 that foreshadows Samson's presumed role as savior of his people. The reader is informed of God's blessing on the child as well as of the beginnings of a stirring of God's spirit within him (compare similar statements made about Samuel in 1 Sam 2:26 and Jesus in Luke 2:40, 52). This ties the birth narrative to the remainder of the story of Samson, in which the infusion of God's spirit is a prelude to action.[312]

CHAPTER 14

(1) Once Samson went down to Timnah, and at Timnah he saw a Philistine woman. (2) Then he came up, and told his father and mother, "I saw a Philistine

---

[307] J. L. Crenshaw, "Samson Saga," *ZAW* 86 (1974): 479.

[308] R. G. Boling, *Judges* (1975): 222.

[309] See the Jacob narrative (Gen 28:10–17; 32:24–30) for two other instances of apparent miraculous survival of a mortal who has had an encounter with God.

[310] V. H. Matthews, "Theophanies Cultic and Cosmic," in *Israel's Apostasy and Restoration* (1988): 309.

[311] Yairah Amit, "'Manoah Promptly Followed His Wife' (Judges 13.11): On the Place of the Woman in Birth Narratives." Pages 149–50 in *A Feminist Companion to Judges*. Edited by Athalya Brenner. Sheffield, Eng.: JSOT Press, 1993.

[312] M. Z. Brettler, *Book of Judges* (2002): 43.

woman at Timnah; now get her for me as my wife." (3) But his father and mother said to him, "Is there not a woman among your kin, or among all our people, that you must go to take a wife from the uncircumcised Philistines?" But Samson said to his father, "Get her for me, because she pleases me." (4) His father and mother did not know that this was from the Lord; for he was seeking a pretext to act against the Philistines. At that time the Philistines had dominion over Israel. (5) Then Samson went down with his father and mother to Timnah. When he came to the vineyards of Timnah, suddenly a young lion roared at him. (6) The spirit of the Lord rushed on him, and he tore the lion apart barehanded as one might tear apart a kid. But he did not tell his father or his mother what he had done. (7) Then he went down and talked with the woman, and she pleased Samson. (8) After a while he returned to marry her, and he turned aside to see the carcass of the lion, and there was a swarm of bees in the body of the lion, and honey. (9) He scraped it out into his hands, and went on, eating as he went. When he came to his father and mother, he gave some to them, and they ate it. But he did not tell them that he had taken the honey from the carcass of the lion. (10) His father went down to the woman, and Samson made a feast there as the young men were accustomed to do. (11) When the people saw him, they brought thirty companions to be with him. (12) Samson said to them, "Let me now put a riddle to you. If you can explain it to me within the seven days of the feast, and find it out, then I will give you thirty linen garments and thirty festal garments. (13) But if you cannot explain it to me, then you shall give me thirty linen garments and thirty festal garments." So they said to him, "Ask your riddle; let us hear it." (14) He said to them, "Out of the eater came something to eat. Out of the strong came something sweet." But for three days they could not explain the riddle. (15) On the fourth day they said to Samson's wife, "Coax your husband to explain the riddle to us, or we will burn you and your father's house with fire. Have you invited us here to impoverish us?" (16) So Samson's wife wept before him, saying "You hate me; you do not really love me. You have asked a riddle of my people, but you have not explained it to me." He said to her, "Look, I have not told my father or my mother. Why should I tell you?" (17) She wept before him the seven days that their feast lasted; and because she nagged him, on the seventh day he told her. Then she explained the riddle to her people. (18) The men of the town said to him on the seventh day before the sun went down, "What is sweeter than honey? What is stronger than a lion?" And he said to them, "If you had not plowed with my heifer, you would not have found out my riddle." (19) Then the spirit of the Lord rushed on him, and he went down to Ashkelon. He killed thirty men of the town, took their spoil, and gave the festal garments to those who had explained the riddle. In hot anger he went back to his father's house. (20) And Samson's wife was given to his companion, who had been his best man.

S amson's involvement with the Timnite woman brings up several questions. Why does he insist on marrying a non-Israelite? Is this another attempt (voiced by his parents) at restoring restrictive (endogamic) marriage practices? If so, the grief of his parents over this seemingly capricious desire could easily be compared to that of Isaac and Rebekah over Esau's marriage to two Hittite women (Gen 26:34–35). Or, is this a further reflection of the anti-Canaanite theme expressed in the *ḥērēm* (holy war) commands of Deut 7:1–10, that they "not make marriages with them" (v. 3) but "utterly destroy them"? One explanation of this latter point is based on the use of a metaphor in which Samson's foreign marriage equals the idolatry of Israel in the Judges period (Judg 3:6).[313] It also functions as a reflection of a world in which values are overturned or reversed.

When he is questioned by his parents, their concern is expressed in a typical negative form found throughout the narrative (see Judg 14:15, 16b; 15:11b, 18; 16:15). The only direct answer they receive is a reiteration by Samson that he wants what pleases him. However, there is an editorial/narrative aside inserted in the text in v. 4 explaining that his parents did not know that this was a result of God's plan to end Philistine dominion. Their lack of knowledge at this point and in the episode involving the slaying of the lion (14:9, 16b) provides still another subtheme (know/not know). Thus one of the literary keys to the construction of the Samson narrative is the signaling to the reader of exactly who knew what and when.[314]

The other literary foundation for the Samson narrative is the "trap motif," a basic framework that contains a series of steps drawing Samson in a web created by his desire for foreign women. This motif is found in chapter 14 and twice in chapter 16.

TRAP MOTIF IN THE SAMSON NARRATIVE

1. Involvement with a Philistine woman: Samson's involvement with women is always portrayed as the result of his own physical desires. He sees the Timnite woman and the prostitute of Gaza and must have them. He falls in love with Delilah and, even in the face of repeated signs of treachery, remains devoted to her.

[handwritten margin note: promiscuous behavior]

---

[313] E. L. Greenstein, "Riddle of Samson," *Proof* 1 (1981): 250.
[314] J. L. Crenshaw, "Samson Saga," *ZAW* 86 (1974): 486–87.

2. A woman entices Samson into a trap: Both the Timnite woman and Delilah are persuaded to entice Samson into revealing information that will harm him. The Gazite prostitute's charms entice the hero and place him in danger.

3. Heroic action leads to escape and revenge against the Philistines: This step figures into each episode, although it is delayed in the final stages of the Delilah story. There are some instances where the "spirit of the Lord" figures into the escape but not in Judg 16.

When Samson's parents see that they cannot change his mind, they travel to the Philistine city of Timnah. On the way to making the actual arrangements for the marriage, Samson demonstrates his great strength against a lion (14:5–6). Curiously, the "young lion" simply roars, and Samson does not react aggressively until the spirit of the Lord "rushed" into him. This is the first time in the narrative that Samson shows his amazing abilities, but they are aided and strengthened by the infusion of God's spirit. As noted in comments on Othniel (3:10), Gideon (6:34), and Jephthah (11:29), the theme of God's spirit "coming upon" or investing judges is intended to provide them with an aura of authority as they are called upon to lead the Israelites in battle. The phrase used in the Samson narrative, however, suggests physical possession by the spirit of God, infusing the hero with superhuman strength. The phrase also appears in slightly varied grammatical form in Samuel's commissioning of Saul in 1 Sam 10:6 as *wĕsālĕhâ ʿālêkā rûᵃḥ yahweh* (the spirit of Yahweh will rush upon you) and again in 1 Sam 11:6 when Saul is informed of the threat to the city of Jabesh-gilead.[315] Unlike Saul, however, Samson will never prophecy or lead the Israelites in battle. The infusion of God's spirit is employed in personal exploits, a sort of berserker frenzy similar to that with which Gilgamesh enflamed himself and became "like a raging bull" (*ANET*, 82: Gilg IV.v.48).

It is possible that the seizing of Samson by God's spirit is an indication of divine sanction for what Samson is about to do. Looking at the episode as a whole, however, this incident can also be identified as an example of a narrative device dividing the tale into three parts. At strategic moments (the lion's attack, the need to repay the bet – 14:19, and the jawbone massacre – 15:14) God's spirit enters Samson and allows him to perform feats of great strength. Interestingly, each of these events also functions as a signal that the

---

[315] See P. Kyle McCarter, *I Samuel: A New Translation with Introduction and Commentary.* AB 8. New York: Doubleday, 1980: 182, 203.

romance is doomed. The escalating rivalry, ordained by God in 14:4, results in fits of violence that allow Samson to vent his emotions but ultimately that frustrate his desire to marry the Timnite woman.[316]

Samson keeps the adventure with the lion a secret from his parents (14:6b). While this may be because it involves a violation of his Nazirite vows, it is also quite likely another example of the knowledge theme used by the writer to build suspense and to introduce the hero as a trickster figure (compare v. 4). Greenstein has argued that as long as Samson did not violate all of his Nazirite obligations he was forgiven and continually empowered by God as his agent.[317] In that sense his "career" serves in microcosm as a parallel to the Israelites throughout the Book of Judges. The people of the covenant, like Samson, continually fail to keep the stipulations of their agreement with God, and God, after a suitable period of instruction/oppression, has mercy on them and allows them to be delivered, however temporarily.

To be sure, there is a place for repentance, and Samson's prayers (16:28–30 more than 15:18–19) may be a reflection of the maxim that anything is possible for the one who recognizes God's power and calls upon him for help.[318] In addition, the Judges period is a time of almost complete lawlessness (Judg 17:6). Samson is as unmindful of the law as any character of this time, but if he is in fact a Nazirite, it can be expected that he is aware of his vows, whether he chooses to obey them or not.

At the wedding feast Samson tells a riddle based on his two encounters with the lion. His use of a personal experience with death and the sweetness garnered from the ripe corpse of the lion is a grim play on what is about to unfold in the story. It is likely that the riddle contest is a part of the evening's entertainment at the marriage celebration and an occasion for those with rhetorical skill to demonstrate their performance abilities.[319] Thus, as Crenshaw suggests, this would serve as a way for Samson "to prove

---

[316] Mieke Bal, *Lethal Love: Feminist Literary Readings of Biblical Love Stories.* Bloomington: Indiana University Press, 1987: 42–48, argues that the violence of the lion's death is the first signal of the demise of Samson's romance and of his eventual rending, in his frustration, of the thirty men of Ashkelon and then, in revenge over the death of his bride, of the Philistines who had burned her father's house down. His frustrated sexuality stands in contrast to the sweetness of the honey taken from the lion's body and is elsewhere (especially in Song of Songs) with the love and the contentment of a young couple. On this point, see Athalya Brenner, "The Food of Love: Gendered Food and Food Imagery in the Song of Songs," *Semeia* 86 (1999a): 109–10.

[317] E. L. Greenstein, "Riddle of Samson," *Proof* 1 (1981): 251.

[318] J. C. Exum, "Aspects of Symmetry and Balance," *JSOT* 19 (1981): 21–24.

[319] Thomas A. Burns, "Riddling: Occasion to Act," *Journal of American Folklore* 89 (1976): 143–45.

his superior wit" in front of the Philistines, who probably considered the Israelites their inferior[320] (see Prov 1:6 for the equation of wisdom with the skill of telling riddles).

Samson's riddle is in the form of a statement, and the answer he eventually receives is in the form of a question, the exact reverse of what might be expected rhetorically.[321] It is possible that the Philistine answer is an attempt to downplay the difficulty of Samson's riddle by responding with a paraphrased version of his original statement, which might also hide the fact that they had forced the answer from his bride.[322]

None of the artful linguistic traps or double entendres in the riddle prove to be effective because ultimately they are all circumvented by the Philistines' coercion of Samson's wife. Samson is enticed by his bride because of the frustration of the wedding "companions" who cannot solve the riddle on their own. Claudia Camp and Carole Fontaine, in their examination of the linguistic structure of this riddle, suggest that Samson, through his use of proverbial wisdom themes, had given the companions clues that made the riddle answerable.[323] However, they note, the companions were blinded by the context of the wedding feast and their inability to go beyond the sexual connotations raised by the ideas of "sweet" and "strong." These men therefore coerce Samson's bride into obtaining the solution by threatening to burn her and her father in their house. Their demand that she "coax [open] your husband" is a wordplay on *pattî*, which can mean "to open" (Prov 20:19) but is translated here in the factitive *piel* form *pattî* as "coax."[324] The Timnite's tears (see Esther 8:3) and continual pleas that he reveal the solution eventually frustrate Samson into giving away his secret.

This contest clearly portrays Samson as a trickster who attempts to ensnare his opponents with his riddle. He is tricked in turn by the Philistines and then turns the tables once again by going to Ashkelon, killing thirty innocent

---

[320] James L. Crenshaw, *Samson, A Secret Betrayed, A Vow Ignored.* Atlanta: Mercer University Press, 1978: 99.

[321] A. Brenner, "Food of Love," *Semeia* 86 (1999a): 109; Edgar Slotkin, "Response to Professors Fontaine and Camp." Page 157 in *Text and Tradition: The Hebrew Bible and Folklore* (*Semeia* 20). Edited by Susan Niditch. Atlanta: Scholars Press, 1990.

[322] Jichan Kim, *The Structure of the Samson Cycle.* Kampen, Neth.: Kok Pharos, 1993: 263.

[323] Claudia Camp and Carole Fontaine, "The Words of the Wise and Their Riddles." Pages 138–40 in *Text and Tradition: The Hebrew Bible and Folklore.* Edited by Susan Niditch. Atlanta: Scholars Press, 1990.

[324] Ibid., 147, n. 11, call this a "triple entendre" since the connotations of the words also allow for the translation "to make a fool of." In this case both Samson and the Philistines will be enticed, the former to give up his riddle solution and the latter to be repaid with bloody garments and an enraged superman.

Philistines and bringing their clothes back to satisfy the bet (14:19). By definition these men are not truly innocent, however, since they are uncircumcised
Philistines (see the continual use of this pejorative term for the Philistines
in 1 Sam 17:26, 36; 31:4). Furthermore, according to the Deuteronomistic
editor (Deut 20:10–18) and the trickster mentality of Samson, they are fair
game because they represent the potential for religious contamination and
idolatry.[325] This is shown by the second infusion of God's spirit into the
hero at this point since it gives the appearance of divine aid and sanction
for Samson's violent actions.

The resolution and escape portion of this episode begins with the statement that when Samson abandoned his wife and returned home she was
given to "his best man" (v. 20). This injury, whether intentional or not, gives
him another opportunity to take revenge on the Philistines. It precipitates a
series of moves and countermoves that ultimately leave Samson triumphant,
although wifeless. The woman had only been a ploy in any case, if the statement in 14:4 is to be taken seriously. She had doubly served her purpose
by posing as bait and then as an object of revenge. Her role also serves to
foreshadow Samson's affair with Delilah.

A CLOSER LOOK AT THE PHILISTINES

The first documentation of the groups that will later be collectively referred
to as the Sea Peoples occurs in the El Amarna documents of Fourteenth
century BCE Egypt. Mention is made of Sherden mercenaries who served in
the Egyptian army at Byblos and the Lukka/Lycians who operated as pirates
in the Mediterranean. Contingents of the Sea Peoples are also recorded in the
account of the Battle of Kadesh (1285 BCE) fighting for Pharaoh Rameses II. A
general collapse of the Aegean cultures resulted in the late thirteenth century
in a general migration of these Sea Peoples, which in turn threatened the
major population centers of the Near East.[326] Various contingents, probably
acting independently of each other, were successful in defeating the Hittite
forces in Anatolia, destroying the seaport city of Ugarit in northern Syria. The
reliefs and inscriptions in the Medinet Habu mortuary temple of Pharaoh

---

[325] R. D. Nelson *Deuteronomy* (2002): 251. Note the continued use of "uncircumcised" as a
term for unclean lands and peoples in the exilic and postexilic prophets (Jer 9:26; Ezek
31:18; Isa 52:1).

[326] William H. Stiebling Jr., "The End of the Mycenean Age," *BA* 43 (1980): 15; Neal Bierling,
Giving Goliath His Due. Grand Rapids, Mich.: Baker, 1992: 65.

Rameses III (1198–1166 BCE) indicate that the Sea Peoples sorely pressed the resources of Egypt before being checked in a naval battle in the 1170s.[327] Seven peoples are listed in the Egyptian record, including the Plst (Philistines), the Tjekel, and the Dnn (Denyen).[328]

Material evidence that the Philistines settled along the coastal plain and in the Shephelah region of southern Canaan can be found in their introduction of Aegean-style pottery, using local clays but with painted designs similar to those found in Mycenaean sites. There are also architectural designs and evidence of goddess cult similar to that found in Greece.[329] During the mid-twelfth century, they founded five major cities (Ashdod, Ashkelon, Gezer, Gath, and Ekron; Josh 13:2–3), displacing some former Canaanite inhabitants and continuing to clash with Egyptian garrisons in the region.[330] In the process of Sea Peoples' settling the area, the Philistine cities and villages such as Timnah (Judg 14:1) came into contact with the Israelite tribes that were settling the Judean Hill Country, and a fierce competition occurred between these peoples for use of the land. To give an idea of seriousness of this rivalry, "enemy" peoples are mentioned 919 times in the biblical narrative and 423 (46%) of these refer to the Philistines.[331] However, it is clear that the Philistines' organizational and technological edge, but not necessarily in the working of iron, gave them a real advantage during the first century of their contact with the Israelites (Judg 15:11; 1 Sam 13:19–20).[332] They maintain their supremacy until the beginning of the tenth century, when pressure from the Egyptian pharaoh Siamun and the emerging Israelite monarchy forces them into a weaker position.[333] It is not surprising that David's first victory, over the Philistine giant Goliath of Gath, takes place in the buffer

---

[327] Trude Dothan, "The 'Sea Peoples' and the Philistines of Ancient Palestine." Pages 1267–69 of vol. 1 in *Civilizations of the Ancient Near East.* Edited by Jack M. Sasson. Peabody, Mass.: Hendrickson, 1995: 1267–69.

[328] See Amihai Mazar, *Archaeology of the Land of the Bible: 10,000–586 B.C.E.* New York: Doubleday, 1990: 302–7; N. Bierling, *Giving Goliath His Due* (1992): 52–62.

[329] Kurt L. Noll, *Canaan and Israel in Antiquity: An Introduction.* London: Sheffield Academic Press, 2001: 147–48.

[330] Lawrence E. Stager, "Forging an Identity: The Emergence of Ancient Israel." Pages 152–54 in *The Oxford History of the Biblical World.* Edited by Michael D. Coogan. New York: Oxford University Press, 1998.

[331] Seymour Gitin, "Philistia in Transition: The Tenth Century BCE and Beyond." Page 163, n. 4 in *Mediterranean Peoples in Transition: Thirteenth to Early Tenth Centuries BCE.* Edited by Seymour Gitin et al. Jerusalem: Israel Exploration Society, 1998.

[332] P. McNutt, *Reconstructing the Society* (1999): 113–14.

[333] T. Dothan, "The 'Sea Peoples' and the Philistines," in *Civilizations of the Ancient Near East* (1995): 1274.

zone of the Elah Valley that had been a center of conflict for decades (1 Sam 17:2).[334]

CHAPTER 15

(1) After a while, at the time of the wheat harvest, Samson went to visit his wife, bringing along a kid. He said, "I want to go into my wife's room." But her father would not allow him to go in. (2) Her father said, "I was sure that you had rejected her; so I gave her to your companion. Is not her younger sister prettier than she? Why not take her instead?" (3) Samson said to them, "This time, when I do mischief to the Philistines, I will be without blame." (4) So Samson went and caught three hundred foxes and took some torches; and he turned the foxes tail to tail and put a torch between each pair of tails. (5) When he had set fire to the torches, he let the foxes go into the standing grain of the Philistines, and burned up the shocks and the standing grain, as well as the vineyards and olive groves. (6) Then the Philistines asked, "Who has done this?" And they said, "Samson, the son-in-law of the Timnite, because he has taken Samson's wife and given her to his companion." So the Philistines came up, and burned her and her father. (7) Samson said to them, "If this is what you do, I swear I will not stop until I have taken revenge on you." (8) He struck them down hip and thigh with great slaughter; and he went down and stayed in the cleft of the rock of Etam. (9) Then the Philistines came up and encamped in Judah, and made a raid on Lehi. (10) The men of Judah said, "Why have you come up against us?" They said, "We have come up to bind Samson, to do to him as he did to us." (11) Then three thousand men of Judah went down to the cleft of the rock of Etam, and they said to Samson, "Do you not know that the Philistines are rulers over us? What then have you done to us?" He replied, "As they did to me, so I have done to them." (12) They said to him, "We have come down to bind you, so that we may give you into the hands of the Philistines." Samson answered them, "Swear to me that you yourselves will not attack me." (13) They said to him, "No, we will only bind you and give you into their hands; we will not kill you." So they bound him with two new ropes, and brought him up from the rock. (14) When he came to Lehi,

---

[334] William M. Schniedewind, "The Geopolitical History of Philistine Gath," *BASOR* 309 (1998): 74.

the Philistines came shouting to meet him; and the spirit of the Lord rushed on him, and the ropes that were on his arms became like flax that has caught fire, and his bonds melted off his hands. (15) Then he found a fresh jawbone of a donkey, reached down and took it, and with it he killed a thousand men. (16) And Samson said, "With the jawbone of a donkey, heaps upon heaps, with the jawbone of a donkey I have slain a thousand men." (17) When he had finished speaking, he threw away the jawbone; and that place was called Ramath-lehi. (18) By then he was very thirsty, and he called on the Lord, saying, "You have granted this great victory by the hand of your servant. Am I now to die of thirst, and fall into the hands of the uncircumcised?" (19) So God split open the hollow place that is at Lehi, and water came from it. When he drank, his spirit returned, and he revived. Therefore it was named Enhakkore, which is at Lehi to this day. (20) And he judged Israel in the days of the Philistines twenty years.

The narrative that follows this initial episode is one of escalating violence. First Samson returns to his father-in-law's house bearing a peace offering. The suggestion that Samson was simply following the conventions of a *tsadiqah* marriage,[335] in which the groom visits his wife in her father's house at particular intervals, is totally out of character for this lusty hero. He had left the feast in a fit of anger over her disloyalty and now was back to reclaim what was his (15:1). In this sense he could be compared to the Levite of Judg 19 who, after a delay of three months, went to fetch his runaway concubine in her father's house (v. 3).

When Samson is offered the younger, fairer sister, he is totally frustrated and blames the Philistines for bringing their punishment upon their own heads (v. 3). He is no more interested at this point in compromise than he was when he first insisted that Manoah arrange the marriage. His revenge satisfies his personal feelings and also hurts the Philistines economically. By tying torches to the tails of 300 foxes, he destroys all facets of their agricultural assets, burning their fields and the stacks of harvested grain, their vineyards and their olive groves (compare 2 Sam 14:30).[336] These three products are the economic and dietary staples of ancient Palestine.[337] By depriving the Philistines of their food and their principal supply of trade goods (wine and

---

335 J. L. Crenshaw, *Samson, A Secret Betrayed* (1978): 82.
336 Othniel Margalith, "Samson's Foxes," *VT* 30 (1980): 224–25.
337 Frank Frick, "'Oil from Flinty Rock' (Deuteronomy 32:13): Olive Cultivation and Olive Oil Processing in the Hebrew Bible – A Socio-Materialist Perspective," *Semeia* 86 (1999): 12–15; Carol L. Meyers, "An Ethnoarchaeological Analysis of Hannah's Sacrifice." Pages 83–85

olive oil), he strips them bare economically in much the same way as he had stripped the bodies of the men he killed in Ashkelon.

It is now the Philistines' turn to respond as part of the alternating vendetta. Upon discovering that Samson is responsible for the loss of their grain, they blame his action on his father-in-law, who "has taken Samson's wife and given her to his companion" (v. 6). This charge provides them with an easy scapegoat, a father who had violated a trust and a wife caught in adultery. Like in the case in Deut 22:13–21, the punishment is carried out at her father's doorstep.[338] In this instance, however, her father as well is consigned to the flames.[339] It also brings them full circle since the threat made by the companions was one of fire if she did not aid them (14:15).

THE RECIPROCATING CYCLE OF REVENGE IN THE SAMSON NARRATIVE

Action	Counteraction
Philistines obtain riddle solution (14:18)	Samson kills 30 Philistines to pay bet (14:19)
Samson's bride given to another man (15:2)	Samson burns the Philistine fields (15:5)
Philistines burn his bride's family (15:6)	Samson slaughters many Philistines (15:8)
Philistines raid Lehi and hunt for Samson (15:9)	Samson kills 1,000 Philistines (15:15)
Philistines prepare trap at Gaza (16:2)	Samson steals Gaza's city gates (16:3)
Philistines capture and blind Samson (16:21)	Samson destroys Dagon temple (16:28–30)[340]

Samson responds to this crime by slaughtering an undetermined number of Philistines "hip and thigh" (v. 7). For his part, Samson must have considered this the highest point of the vendetta since he says that after this "I will quit." Feuds do not end quite so easily, however. Samson has not yet reached a crisis point. Neither in the incident with the foxes nor in this latest

in *Pomegranates and Golden Bells*. Edited by David P. Wright et al. Winona Lake, Ind.: Eisenbrauns, 1995.

[338] Victor H. Matthews, "Entrance Ways and Threshing Floors: Legally Significant Sites in the Ancient Near East," *Fides et Historia* 19 (1987): 32.

[339] E. L. Greenstein, "Riddle of Samson," *Proof* 1 (1981): 248, also notes the fiery threat made by the Ephraimites against Jephthah in Judg 12:1.

[340] This list is based in part on Hartmut Gese, "Die ältere Simsonüberlieferung (Richter c. 14–15)," *Zeitschrift für Theologie und Kirche* 82 (1985): 265–68; J. Kim, *Structure of Samson Cycle* (1993): 322.

encounter with the Philistines has God's spirit entered him. That is reserved for the finale.

The conclusion of this episode and the escape are tied once again to the political reality of the times (i.e., Philistine domination – see 13:1 and 14:4). A Philistine posse is formed to trap Samson in his hiding place. By raiding in their territory, the Philistines enlist the reluctant services of the men of Judah to bind him "to do to him as he did to us" (compare this to the enlistment of Samson's Timnite wife, 14:15, and Delilah to betray him, 16:5).

The key word here is "bind." It will be used repeatedly in the dialogue of the Delilah story (16:4–21) and as a reminder that Samson in bondage is a symbol of the nation in bondage to the Philistines.[341] To bind him is a basic violation of Samson's freedom, but his ability to escape bondage is tied directly to his recognition of Yahweh as his source of strength and thus is a source of hope to the nation if it will return to the worship of Yahweh. It is to be understood, however, that freedom from bondage here does not include freedom from God's design.

Negotiations over Samson's surrender are contained in a series of dialogues between the hero and 3,000 men of Judah. In this period, when the tribes seldom seem to cooperate, it is significant that Samson is a member of the tribe of Dan and is therefore less likely to receive aid from the men of Judah. They sadly admit their own powerlessness in relation to the Philistines and show a desire not to come to the attention of their masters and thus incur their wrath.[342] Resolution comes with Samson agreeing to be bound and their taking an oath not to harm him if he surrenders. By not having to fight the men of Judah, Samson (like David in 1 Sam 29:6–11) was able to remain true to his own people. It also allowed him to focus his power on the real enemy, the Philistines.

Samson's escape from this trap is once again the result of divine empowerment, and it provides yet another series of climactic moments in the narrative.[343] Ironically, it occurs at the moment of greatest triumph for the Philistines (see similar reversals in 1 Sam 7:7–11 and 2 Kings 3:21–24). They shout, and immediately the third infusion of power from the Lord's spirit enters Samson, signifying once again his special, God-given abilities in times of personal crisis (compare Elijah's miraculously strengthened running ability in 1 Kings 18:46 when "the hand of the Lord" was upon him). In a superhuman flexing of his muscles, Samson snaps the two "new" (not

341 J. Kim, *Structure of Samson Cycle* (1993): 329–33.
342 C. Smith, "Samson and Delilah," *JSOT* 76 (1997): 50.
343 R. H. O'Connell, *Rhetoric of the Book of Judges* (1996): 221.

brittle) ropes binding him and lays about him with the "fresh" (not brittle) jawbone of an ass (vv. 14–15). In victory, however, Samson once again
demonstrates either a lack of understanding for his Nazirite obligations or
a total disregard for them.[344]

how so?

The real significance of his victory comes in vv. 17–20. An acknowledgment of Samson's power source is found in this etiological story of the
Enhakkore spring at Lehi. Samson's prayer, despite its negative rhetoric
(compare 14:3 and 15:11b) and its coming on the heels of the victory, is a
definitive reminder for the reader of God's role in these events.[345] Samson
may be able to kill a thousand Philistines, but he cannot save his own life in
the desert without God's help (compare the events at Meribah in Exod 17:1–7
and Num 20:2–13). He remains a part of God's plan to free the people from
the Philistines and is spared from death to fulfill that mission. His call for
help foreshadows a similar plea in Judg 16:28, which asks for one final infusion of strength so that he can gain revenge for being blinded and take a
large number of Philistines with him in his suicide demolition of the Dagon
temple.

CHAPTER 16

EPISODE FOUR: THE GAZITE PROSTITUTE

(1) Once Samson went to Gaza, where he saw a prostitute and went in to her.
(2) The Gazites were told, "Samson has come here." So they circled around and
lay in wait for him all night at the city gate. They kept quiet all night, thinking,
"Let us wait until the light of morning; then we will kill him." (3) But Samson
lay only until midnight. Then at midnight he rose up, took hold of the doors
of the city gate and the two posts, pulled them up, bar and all, put them on his
shoulders, and carried them to the top of the hill that is in front of Hebron.

Crenshaw sees this short episode with the Gazite prostitute as Samson
responding on the rebound.[346] He has lost his wife and now seeks solace
and sexual satisfaction in a relationship without emotional or legal ties. There
is no necessity, however, for this story to be sequential to that of chapters 14

---

[344] J. Kim, *Structure of Samson Cycle* (1993): 291–92.
[345] J. C. Exum, "Theological Dimension," *VT* 33 (1983): 34.
[346] J. L. Crenshaw, "Samson's Saga," *ZAW* 86 (1974): 497–98.

and 15.[347] It can stand on its own, having all the elements of the trap motif as outlined earlier. The entire chapter, containing two escape episodes, follows this pattern, although it does not include one of the main ingredients of the Timnite narrative – the infusion of God's spirit into Samson. Perhaps this is due to the nature of his sexual affairs, or perhaps this is an indication of a separate tradition (using basically the same narrative pattern), which has been fused onto the earlier tale and is not dependent on the injection of the spirit of God as the catalyst for Samson's actions.[348]

Samson's involvement with the prostitute of Gaza is based on his physical desire for her. This could be compared to the story of the Timnite woman whom he also saw and therefore wanted (14:1). His brazen entrance into Gaza, a major Philistine city, can be compared to the act of going to Timnah, also a Philistine settlement. The reaction of the men of Gaza could thus be explained either in reference to Samson's previous actions against the Philistines (if these stories are sequential) or simply as the reaction of the locals to an Israelite who had no right to simply to walk in and use the "facilities" of their city. His actions, based on instances from the earlier narrative, can also be interpreted as a part of a conscious plan to force confrontation with the enemy by a trickster figure. However, this argument is not in line with the editorial notation found in 14:4 that God is directing Samson's actions.

The trap is set by the men of Gaza, who assume Samson will spend the entire night with the prostitute and in the morning will be too fatigued to resist. They set their "quiet" watch at the gate in the hope of killing him. As it turns out, however, escape in this case is almost too easy. Samson simply rises earlier than expected, catches his "captors" by surprise and with impunity carries away the city gates, "bar and all," as a souvenir (v. 3).[349] There is no hint in the text that the men of Gaza tried to or could stop Samson. The folkloristic character of the narrative centers on the superhuman act of uprooting and transporting the gates.

[347] J. A. Soggin, *Judges* (1987): 230–31.

[348] Yair Zakovitch, "The Double Ending Formula in the Samson Stories and Its Meaning for the Ending of the Cycle," *Heger Veiyum* (1976): 95–102 (Hebrew).

[349] Othniel Margalith, "The Legends of Samson/Heracles," *VT* 37 (1987): 69, attempts to show the impossibility of carrying this out without being noticed. However, it is more likely that Samson wanted an audience for his feat. As J. Vickery, "In Strange Ways," in *Images of Man and God* (1981): 72, notes, this action is a "marvel" typical of the exaggerated nature of folklore and is therefore to be "noticed." Stanislav Segert, "Paronomasia in the Samson Narrative in Judges xiii–xvi," *VT* 34 (1984): 457, also suggests a pun here with *bᵉrîaḥ* comparable to *bᵉrîḥeha* (one who has escaped) in Isa 15:5 as a further indication of Samson's easily avoiding the Gazite trap.

But what symbolism, if any, is embodied in the theft of the gates? It could simply be an act of revenge, perhaps comparable to Rachel's theft of her father's teraphim, without Jacob's knowledge (Gen 31:14–19), against the city that had tried to trap him. That the men of Gaza were surprised by Samson's early rising is yet another example of the knowledge theme that runs throughout his narrative. It also serves as his dramatic way of demonstrating that the Philistine cities were not closed to him. He acts as if he were a free citizen of Gaza, and he claims the right to go "in" or "out of the city gate" (Gen 23:10; 34:24).[350]

Since the gates represented, in both real and symbolic terms, the safety of the city, Samson's theft is a figurative reversal. As an enemy of the Philistines, he was not safe in the city of Gaza, and now, without their gates, the people of Gaza were no longer free from attack. Furthermore, that Samson carried the gates to a hilltop overlooking Hebron, forty miles east of Gaza and continuously uphill (3,350 feet in elevation), may be both a public display of his immense strength and a political statement. Hebron was in the tribal allotment of Judah (Josh 15:1–13), and it is therefore ironic that Samson returned these pilfered gates to the men of Judah, who had helped the Philistines capture him in 15:9–13. Perhaps by defiantly carrying the gates toward Hebron Samson was calling on the men of Judah to resist Philistine domination – to be free. In any case his actions are not reinforced by divine action. The spirit of the Lord does not enter him and help with this feat of strength, as in the case in 15:1–8. This may be due to a separate literary tradition that does not employ the infusion of the spirit of the Lord as key to Samson's bursts of energy.

(4) After this he fell in love with a woman in the valley of Sorek, whose name was Delilah. (5) The lords of the Philistines came to her and said to her, "Coax him, and find out what makes his strength so great, and how we may overpower him, so that we may bind him in order to subdue him; and we will each give you eleven hundred pieces of silver." (6) So Delilah said to Samson, "Please tell me what makes your strength so great, and how you could be bound, so that one could subdue you." (7) Samson said to her, "If they bind me with seven fresh bowstrings that are not dried out, then I shall become weak, and be like anyone else." (8) Then the lords of the Philistines brought her seven fresh bowstrings that had not dried out, and she bound him with them. (9) While

---

[350] See Ephraim A. Speiser, "'Coming' and 'Going' at the City Gate," *BASOR* 144 (1956): 20–23.

men were lying in wait in an inner chamber, she said to him, "The Philistines are upon you, Samson!" But he snapped the bowstrings, as a strand of fiber snaps when it touches the fire. So the secret of his strength was not known. (10) Then Delilah said to Samson, "You have mocked me and told me lies; please tell me how you could be bound." (11) He said to her, "If they bind me with new ropes that have not been used, then I shall become weak, and be like anyone else." (12) So Delilah took new ropes and bound him with them and said to him, "The Philistines are upon you, Samson!" (The men lying in wait were in an inner chamber.) But he snapped the ropes off his arms like a thread. (13) Then Delilah said to Samson, "Until now you have mocked me and told me lies; tell me how you could be bound." He said to her, "If you weave the seven locks of my head with the web and make it tight with the pin, then I shall become weak, and be like anyone else." (14) So while he slept, Delilah took the seven locks of his head and wove them into the web, and made them tight with the pin. Then she said to him, "The Philistines are upon you, Samson!" But he awoke from his sleep, and pulled away the pin, the loom, and the web. (15) Then she said to him, "How can you say, 'I love you,' when your heart is not with me? You have mocked me three times now and have not told me what makes your strength so great." (16) Finally, after she had nagged him with her words day after day, and pestered him, he was tired to death. (17) So he told her his whole secret, and said to her, "A razor has never come upon my head; for I have been a Nazirite to God from my mother's womb. If my head were shaved, then my strength would leave me; I would become weak, and be like anyone else." (18) When Delilah realized that he had told her his whole secret, she sent and called the lords of the Philistines, saying, "This time come up, for he has told his whole secret to me." Then the lords of the Philistines came up to her, and brought the money in their hands. (19) She let him fall asleep on her lap; and she called a man, and had him shave off the seven locks of his head. He began to weaken, and his strength left him. (20) Then she said, "The Philistines are upon you, Samson!" When he awoke from his sleep, he thought, "I will go out as at other times, and shake myself free." But he did not know that the Lord had left him. (21) So the Philistines seized him and gouged out his eyes. They brought him down to Gaza and bound him with bronze shackles; and he ground at the mill in the prison. (22) But the hair of his head began to grow again after it had been shaved. (23) Now the lords of the Philistines gathered to offer a great sacrifice to their god Dagon, and to rejoice; for they said, "Our god has given Samson our enemy into our hand." (24) When the people saw him, they praised their god; for they said, "Our god has given our enemy into our hand, the ravager of our country, who has killed many of us." (25) And when their hearts were merry, they said, "Call Samson, and let him entertain us." So they called Samson out of the prison, and he performed for them. They made him stand between the pillars; (26) and Samson said to the attendant who held him by the hand, "Let me feel the pillars on which the house rests, so that I may lean against them." (27) Now the house was full of men and women; all the lords of the Philistines were there, and on the roof there were about three thousand men and women, who looked on while Samson performed. (28) Then Samson called on the Lord and said, "Lord God, remember me and strengthen me only this once, O God, so that with this one act of revenge I may pay back the Philistines for my two eyes." (29) And Samson grasped the two middle pillars on which the house rested, and he leaned his weight against them, his right hand on the one and his left hand on the other. (30) Then Samson said, "Let me die with the Philistines." He strained with all his might; and the house fell on the lords and all the people who were in it. So those he killed at his death were more than those he had killed during his life. (31) Then his brothers and all his family came down and took him and brought him up and buried him between Zorah and Eshtaol in the tomb of his father Manoah. He had judged Israel twenty years.

The final entrapment episode begins with the simplest of literary transitions, "after this."[351] A sense of the passage of time is achieved without the necessity of directly tying the previous narrative to this one. Again, then, this could be seen as an isolated narrative, fused to the others, and not dependent upon them for anything other then narrative pattern. Although the established pattern is followed throughout, there is more reliance on dialogue than in the previous episodes.

Introducing Samson's latest amorous involvement is the statement, "he fell in love with a woman in the valley of Sorek, whose name was Delilah" (v. 4). There are two remarkable things about this introduction; Delilah is the first of Samson's women to be given a name by the storyteller, and this is the first time it is said explicitly that he "loves" anyone.[352] This heightened emotional state will simply make him even more vulnerable in the midst of their relationship.[353]

---

[351] "After this" functions as an idiomatic transition marker that is used elsewhere by the Deuteronomistic Historian (2 Sam 2:1; 8:1; 10:1; 13:1; 15:1; 21:18; 2 Kings 6:24). It both introduces and links a new episode with what has gone before.

[352] Jack M. Sasson, "Who Cut Samson's Hair? (And Other Trifling Issues Raised by Judges 16)," *Proof* 8 (1988): 334.

[353] M. Greene, "Enigma Variations," *Vox Evangelica* 21 (1991): 71.

The Sorek Valley leads into the northern end of the Philistine plain and was known for its production of red grapes, and the location hints at Delilah's foreign origins although she is never actually said to be a Philistine. Segert postulates that a double entendre is to found in the name Sorek: (1) a *nazir* "should have been warned by this name and should have avoided this place of renowned grape vines," and (2) the root *srq* also has the meaning "to comb," which is one of the steps taken prior to cutting hair.[354] Setting this episode in the valley of Sorek would thus be a signal to the reader of Samson's ultimate fate.

As for Delilah, the text is not explicit regarding her origins, and it is not possible to identify her unquestionably as a Philistine.[355] However, if her apparent role as seductress and agent for the Philistines is to be taken seriously, then she seems more than just another prostitute who has caught Samson's eye. Like Rahab (Josh 2:1), she has her own house and is not defined as a member of any male's household, which gives her a measure of independence unusual for women in the biblical world and may indicate a particularly strong personality.[356] Her persistence, ingenuity, and determination suggest not only that she is working for the Philistines for monetary gain, but that, from a Philistine perspective, she might actually be termed a patriot,[357] making her intellectually distinct from Samson's nagging wife in Judg 14:17.

Despite these apparently positive characteristics, it is unlikely that the biblical writer was trying to portray Delilah as a heroine. What she is doing in the story is endangering the life of an Israelite hero, drawing him into a trap made of words and female guile. This picture approaches that of Jezebel, another foreign woman who seduces and manipulates an Israelite leader, her royal husband Ahab. Delilah has a name but not a social location. She has a task, but her motivation, other than the money offered by the "lords of the Philistines," is unclear. The ambiguities seem to provide a woman who otherwise might be considered in a weak position with great power over the

---

354 S. Segert, "Paronomasia in the Samson Narrative," *VT* 34 (1984): 458.

355 J. Cheryl Exum, *Fragmented Women: Feminist (Sub)versions of Biblical Narratives.* JSOTSup 163. Sheffield, Eng.: JSOT Press, 1993: 69.

356 J. Cheryl Exum, *Plotted, Shot, and Painted.* JSOTSup 215. Sheffield, Eng.: Sheffield Academic Press, 1996: 181.

357 Lillian R. Klein, "The Book of Judges: Paradigm and Deviation in Images of Women." Pages 65–66 in *A Feminist Companion to Judges.* Edited by Athalya Brenner. Sheffield, Eng.: JSOT Press, 1993; Carol Smith, "Delilah: A Suitable Case for (Feminist) Treatment?" Page 109 in *Judges: A Feminist Companion to the Bible,* 2nd series. Edited by Athalya Brenner. Sheffield, Eng.: Sheffield Academic Press, 1999.

most powerful of the Israelites.[358] In this way it fits nicely into the topsy-turvy world of the judges.

As in 14:15, Samson will be enticed to reveal a secret, in this case the source of his great strength. The lords of the Philistines each offer Delilah a hefty sum of 1,100 pieces of silver to obtain this information. There is no sense of coercion, or, for that matter, of any reluctance by Delilah to betray her lover. Nor is there any real malice on her part either. It is simply a matter of business for this very business-like woman.

The offer of a bounty is predicated on her learning "what makes his strength so great, and how we may overpower him, so that we may bind him in order to subdue him." Having seen that ordinary measures (ropes, 15:13–14, and ambushes, 16:2–3) do not work, they must have assumed that magic or some other force was protecting this hero. Perhaps this explains the ritualistic pattern of question, answer, test, and recrimination followed by Delilah and Samson in the narrative.[359]

PATTERN OF THE SAMSON/DELILAH RIPOSTE

1. Delilah asks Samson the basis of his strength and how he could be bound and made helpless. This is prefaced in the final three attempts by rebuking his previous deception of her.
2. Samson responds to Delilah with explicit instructions. He lies the first three times. The fourth time he tells her the truth.
3. Delilah follows Samson's instructions and tests them by crying out "the Philistines are upon you."
4. Samson's deception allows him to escape three times. The fourth time he reveals his secret and is taken captive. The pattern of question/answer may require the truth in the fourth asking.[360]

Their rhetorical contest, a form of communicative strife, is initiated when Delilah boldly asks Samson the dual question of where his great strength lies and how he might be bound so that one could subdue him (16:6). Given

---

[358] C. Smith, "Samson and Delilah," *JSOT* 76 (1997): 48–49.

[359] This structured approach is based in part on J. Cheryl Exum, "Harvesting the Biblical Narrator's Scanty Plot of Ground: A Holistic Approach to Judges 16:4–22." Pages 41–42 in *Tehillah le-Moshe: Biblical and Judaic Studies in Honor of Moshe Greenberg*. Edited by Mordechai Cogan et al. Winona Lake, Ind.: Eisenbrauns, 1997.

[360] J. Blenkinsopp, "Structure and Styles in Judges 13–16," *JBL* 82 (1963): 73–74, refers to this intentional diversion from a more regular threefold literary pattern as one of the "tricks of the trade" used by the Israelite writer, as in the 3 + 1 pattern in Jotham's fable in Judg 9:8–15. It also is used in Wisdom literature (Prov 6:16; Eccles 11:2).

the problems he has faced in the past with keeping his secrets, it seems odd that he should so readily respond to Delilah's question. However, Samson's answer is the first of three deceptions he will use to frustrate her attempt to trap him.[361] He says that if he is bound with seven "fresh" bowstrings he "shall become weak, and be like anyone else" (v. 7). This response, using the significant number seven, plays on the supposition by the Philistines that Samson's strength is based on magic. Fresh bowstrings would still be moist and too easily stretched to serve as normal bonds. The ease with which Samson snaps the bowstrings, "as a strand of fiber snaps when it touches the fire," can be compared to the similar action in 15:14.[362]

Samson is clearly playing the role of a trickster in this scene. He goes along with the test and allows Delilah to bind him, apparently thinking himself to be very clever. Then, when she cries, "The Philistines are upon you," he breaks his bonds, thereby frustrating Delilah's intentions. To ensure that readers catch the irony of the deceiver being deceived, it is explained in v. 9b that "the secret of his strength was not known." At this point, the only truly wise characters in the episode seem to be the Philistines waiting in the back room. They have learned to be cautious of Samson's strength and apparently are not lured into combat with him as long as he shows he is still in full control of his powers.

This phase of the cycle then ends, and another phase begins with Delilah reproaching Samson for mocking her with his lies and asking him again how he might be bound (16:10, 13). Delilah, it seems, did not notice (i.e., was deceived herself) that Samson had given her only a partial answer to her original question. She may have also been blinded by her conviction that the key to his strength was in a magical set of bonds since she is apparently unaware of the significance of his hair.[363]

The second test (16:10–12) is so similar to the escape in 15:13–14 (both involve the use of new ropes) that it seems unrealistic for the conspirators

---

[361] Note the similar use of three dialogues in the contest of Darius's guards in 1 Esd 3:1–5:3 (see James L. Crenshaw, "The Contest of Darius's Guards in 1 Esdras 3:1–5:3." Pages 222–34 in *Urgent Advice and Probing Questions*. Macon, Ga: Mercer University Press, [1995]). Although this verbal contest is more philosophical than lethal, it includes the same sense of intense competition as that between Samson and Delilah.

[362] Once again there is a pun here based on the assonant quality of the word *patti* (entice). Samson is enticed by Delilah's charms, but he broke his bonds as if they were only string (*pᵉtil*).

[363] See Othniel Margalith, "Samson's Riddle and Samson's Magic Locks," *VT* 36 (1986): 229–31; idem, "Legends of Samson/Heracles," *VT* 37 (1987): 64.

to try this again. If, however, these are separate traditions, that problem disappears. Also, this episode is somewhat fragmentary. It lacks any specified number of ropes to bind him and fails to include the formula statement that these bonds would cause him to "become weak, and be like any other man." Plus the mention of the hiding Philistines is now reduced to a parenthetical gloss (16:12b), just to remind the reader of their continued presence. The pattern of ritual questioning may have demanded that Delilah ask how he might be bound three times before again asking the full question of the source of his strength.

In the third round of questioning, we once again have a full narrative episode that includes all of the necessary stages of the cycle, although there are some variations this time that may signal the approaching climax of the tale to the reader.[364] Thus there is no mention of the Philistines lying in wait or that Samson will become weak when he is bound. The form of his "bonds" in this case is also unusual. After she berates him for lying, Samson tells her that she is to weave the seven locks of his head into the web of the loom.[365] He then goes to sleep, and she weaves his hair into the web (v. 14). Delilah's cry of approaching Philistines awakens Samson, and he frees himself by pulling out the embedded poles of the loom from the floor. The various pieces of the loom trailing behind him are reminiscent of the gates of Gaza that he uprooted and carried away (16:3).

As so often happens to tricksters, however, Samson runs afoul of his own tricks. He has "enticed" the enticer into wrong actions. Now, with tension rising, and having experienced three failures to subdue Samson, Delilah emotionally loads her inquiry, making two critical points: (1) "How can you say, 'I love you,' when your heart is not with me?" and, returning to her original question in v. 6, (2) "you have not told me what makes your strength so great" (16:15). Almost as if this were what he was waiting for,[366] the spell of deception is broken and the thoroughly frustrated Samson is compelled to reply that his strength is based on his status as a Nazirite. If his hair is shaved, then he will become like "any other man" (v. 17). In so doing,

---

[364] J. C. Exum, "Harvesting the Biblical Narrator's Scanty Plot," in *Tehilla le-Moshe* (1997): 44–45.

[365] The LXX has a fuller version of this verse, adding after the verb "and make it tight with the pin." The Greek version also contains the stock phrase that Samson will be weakened by this procedure.

[366] It is possible that a literary feature of this question contest is what might be termed an X + 1 progression similar to that found in Prov 6:16 and Mic 5:5. In each of these cases a number is used and then is augmented by one more (3 + 1; 6 + 1; 7 + 1). The extra time therefore is the operative one that requires a new action be taken.

Samson's fatal flaw is once again revealed (see 14:16); he cannot bear to be accused of failing to love.[367]

Having given away his ultimate secret to Delilah, Samson seems to have exhausted all his physical and mental reserves and once again falls asleep with his head secure on Delilah's knees (compare the exhausted Sisera lying at Jael's feet in Judg 4:21). He has trapped himself by playing his game once too often. Delilah, whom he had hoped to confuse by his many false answers, now realizes that Samson at last has told her the truth. She calls on the Philistines, who had ceased to inhabit her back room, to come once again to bind Samson. Preparatory to shaving his locks, she shouts loud enough to determine that Samson is truly sound asleep.[368] Samson's subsequent attempt to escape from the Philistines fails, and he at last is bound in bronze fetters and blinded.

It is interesting to note how surprised Samson was that he was not able to "go out as at other times" (v. 20). Boling suggests that Samson's failure to realize that Yahweh had left him was a means of building suspense.[369] It seems more likely, however, that this is a play on the theme found in 14:6 and 15:14 in which Yahweh's spirit entered Samson and aided him to perform extraordinary feats. The present reversal of fortunes also reinforces the point that Samson's strength and his role as Nazirite and judge originated with the statement made to his mother by the angel in 13:7.[370] Samson's failure to keep the secret or the terms of his Nazirite vows, like the unfaithful Israelites who cannot obey the covenant, is the basis for being left in the clutches of the Philistines (compare Saul, who had previously been filled with God's spirit in 1 Sam 10:6, 10 and 11:6, but whose inquiries of the Lord go unanswered in 1 Sam 28:6 because of his disobedience). Samson's surprise at the changes in circumstances may be due to his reasoning that he had previously violated Nazirite obligations and that he really did not believe that he would lose his strength if his hair is cut.[371] He learns (as do the Philistines when they allow

[367] J. L. Crenshaw, "Samson's Saga," *ZAW* 86 (1974): 498; Nahum M. Waldman, "Concealment and Irony in the Samson Story," *Dor le Dor* 13 (1984–85): 74.

[368] J. M. Sasson, "Who Cut Samson's Hair?" *Proof* 8 (1988): 338. This interpretation does not follow the NRSV translation, but it makes more physical sense based on the Hebrew text. It also removes the necessity of drawing another character into the story when it is simpler for it to be Delilah who cuts Samson's hair while he remains in her lap.

[369] R. G. Boling, *Judges* (1975): 230.

[370] J. C. Exum, "Harvesting the Biblical Narrator's Scanty Plot," in *Tehilla le-Moshe* (1997): 45.

[371] David M. Gunn, "Samson of Sorrows: An Isaianic Gloss on Judges 13–16." Pages 244–47 in *Reading between Texts: Intertextuality and the Hebrew Bible.* Edited by Danna N. Fewell. Louisville, Ky.: Westminster/John Knox, 1992.

his hair to grow back) that it is Yahweh who determines events, not Samson alone.

The pattern of trap and escape has now seemingly been broken. Samson is blinded and put to work like a slave, grinding grain in the prison house at Gaza (v. 21). This is only the setting, however, for the final stage in the Samson narrative. His captors have made a crucial error by falling into a trap laid for them by Yahweh. They had believed that there was a "secret" to Samson's feats of strength and that once it was learned he could be neutralized for good.[372] Thus they took no notice of Samson's hair growing back, and as a result a final reversal occurs. It seems curious that after going to such lengths to capture Samson the Philistines would have allowed this to happen. Perhaps they were now secure in their own strength (just as Samson had been before his capture) and did not believe their blinded captive could harm them anymore than Samson believed that his strength would ever fail him.[373] However, the text never mentions that Delilah actually told the Philistines the source of Samson's strength. She exclaims that she has learned his secret, but she does not repeat Samson's words, a standard rhetorical device in every other section of the narrative. The Philistines, who have temporarily overpowered Samson, in a final ironic twist to this story will now be overpowered in turn, along with their god Dagon, for lack of basic curiosity on their part. They paid Delilah, took their captive, but did not ask how she had accomplished her task.

The final scene then unfolds as the Philistines display what they believe is a helpless prisoner. They call him to a celebration in the temple of Dagon, where he can be shown to the crowd in all his ignominy. He is a trophy of war, laid at the "feet" of their god in much the same way as the Ark of the Covenant will be in 1 Sam 5:1–2. Supported by a young boy, Samson steadies himself between two pillars of the temple. He then calls on the last deception in his trickster's arsenal, a prayer of vindication to Yahweh. Despite his past failures, Samson is confident, although a good deal more humble than in his prayer in 15:18, asking Yahweh "only this once" to strengthen him. His cry is Israel's cry and his triumphal, suicidal act contains within it the common idea in the Judges narrative (3:15–26; 5:24–27; 7:9–22) that a blow struck against the enemy is worth any personal risk.

Samson's moment and place of opportunity were also perfect. Yahweh apparently could not resist his call to "trial by ordeal," and the setting within

---

[372] Ibid., 247.
[373] C. Smith, "Samson and Delilah," *JSOT* 76 (1997): 55.

the temple of Dagon makes it that much more enticing.[374] All the conditions were therefore right to complete the cycle: (1) Samson's hair, the sign of his original vow and entrapment by Yahweh, was restored; (2) Samson once again acknowledged the true source of his strength, Yahweh; and (3) an opportunity existed publicly to vindicate Yahweh as the one true God within the holy precincts of the Philistines' deity (compare 1 Sam 5:1–5 where the ark brings Dagon down).

The collapse of the building is almost anticlimactic. The reader knows that Samson will be heard and that at last he will be allowed to achieve his freedom. His death, in the midst of his enemies, frees him from all vows, plans, and traps. His service is complete and he is buried in his father's tomb, as was another trap-ridden suicide, Saul.

BRIDGING THE HORIZONS

The Samson episodes constitute the longest extended narrative in the Book of Judges. Clearly, this hero or antihero captured the ancient imagination. His exploits are amusing and shocking, and his failure to recognize or fulfill his potential is disappointing. The issues that are raised by his stories follow:

(1) When the story of a prominent individual begins with a miraculous birth narrative, the reader is filled with expectations for that person's future career. Thus when the narrator spends a great deal of time describing the events surrounding the births of Moses (Exod 2:1–10) and Samuel (1 Sam 1:3–20) it seems only natural that they will eventually rise to positions of leadership and authority. God has taken a hand in their preservation or conception, and this signals greatness to come. A similar sentiment is raised by the annunciation story associated with Samson's birth to a previously barren couple. The extra dimension of Nazirite restrictions placed on both the mother and the child plays up his importance, and it is therefore startling when this divinely heralded child becomes a headstrong, self-indulgent young adult in the next chapter. This dissonance may be part of the thematic character of Judges, always presenting reversals to readers. It may also serve as a reminder that children do not always meet their parents' expectations (see Hos 11:1–4).

(2) One question that arises from reading the Samson cycle of stories is whether he was free to make his own choices or whether he was simply

---

[374] Frederick E. Greenspahn, "The Theology of the Framework of Judges," *VT* 36 (1986): 395.

following a path laid out for him by God. Because Samson was proclaimed a Nazirite from birth there were greater restrictions on him than there were on others. In addition, the "rush" of the divine spirit into his body during times of extreme danger (14:6, 19; 15:14) must have given him great confidence to overcome any obstacle. Was this too much for him? Is this why he courts danger so often (16:1–3 and the contest with Delilah in 16:6–22)? Are superhuman heroes always destined to be brought down by their own hubris (see Gilgamesh and Hercules for other examples)?

(3) Despite the extremely high level of violence in the Samson narrative, there are also comedic aspects that make it entertaining, at least for the Israelite audience. Are these stories to be considered a form of nationalistic propaganda, portraying the enemy as too dense to answer a riddle without cheating (14:12–18), too inept to prevent Samson from stealing the city gates of Gaza (16:3), and, after shaving his head, too forgetful to remember that Samson's source of power is his hair (16:19–22)? Samson's use of unorthodox weapons (15:15–16) and his bare hands to kills thousands of Philistines must have also delighted the listeners and readers who were aware of the Philistines' superior material culture (1 Sam 13:19–21).

CHAPTER 17

(1) There was a man in the hill country of Ephraim whose name was Micah. (2) He said to his mother, "The eleven hundred pieces of silver that were taken from you, about which you uttered a curse, and even spoke it in my hearing – that silver is in my possession; I took it; but now I will return it to you." And his mother said, "May my son be blessed by the Lord!" (3) Then he returned the eleven hundred pieces of silver to his mother; and his mother said, "I consecrate the silver to the Lord from my hand for my son, to make an idol of cast metal." (4) So when he returned the money to his mother, his mother took two hundred pieces of silver, and gave it to the silversmith, who made it into an idol of cast metal; and it was in the house of Micah. (5) This man Micah had a shrine, and he made an ephod and teraphim, and installed one of his sons, who became his priest. (6) In those days there was no king in Israel; all the people did what was right in their own eyes. (7) Now there was a young man of Bethlehem in Judah, of the clan of Judah. He was a Levite residing there. (8) This man left the town of Bethlehem in Judah, to live wherever he could find a place. He came to the house

of Micah in the hill country of Ephraim to carry on his work. (9) Micah said to him, "From where do you come?" He replied, "I am a Levite of Bethlehem in Judah, and I am going to live wherever I can find a place." (10) Then Micah said to him, "Stay with me, and be to me a father and a priest, and I will give you ten pieces of silver a year, a set of clothes, and your living." (11) The Levite agreed to stay with the man; and the young man became to him like one of his sons. (12) So Micah installed the Levite, and the young man became his priest, and was in the house of Micah. (13) Then Micah said, "Now I know that the Lord will prosper me, because the Levite has become my priest."

OVERVIEW OF CHAPTERS 17–21

The final five chapters of Judges accelerate the pace of idolatry, disobedience to the covenant with Yahweh, and general lawlessness. While there is no direct link between these stories and the remainder of the Book of Judges, there are enough common themes (hospitality, idolatry, civil strife) and indirect references (1,100 pieces of silver in Judg 16:5; 17:2; polemics against Ephraim; tenuous situation for the tribe of Dan) to suggest that they are more than just appended stories.[375] In fact, they function as an appropriate and climactic ending to an extended narrative highlighted by extreme behavior and the recurrent realization that the Israelites cannot succeed without resort to their God.

The cycle that had introduced the stories about the various judges in chapters 3–16 is not found here; no judge appears in any of these episodes, marking a distinct narrative break. Instead each episode is given a dark political and social tone and is tied with the others with the recurrent phrase, "In those days there was no king in Israel" (Judg 17:6; 18:1; 19:1; 21:25). The phrase serves as both a structural link holding the stories together and a reminder to the reader that anarchy is bred in the "extreme individualism" portrayed in these tales.[376] However, it is not necessary to see an original literary or historical connection between chapters 17–18 and chapters 19–21. The first section concerns itself with cultic violations while the latter section is built around civil unrest. Although both contain a Levite, that does not mean that they necessarily developed at the same time or for the same purpose.[377] The editor, in linking them into this final portion of the

[375] M. A. Sweeney, "Davidic Polemic," *VT* 47 (1997): 524–26.

[376] William J. Dumbrell, "'In Those Days There Was No King in Israel; Every Man Did What Was Right in His Own Eyes': The Purpose of the Book of Judges Reconsidered," *JSOT* 25 (1983): 31–32.

[377] Y. Amit, *Book of Judges* (1999): 351–57.

settlement "history," infuses them with a common theological goal of the need to seek direction from Yahweh, but this does not mean that the social or historical premise that they represent is the same.[378]

Given this editorial artistry as the basis for the current version of the text, many scholars date the edited form of the materials in chapters 17–18 to the time of the Josianic reform (late seventh century) or the early exilic period (sixth century).[379] The use of spies (Judg 18:2–6),[380] overt violations of the Decalogue (theft, idolatry), and the hiring of an itinerant Levite from Bethlehem in the tribal territory of Judah to serve as a priest in a local shrine provide excellent backdrops to the centralization of worship in Jerusalem in Josiah's time and the stricter attention to the law in that era (see Deut 12:8). The injection of the phrase "in those days there was no king in Israel" only adds to the importance of Josiah's reign (640–609 BCE) as the first strong king of Judah in a century and the first to be free of foreign influence since the time of Solomon.[381] If the Josianic reform movement is indeed a part of the Deuteronomistic Historian's agenda, it is still necessary to remember these stories may have resonated to an exilic audience less in terms of monarchic leadership than to the strength that comes from adherence to the covenant.[382]

The story found in Judg 19, a literary parallel to Gen 19, can also stand alone as an independent narrative.[383] The material in chapters 20–21 may have been appended later to bolster the claims of the Davidic dynasty and to add to the "disqualification story" attached to Saul and his family.[384] However, by the time that the stories are edited and compiled into their Deuteronomistic form, the Judean monarchy has been demolished by the

[378] D. H. Mayes, "Deuteronomistic Royal Ideology in Judges 17–21," *BibInt* 9 (2001): 254.

[379] See E. Aydeet Mueller, *The Micah Story: A Morality Tale in the Book of Judges.* New York: Peter Lang, 2001: 16–26, for a summary of the scholarly debate on the extent of Deuteronomistic influence on these stories.

[380] Abraham Malamat, "The Danite Migration and the Pan-Israelite Exodus-Conquest: A Biblical Narrative Pattern," *Bib* 51 (1970): 1–7, ties the Danite's use of spies to the Deuteronomistic account of the Israelites' use of spies in Num 13–14 and Deut 1:19–46. R. H. O'Connell, *Rhetoric of the Book of Judges* (1996): 235, n. 346, expands upon this to suggest that the conquest of Laish by the Danites may serve as a broad analogy to the conquest accounts found in these passages.

[381] See Baruch Halpern, "Levitic Participation in the Reform Cult of Jeroboam I," *JBL* 95 (1976): 38.

[382] See E. A. Mueller, *The Micah Story* (2001): 34.

[383] H. Becker, *Richterzeit und Königtum* (1990): 257–66.

[384] A. D. H. Mayes, "Deuteronomistic Royal Ideology," *BibInt* 9 (2001): 254; Victor H. Matthews and James C. Moyer, *The Old Testament: Text and Context.* Peabody, Mass.: Hendrickson, 1997: 93–98.

Babylonians and thus the cry that "in those days there was no king in Israel" is quite correct. Only an idealized version of the kingship was possible for the exilic audience to contemplate.[385]

COMMENTS ON CHAPTER 17

Chapter 17 concerns itself with two stories that may not have been originally related. The tale of Micah's theft of his mother's silver, the manufacture of a group of cultic objects, and the construction of a household shrine could easily stand alone, ending at 17:6. Perhaps alarmed at the curse uttered by his mother over the theft of her property, Micah admits his crime, and she is impressed enough to consecrate a portion of the silver to God (vv. 2–3). Such a gracious action on her part might be seen as a parallel to God's willingness to note true repentance and to remit any further punishment on the sinner (see Judg 10:10–16). But the scene is "spoiled" or characteristically reversed by the storyteller, when his mother commissions the creation of a "molten image" (*pesel ûmassēkâ*), and it is placed in a portion of Micah's house that is set aside as a shrine, making it the *bêt mîkāyĕhû* (17:4). In this way an ironic pun occurs based on Micah's name. In the Hebrew, he is initially referred to as Mîkāyĕhû (Who Is Like Yahweh). Clearly, the idol is "like Yahweh" in the minds of Micah and his mother.[386] Then at v. 5 the writer shortens his name to Mîkâ, diminishing the status of the character to an unruly child.

The Deuteronomistic judgment of Micah's actions becomes clear when this self-centered man further enhances his private shrine, now referred to as a *bêt 'ĕlōhîm*, with the addition of several other cultic items, including an ephod and teraphim, and the installation of one of his sons as his "priest." It is exactly this type of individualistic and unsanctioned form of cultic activity that would be condemned by the Deuteronomistic editor whose loyalties are to the central shrine in Jerusalem.[387] It is likely that each of these features of the story is a progressive signal on the Deuteronomistic Historian's part

---

[385] Norbert Lohfink, "Distribution of the Functions of Power: The Laws Concerning Public Offices in Deuteronomy 16:18–18:22." Pages 345–46 in *A Song of Power and the Power of Song: Essays on the Book of Deuteronomy.* Edited by Duane L. Christensen. Winona Lake, Ind.: Eisenbrauns, 1993; A. D. H. Mayes, "Deuteronomistic Royal Ideology," *BibInt* 9 (2001): 257.

[386] E. Theodore Mullen Jr., *Narrative History and Ethnic Boundaries.* Atlanta: Scholars Press, 1993: 166.

[387] Ibid., 166–67.

to indicate movement away from adherence to the covenant and toward idolatry.[388]

The continuation of the narrative with the introduction of the itinerant Levite from Judah may be a separate story or simply a further step in this tale of idolatry.[389] Thus the civil and cultic infractions escalate from the acts of individuals to those of an entire household, which is misdirected by its head. Micah's attempt to certify his actions by adding a Levite priest only makes matters worse according to the statutes of the Deuteronomic Code, which condemn both idolatry and the enticing of others into false worship (Deut 12:29–13).

The Deuteronomistic Historian thereby creates a clear comparison between Micah's actions and those described as "Jeroboam's Sin" in 1 Kings 12:26–33, which included the official sanctioning of shrines at alternative cultic sites (Dan and Bethel) as well as on local high places. This is then contrasted with the religious reforms of Josiah, who ordered the destruction of all shrines outside of Jerusalem and thereby obtained a fiscal advantage for his capital city and his regime.[390] Micah, whose very name swears allegiance to the supremacy of Yahweh, ironically provides a shrine for his molten image and cult objects. This act stands in direct contrast to the injunction in Deut 12:2–20 to establish a central shrine for the worship of Yahweh and to destroy all idols so that the people would not fall into false religious practices.[391]

Additional aspects of chapter 17 that should be considered include the possible identity of Micah's mother. Like all other characters in chapters 17–21, except for Micah, this woman in nameless.[392] This lack of names possibly indicates an attempt on the part of the editor to focus on "categories of people" (i.e., their societal roles such as mother, priest, spy, tribesman) rather than on individuals.[393] Given the desire to put a name to characters,

[388] E. A. Mueller, *The Micah Story* (2001): 53.

[389] R. G. Boling, *Judges* (1975): 40–41; H. Becker, *Richterzeit und Königtum* (1990): 227–28.

[390] Gale A. Yee, "Ideological Criticism: Judges 17–21 and the Dismembered Body." Pages 153–56 in *Judges and Method: New Approaches in Biblical Studies.* Edited by Gale Yee. Minneapolis: Fortress Press, 1995. B. Halpern, "Levitic Participation," *JBL* 95 (1976): 34–38, identifies Micah's shrine as Bethel and the molten image as a bull in making the alternative argument that this story is originally of northern or Israelite origin and intended to provide an earlier provenance for Jeroboam's choice of Bethel over Shiloh as one of his royal shrines.

[391] R. H. O'Connell, *Rhetoric of the Book of Judges* (1996): 237–41.

[392] E. John Revell, *The Designation of the Individual: Expressive Language in Biblical Narrative.* Kampen, Neth.: Kok Pharos, 1996: 190–94.

[393] J. Marais, *Representation in Old Testament* (1998): 133.

however, and seeing possible connections between this story and that of Samson, Schneider makes the case for the possibility that she is Delilah.[394] This is based on the coincidence of the amount of silver (1,100 pieces) that Delilah is paid by the Philistines and the amount stolen by Micah. Such a connection would help to draw these stories together and to provide an epilogue to Samson's narrative, demonstrating how the blood money is further degraded by its use in the manufacture of an idol.

The mother's curse called down upon the thief and the subsequent blessing of her son for returning the stolen goods are quick and ironic twists, necessitated by a fear of God, whose name has been invoked in the curse.[395] This curse stands in contrast to the emphasis placed earlier on fulfilling an oath in the Jephthah story (Judg 11:30–36) and to the similarly hasty vow taken by the men of Israel as they prepared to fight the Benjaminites in Judg 21:1.[396] In each case the individuals cannot forswear themselves, but Micah's mother's action seems to be more of a countermeasure negating the curse with a blessing, somehow cooling God's anger by consecrating the silver to the deity. However, in what is a real irony, she and Micah see nothing wrong in using the silver to cast an idol. Such a flagrant violation of Exod 20:4–5 and Deut 12:2–4 is almost comic – a masterful use of humor to indicate once again how the thinking of the Israelites is backward and illegitimate.[397]

There also exists the likelihood that these initial episodes have been crafted by the editor to foreshadow the story of the migration of the tribe of Dan, which dominates chapter 18. Just as the Levite is looking for a place to live, the Danites are actively searching for a territory that they can claim for their own. In addition, the Levite first serves Micah's shrine as its priest and subsequently performs these duties for the high place constructed at the city of Dan to house the idol appropriated by the migrating Danites. The literary path thus becomes clear, with the Levite and the idol tying the two

---

[394] T. J. Schneider, *Judges* (2002): 231–32.

[395] M. Bal, *Death and Dissymmetry* (1988b): 197. The Israelites were admonished in Exod 20:7 not to make "wrongful use" of the name of God. Therefore a curse or a vow, such as Jephthah's in Judg 11:30–31, is very serious business and subject to divine wrath if taken frivolously or without a clear thought for what is at stake. For example, in the case of the blasphemous son in Lev 24:10–12, the episode hinges on his using God's name in a curse in the heat of a fight with another man. Micah's concern over his mother's curse is therefore quite understandable, if somewhat ironic, in the face of his violation of the statute against theft (Exod 20:15) and their subsequent violation of the statute against idolatry (Exod 20:4–6).

[396] L. R. Klein, *The Triumph of Irony* (1989): 186–87.

[397] Michael K. Wilson, "'As you Like it': The Idolatry of Micah and the Danites (Judges 17–18)," *RTR* 54 (1995): 81.

chapters together as common features and forming a comparison with Deut 12:2–20.

DEUT 12:2–20 ON IDOLATRY AND THE LAND	MICAH'S IDOLATRY AND DAN'S LACK OF LAND
High places are to be destroyed (Deut 12:2)	Micah constructs a high place shrine (Judg 17:5)
Idols are to be destroyed (Deut 12:3)	Micah manufactures an idol (Judg 17:4)
A central shrine is endorsed (Deut 12:5–7)	Micah's story repeatedly ignores the call for a central shrine (Judg 17:2–5, 13; 18:31)
Israel has not come into its inheritance as yet (Deut 12:9–10)	Dan fails to settle in its tribal allotment (Judg 18:1)
Yahweh promises that Israel will live in safety after entering the land (Deut 12:10)	Dan is unsettled while the people of Laish are living in comfort (Judg 18:7, 10, 27)
Yahweh promises to extend the territory of Israel in the future (Deut 12:20)	Dan is landless while the people of Laish have connections to Sidon (Judg 18:7, 10)[398]

CHAPTER 18

(1) In those days there was no king in Israel. And in those days the tribe of the Danites was seeking for itself a territory to live in; for until then no territory among the tribes of Israel had been allotted to them. (2) So the Danites sent five valiant men from the whole number of their clan, from Zorah and from Eshtaol, to spy out the land and to explore it; and they said to them, "Go, explore the land." When they came to the hill country of Ephraim, to the house of Micah, they stayed there. (3) While they were at Micah's house, they recognized the voice of the young Levite; so they went over and asked him, "Who brought you here? What are you doing in this place? What is your business here?" (4) He said to them, "Micah did such and such for me, and he hired me, and I have become his priest." (5) Then they said to him, "Inquire of God that we may know whether the mission we are undertaking will succeed." (6) The priest replied, "Go in peace. The mission you are on is under the eye of the Lord." (7) The

---

[398] This chart is based in part on the discussion in R. H. O'Connell, *Rhetoric of the Book of Judges* (1996): 238–41, and the summary in E. A. Mueller, *The Micah Story* (2001): 20.

five men went on, and when they came to Laish, they observed the people who were there living securely, after the manner of the Sidonians, quiet and unsuspecting, lacking nothing on earth, and possessing wealth. Furthermore, they were far from the Sidonians and had no dealings with Aram. (8) When they came to their kinsfolk at Zorah and Eshtaol, they said to them, "What do you report?" (9) They said, "Come, let us go up against them; for we have seen the land, and it is very good. Will you do nothing? Do not be slow to go, but enter in and possess the land. (10) When you go, you will come to an unsuspecting people. The land is broad – God has indeed given it into your hands – a place where there is no lack of anything on earth." (11) Six hundred men of the Danite clan, armed with weapons of war, set out from Zorah and Eshtaol, (12) and went up and encamped at Kiriath-jearim in Judah. On this account that place is called Mahaneh-Dan to this day; it is west of Kiriath-jearim. (13) From there they passed on to the hill country of Ephraim, and came to the house of Micah. (14) Then the five men who had gone to spy out the land (that is, Laish) said to their comrades, "Do you know that in these buildings there are an ephod, teraphim, and an idol of cast metal? Now therefore consider what you will do." (15) So they turned in that direction and came to the house of the young Levite, at the home of Micah, and greeted him. (16) While the six hundred men of the Danites, armed with their weapons of war, stood by the entrance to the gate, (17) the five men who had gone to spy out the land proceeded to enter and take the idol of cast metal, the ephod, and the teraphim. The priest was standing by the entrance of the gate with the six hundred men armed with weapons of war. (18) When the men went into Micah's house and took the idol of cast metal, the ephod, and the teraphim, the priest said to them, "What are you doing?" (19) They said to him, "Keep quiet! Put your hand over your mouth, and come with us, and be to us a father and a priest. Is it better for you to be priest to the house of one person, or to be priest to a tribe and clan in Israel?" (20) Then the priest accepted the offer. He took the ephod, the teraphim, and the idol, and went along with the people. (21) So they resumed their journey, putting the little ones, the livestock, and the goods in front of them. (22) When they were some distance from the home of Micah, the men who were in the houses near Micah's house were called out, and they overtook the Danites. (23) They shouted to the Danites who turned around and said to Micah, "What is the matter that you come with such a company?" (24) He replied, "You take my gods that I made, and the priest, and go away, and what have I left? How then can you ask me, 'What is the matter?'" (25) And the Danites said to him, "You had better not let your voice be heard among us or else hot-tempered fellows will attack you, and you will lose your life and the lives of your household." (26) Then the Danites went their way. When Micah saw that they were too strong for him, he turned and went back to his home. (27) The Danites, having taken what Micah had made, and the priest who belonged to him, came to Laish, to a people quiet and unsuspecting, put them to the sword, and burned down the city. (28) There was no deliverer, because it was far from Sidon and they had no dealings with Aram. It was in the valley that belongs to Beth-rĕḥôb. They rebuilt the city, and lived in it. (29) They named the city Dan, after their ancestor Dan, who was born in Israel; but the name of the city was formerly Laish. (30) Then the Danites set up the idol for themselves. Jonathan son of Gershom, son of Moses, and his sons were priests to the tribe of the Danites until the time the land went into captivity. (31) So they maintained as their own Micah's idol that he had made, as long as the house of God was at Shiloh.

The opening of this chapter repeats the phrase first used in Judg 17:6, thus indicating to the reader that the episodes are related, at least to the extent of sharing a common social and political setting, much like the phrase "once upon a time, long, long ago" does in fairy tales. The reference to the landless condition of the tribe of Dan contradicts the situation in the Samson narrative (Judg 13–16) and the list of tribal allotments found in Josh 19:40–48. If chapter 18 is connected to the Samson story, it may be in the decision by the Danites to leave their assigned territory under pressure from the Philistines (compare Judg 5:17, which associates them with ships and thus suggests a northern location). It is also possible that the editor/storyteller is more concerned with paralleling the Levite's need of a place and, on a microlevel, the need of the Israelites prior to the conquest to acquire a homeland.[399]

The dominant story element in this tale is the expedition of the spies and the aftermath of their discovery. Standard spy stories are a recurrent motif prior to the settlement of the Israelites in Canaan (see Num 13–14; 21:32–35; Deut 1:19–46; Josh 2; 7:2–4; 14:7–8). They have a distinctive structure that can be traced in each of these examples.

LITERARY STRUCTURE OF SPY STORIES
1. Spies chosen or appointed
2. Mission of the spies described
3. General report on the spies' mission for the reader
4. Return of spies and recitation of their report

---

[399] A. Malamat, "Danite Migration," *Bib* 51 (1970): 1–2.

5. Yahweh declares the gift of the land
6. Summation and commencement of immigration or conquest[400]

However, the spy account in Judg 18 does not follow this basic outline, and like so many other stories in the Book of Judges, it seems to relish the large number of violations of the literary protocol.[401] For instance, there is never any direct mention of divine aid or sanction for the activities of the spies or for the immigration of the tribe of Dan. The consultation with Micah's Levite, at his illegitimate, idol-based shrine, confirms only the desires of the spies, not Yahweh's approval. In addition, the city of Laish and its inhabitants are described as peaceful people, lacking any close allies who could come to their aid (compare Joshua's and Caleb's assessment of the prospects of conquering the Canaanites in Num 14:6–9). In all the other accounts Yahweh directs the Israelites not to fear their opponents and their walled cities. These people of Canaan are marked for destruction because they stand in the way of the Israelite invasion of their Promised Land. The citizens of Laish are victimized by an opportunistic, calculating group of 600 Danites who are armed to the teeth.[402]

[Margin note: not, quite true — see v. 5) oh, ok.]

The observations of the spies regarding the people of the city Laish, recorded in v. 7, might be better translated, "They had no king over them and no one to take control of the kingship."[403] This would in turn parallel the assessment of the Israelites that is repeated several times, that "there was no king in Israel." Thus the people of Laish are vulnerable because they lack leadership and because they are in the predatory path of a people who do "what is right in their own eyes."

The other theme in this chapter is the theft of Micah's idol and the hiring away of his Levite priest. It is interesting to note the reuse of terminology in Judg 17:10 and 18:19. As the Danites negotiate to hire the itinerant Levite, both Micah and the men of Dan request that he become "a father and a priest" to them. After raising only a minimal objection to this callous offer by the spies, the Levite happily accepts the opportunity presented him of serving a whole tribe rather than a local house shrine.[404]

---

[400] This list is based in part on Uwe F. W. Bauer, "Judges 18 as an Anti-Spy Story in the Context of an Anti-Conquest Story: The Creative Usage of Literary Genres," *JSOT* 88 (2000): 38.

[401] Ibid., 38–39.

[402] B. G. Webb, *Book of Judges* (1987): 186.

[403] Andrew A. MacIntosh, "The Meaning of *MKLYM* in Judges XVIII 7," *VT* 35 (1985): 73.

[404] J. C. Exum, "The Centre Cannot Hold," *CBQ* 52 (1990): 427; Robert Polzin, *Moses and the Deuteronomist: A Literary Study of the Deuteronomic History. Part One: Deuteronomy, Joshua, Judges.* New York: Seabury, 1980: 198.

A CLOSER LOOK AT LEVITES IN JUDGES

There has been a long debate among scholars over whether the mention of Levites in the settlement materials of Exodus, Leviticus, Joshua, and Judges reflects this early stage of Israelite history or is more reflective of the divided monarchy or postexilic period.[405] In more recent literature, greater credence is given to the likelihood that at least some of this material does correspond to the situation in the settlement period. The itinerant nature of the Levites in Judg 17–21 could signal a time when small villages could not support more than one or two cultic figures, and thus the surplus Levites were forced to seek employment elsewhere. Of course, that could also easily fit the situation in Josiah's time, when all the local high places and shrines were closed down and worship was centralized in Jerusalem (2 Kings 23:8–9).[406] The cupidity of the Levite who accepts the offers of employment in Judg 17:7–13 and 18:19–20 might also be compared to the actions of the "prophets" who are condemned by the prophet Micah for selling their services to who's willing to "feed" them (Mic 3:5–7).

Micah's joy at having the opportunity to hire a Levite to serve in his personal shrine clearly signals both the prestige attached to the Levitical priests as the official practitioners of religious rites and the shortage of such personnel in his vicinity (Judg 17:13). The Levite's abilities are also appreciated by the Danites, and they are eager to add his authority and skills in divination to their shrine at Dan (18:3–6, 19–20).[407] Yet this Levite from Bethlehem of Judah (17:9) is said to be the grandson of Moses (18:30), and his line of the priesthood is tied to the shrine at Shiloh (Josh 18:1), a community that would not have acknowledged the authority or validity of either private shrines or ones centered around idol worship (see 1 Sam 1:3).[408]

[405] Merlin D. Rehm, "Levites and Priests." Pages 297–302 of vol. 4 in *The Anchor Bible Dictionary*. Edited by David N. Freedman. New York: Doubleday, 1992.

[406] J. C. McCann, *Judges* (2002): 121–22.

[407] Joseph Blenkinsopp, *Sage, Priest, Prophet.* Louisville, Ky.: Westminster/John Knox, 1995: 73.

[408] See Frank M. Cross, *Canaanite Myth and Hebrew Epic.* Cambridge, Mass.: Harvard University Press, 1973: 197–99, for a discussion of the golden calf story in Exod 32:1–35 as the basis of Bethel being a center of activity by the Aaronid priesthood and Shiloh and Dan as shrines associated with the Mushite (those tied to Moses) priests. B. Halpern, "Levitic Participation," *JBL* 95 (1976): 33–34, adds to this position by pointing out the anti-Aaron rhetoric in Deut 9:20 making him the creator of the idol and thereby condemning his line of the priesthood. Thus the Mushites of Shiloh polemicized Aaron's role in both passages and made it quite clear that Moses never worshiped the golden calf.

Despite the historical connections to Dan, it is therefore possible that the Levite's acquiescence to service in shrines featuring an idol, possibly a bull image,[409] is another indication to later readers of the world-turned-upside-down theme so pervasive in the Book of Judges.

The Levite in Judg 19–21 takes on a cultic character only when he calls on the tribes to assemble and to consider the crime committed against him by Gibeah and the Benjaminites. He is overshadowed as a priestly figure, however, by Phineas son of Eleazar, son of Aaron (20:28), who is said to "minister before" (*lipnê*) the ark at Bethel. In this official capacity, he is the one consulted and asked to divine God's intention during the civil war against the tribe of Benjamin. Only a divinatory priest, tied to the ark and with the proper authority and ritual skills, could be called upon "to inquire of the Lord," and thus the unnamed Levite is not consulted in this matter.[410] Furthermore, the mention of Bethel and then later of Shiloh (21:19) as the site of the "yearly festival of the Lord" (*hag yhwh běšilô miyyāmîm yāmîmâ*) attests that there were several cultic sites recognized as Yahweh centers during settlement period and thus also provides a narrative strand introducing the Shiloh shrine in 1 Sam 1.

The story of a thief (Micah) who has his dearest possessions stolen duly complements the capture of Laish since in both cases a weaker opponent is stripped of its property. It is almost comical to hear Micah complain to the Danites that they have taken his cult objects and his Levite, and is reminiscent of the scene in which Laban confronts Jacob for absconding with his daughters and stealing his teraphim in Gen 31:26–30. However, the answer Micah receives from the Danites is not as civil as Jacob's. Like Paltiel son of Laish,[411] who was told to go home and stop pursuing the men who had taken Saul's daughter Michal from him (2 Sam 3:15–16), Micah is also advised to hold his tongue and accept his losses or face even worse consequences from a superior power.

---

[409] B. Halpern, "Levitic Participation," *JBL* 95 (1976): 34.
[410] E. T. Mullen, *Narrative History* (1993): 178.
[411] There is an interesting coincidence of names in these two texts. The Danites, after taking Micah's idol, capture and rename the city of Laish (Judg 18:27–31), and Paltiel son of Laish is stripped of his wife Michal by David's command. The irony attached to the name of a place that suffers such loss and a similarly named man in later Israelite history who experiences a devastating loss may only be coincidence, but it is the sort of wordplay that may have been attractive to the biblical writers. There is no geographic connection since Paltiel is said to be from Gallim, a town just north of Jerusalem, and Laish is located north of the Sea of Galilee.

The final section of chapter 18 provides a historical coda to the events that have just transpired. Through violent means the Danites have obtained both a new homeland and a sacred image. They rebuild the destroyed city of Laish, renaming it for their tribal ancestor, and establish long-term presence in the land, according to the editorial formula "until the time the land went into captivity." This latter statement may indicate that the people of the northern kingdom had a period of time to reform their religious and political practices but chose not to and ultimately succumbed to foreign conquest.[412] Furthering this idea is the apparent legitimacy gained by tying their shrine to Moses' grandson Gershom.[413] It may have been expected that such a lineage would eventually draw the people back into compliance with the covenant.[414] However, they are said to be adamant in their idolatry until the shrine at Shiloh was destroyed at the time of the Assyrian invasion of the northern kingdom in the latter part of the eighth century BCE.[415]

CHAPTER 19

Septuagint & the Vulgate

Hebrew text: "prostituted herself / played the harlot"

(1) In those days, when there was no king in Israel, a certain Levite, residing in the remote part of the hill country of Ephraim, took to himself a concubine from Bethlehem in Judah. (2) But his concubine became angry with him, and she went away from him to her father's house at Bethlehem in Judah, and was there some four months. (3) Then her husband set out after her, to speak tenderly to her and bring her back. He had with him his servant and a couple of donkeys. When he reached her father's house, the girl's father saw him and came with joy to meet him. (4) His father-in-law, the girl's father, made him stay, and he remained with him three days; so they ate and drank, and he stayed there. (5) On the fourth day they got up early in the morning, and he prepared to go; but the girl's father said to his son-in-law, "Fortify yourself with a bit of food, and after that you may go." (6) So the two men sat and ate and drank together; and the girl's father said to the man, "Why not spend the night and

---

[412] Philip Satterthwaite, "'No King in Israel': Narrative Criticism and Judges 17–21," *TynBul* 44 (1993): 85.

[413] See T. J. Schneider, *Judges* (2000): 242, for a discussion of the variant reading in the MT that may actually tie this Gershom to the apostate Judahite king Manasseh rather than to Moses.

[414] E. A. Mueller, *The Micah Story* (2001): 73–74.

[415] Donald G. Schley, *Shiloh: A Biblical City in Tradition and History*. JSOTSup 63. Sheffield, Eng.: JSOT Press, 1989: 200–201.

enjoy yourself?" (7) When the man got up to go, his father-in-law kept urging him until he spent the night there again. (8) On the fifth day he got up early in the morning to leave; and the girl's father said, "Fortify yourself." So they lingered until the day declined, and the two of them ate and drank. (9) When the man with his concubine and his servant got up to leave, his father-in-law, the girl's father, said to him, "Look, the day has worn on until it is almost evening. Spend the night. See, the day has drawn to a close. Spend the night here and enjoy yourself. Tomorrow you can get up early in the morning for your journey, and go home." (10) But the man would not spend the night; he got up and departed, and arrived opposite Jebus (that is Jerusalem). He had with him a couple of saddled donkeys, and his concubine was with him. (11) When they were near Jebus, the day was far spent, and the servant said to his master, "Come now, let us turn aside to this city of the Jebusites, and spend the night in it." (12) But his master said to him, "We will not turn aside into a city of foreigners, who do not belong to the people of Israel; but we will continue on to Gibeah." (13) Then he said to his servant, "Come let us try to reach one of these places, and spend the night at Gibeah or at Ramah." (14) So they passed on and went their way; and the sun went down on them near Gibeah, which belongs to Benjamin. (15) They turned aside there, to go in and spend the night at Gibeah. He went in and sat down in the open square of the city, but no one took them in to spend the night. (16) Then at evening there was an old man coming from his work in the field. The man was from the hill country of Ephraim, and he was residing in Gibeah. (The people of the place were Benjaminites.) (17) When the old man looked up and saw the wayfarer in the open square of the city, he said, "Where are you going and where do you come from?" (18) He answered him, "We are passing from Bethlehem in Judah to the remote parts of the hill country of Ephraim, from which I come. I went to Bethlehem in Judah; and I am going to my home. Nobody has offered to take me in. (19) We your servants have straw and fodder for our donkeys, with bread and wine for me and the woman and the young man along with us. We need nothing more." (20) The old man said, "Peace be with you. I will care for all your wants; only do not spend the night in the square." (21) So he brought him into his house, and fed the donkeys; they washed their feet, and ate and drank. (22) While they were enjoying themselves, the men of the city, a perverse lot, surrounded the house, and started pounding on the door. They said to the old man, the master of the house, "Bring out the man who came into your house, so that we may have intercourse with him." (23) And the man, the master of the house, went out to them and said to them, "No, my brothers, do not act so wickedly. Since this man is my guest, do not do this vile thing. (24) Here are my virgin daughter and his concubine; let me bring them out now. Ravish them and do whatever you want to them; but against this man do not do such a vile thing." (25) But the men would not listen to him. So the man seized his concubine, and put her out to them. They wantonly raped her, and abused her all through the night until the morning. And as the dawn began to break, they let her go. (26) As morning appeared, the woman came and fell down at the door of the man's house where her master was, until it was light. (27) In the morning her master got up, opened the doors of the house, and when he went out to go on his way, there was his concubine lying at the door of the house, with her hands on the threshold. (28) "Get up," he said to her, "we are going." But there was no answer. Then he put her on the donkey; and the man set out for his home. (29) When he had entered his house, he took a knife, and grasping his concubine he cut her into twelve pieces, limb by limb, and sent her throughout all the territory of Israel. (30) Then he commanded the men whom he sent, saying, "Thus shall you say to all the Israelites, 'Has such a thing ever happened since the day that the Israelites came up from the land of Egypt until this day? Consider it, take counsel, and speak out.'"

The narrative in Judg 19 begins with the now familiar phrase, "In those days, when there was no king in Israel. . . ." This will form an inclusio with the similar phrase that concludes the set of episodes found in Judges 19–21: "In those days there was no king in Israel. . . ." (21:25). There is, however, a further ironic phrase added to the latter verse: "all the people did what was right in their own eyes." This may serve in a narrative that is otherwise relatively free of judgmental statement or tone to pass judgment on the entire story, and in a way to provide some small justification for the lawlessness found there.[416]

With the basic anarchy of the times established, the reader is introduced to a Levite from the Ephraimite hill country and his Bethlehemite concubine. Her status as a secondary wife (i.e., one without a dowry) may contribute to her alienation from her husband, her flight, and her silence throughout the narrative.[417] Her flight, possibly in an attempt to divorce the Levite,[418]

---

[416] Kenneth A. Stone, "Gender and Homosexuality in Judges 19: Subject-Honor, Object-Shame?" *JSOT* 67 (1995): 90.

[417] M. Bal, *Death and Dissymmetry* (1988b): 89, attempts to classify a concubine as a wife who lives in her father's house. J. C. Exum, *Fragmented Women* (1993): 177, n. 13, demonstrates such a living situation is unlikely given other examples, such as 2 Sam 16:20–22.

[418] Yair Zakovitch, "The Woman's Rights in the Biblical Law of Divorce," *Jewish Law Annual* 4 (1981): 39.

initiates the story, and ultimately her husband's flight from the dangers of the night in Gibeah is her undoing.

Issues of hospitality (see the discussion on Judg 4) and the close parallels between this narrative and Gen 19 are quite obvious. They begin when the Levite travels to his father-in-law's house in Bethlehem to retrieve his wife. The standard Hebrew text (Massoretic text [MT]) suggests she has "played the harlot," while the Greek version of the Hebrew Bible (Septuagint [LXX], created between the third century BCE and the first century CE) and the Latin Vulgate translation simply state that she "became angry" with him. However, this would seem unlikely since a woman who had played the harlot would hardly be welcomed back to her father's house. Such a woman, based on Deut 22:13–21, would be stoned at her father's door or would go to live, as Hosea's wife Gomer did, with her lovers (Hos 2:5). It is possible that the text is actually expressing a negative judgment on the woman for having taken an action considered either unjustified or unacceptable to the editor as well as to the reader who have a particular view of male control over the women of their household.[419]

The translations once again vary in Judg 19:3c, and the MT is preferable, saying "she brought him to her father's house." This would parallel the statement at the beginning of the verse that the Levite's intention was "to speak kindly to her and bring her back." Reconciliation appears to be the order of the day between them, although he never speaks directly to her in this episode. Once he arrives, she becomes part of his entourage once more, reclaimed as his property, and packed away when he is ready to leave.[420] There will be an ironic and gruesome encore of this idea of packed baggage in v. 28.

The father's joy on the arrival of his son-in-law may be due to the father putting on a host's face to adhere to the regime of hospitality. It may also reflect the father's concern over the break in relations between his daughter and the Levite. A bride-price may have been paid or at least gifts exchanged – neither of which the father would wish to return to the Levite. Furthermore, his hospitable actions stand in stark contrast to those of the citizens of Gibeah later in the narrative.[421] They will also delay the Levite's departure,

---

[419] K. A. Stone, "Gender and Homosexuality," *JSOT* 67 (1995): 91, 96.

[420] K. G. Bohmbach, "Conventions/Contraventions," *JSOT* 83 (1999): 87.

[421] Susan Niditch, "The 'Sodomite' Theme in Judges 19–20: Family, Community, and Social Disintegration," *CBQ* 44 (1982): 366–67.

forcing him to leave in late afternoon and to stop that evening at Gibeah as he made his way toward home.[422]

For three days (19:4) the Levite lodged with his father-in-law. On the fourth day he prepared to depart but was convinced to eat first before leaving and then as the day waned to spend the night (vv. 5–7). The fifth day began like the fourth with an offer of food before departure. Once again the offer is accepted, but this time, when the father uses the same ritual formula, calling on him to remain yet another night, the Levite refuses further hospitality and departs with his concubine and servant in the late afternoon (vv. 8–9). This is his right since the host, after the initial period of hospitality, cannot force his guest to remain. He may request an extension, but it is up to the guest to decide whether to stay. In this case the Levite may have grown tired of the continual delays, or he may have felt that he would not be able to match the generosity of his host if the stay was extended any longer.[423]

Certainly, there is a rivalry between males in these repeated requests to stay. However, the statement by the father that makes an unfavorable comparison between his house and the potential dangers of the night (19:9e) can be construed as part of the hospitality ritual. Host and guest are never to be equal, for this in fact breeds rivalry and endangers the hospitality situation.[424] For example, the disparaging statement by the Levite in 19:19, in which he claims to need nothing from Gibeah other than shelter, having all the provisions he requires, places the guest above his host, setting the stage for a deadly rivalry to come.

The second episode now begins with the departure of the Levite and his concubine. Because they have started out so late in the day, they have to seek shelter for the night along the way. They reach the vicinity of Jebus (Jerusalem) and are faced with a choice of either staying in that Canaanite city or traveling on to the nearby villages of Gibeah and Ramah, which were in the tribal territory of Benjamin. The irony of this decision becomes evident,

---

[422] Stuart Lasine, "Guest and Host in Judges 19: Lot's Hospitality in an Inverted World," *JSOT* 29 (1984): 56–57, n. 34, refers to this as an example of "comic repetition."

[423] Dennis P. Cole, *Nomad of the Nomads: The Al Murrah Bedouin of the Empty Quarter*. Chicago: Aldine, 1975: 67. This can be compared to Gen 24:54–61, in which Abraham's servant requests leave of Laban in order to depart for Canaan. His request may be part of a ritual but may also reflect a break in protocol in which a certain number of days was expected during which the betrothed would make her preparations and good-byes and the family would stage a feast (see S. Greengus, "Old Babylonian Marriage Ceremonies and Rites," *JCS* 20 [1966]: 62). That could then explain why Rebekah was consulted since it was her schedule that was being disrupted.

[424] J. Pitt-Rivers, "The Stranger, the Guest, and the Hostile Host," in *Contributions to Mediterranean Sociology* (1968): 21.

since the Levite's explanation for rejecting his servant's suggestion that they stay in Jebus was that it is a "city of foreigners, who do not belong to the people of Israel" (19:11–12). When they reach an Israelite village the Levite and his company are treated like hostile "foreigners" and will be hosted by a "sojourner."[425]

Implied in Judg 19:15 is that no one met them as they entered the village, unlike in Gen 19:1, and they were forced to seek shelter in the *rĕḥôb*. This is an interesting twist on the narrative in Gen 19, where Lot meets the strangers at the gate and repeatedly and forcefully invites them to his home, but at first they refuse, saying they will spend the night in the *rĕḥôb* (Gen 19:2b), which is a poor refuge for travelers.[426] Having to spend the night there would be their last choice, and it would reflect on the poor hospitality of the town that strangers would have to shelter there. In Gen 19, the angels' intention to go to the *rĕḥôb* suggests a testing of the community. That the Levite in Judg 19 is forced to go to the *rĕḥôb* demonstrates a basic failure on the part of the citizens of Gibeah and a general lack of respect for the Levite.

Judg 19:16 sets the stage for the parallel with Gen 19:3–11. The narrator is very careful to define the old man as a sojourner from the hill country of Ephraim and to explain once again that the city of Gibeah was inhabited by Benjaminites. Such attention to detail suggests a strategy found in both of these narratives to show that the invitation of hospitality is made improperly by the one person in the city who had no legal right to make it.[427] It also indicts a town, specifically one in the tribal territory of Benjamin,[428] that fails to honor its obligation (Exod 23:9) not to "oppress a stranger" (see also Heb 13:2).

The label "wayfarer" (*hā'ōrēah*) for the Levite is also a legal term. In Jer 14:9 the "helpless stranger and wayfarer" who must "turn aside to tarry for a night" gives himself up to the hospitality of the people – guested optimally with both safe lodging and a meal. For instance, in 2 Sam 12:4 the wayfarer was given a lamb for dinner by the rich man, at the expense of his poor neighbor.

---

[425] P. Trible, *Texts of Terror* (1984): 71.
[426] C. A. O. Van Nieuwenhuijze, *Sociology of the Middle East* (1971): 693.
[427] Ibid., 287.
[428] Simcha S. Brooks, "Was There a Concubine at Gibeah?" *Bulletin of the Anglo-Israel Archaeological Society* 15 (1996–97): 32, ascribes this to a deliberate effort on the part of the editor to "besmirch" the reputation of the men of Saul's hometown.

Perhaps it is surprise that is being expressed in the story when the Ephraimite approaches the stranger and asks his questions. It may have been unusual for a visitor to be found in the *rĕḥôb* after dark. Whatever the case, the systematic violation of the hospitality code now begins with these questions. It is totally inappropriate for the potential or actual host to ask questions of his guest.[429] To do so demonstrates a lack of tact within the ritual of hospitality.[430]

The obvious frustration of the Levite comes out in his boastful and preemptory speech (Judg 19:18–19). He is feeling neglected and scorned by the people of Gibeah. He may also consider that he is being insulted by being questioned, since that clearly is not proper protocol. In the heat of his anger, this violation breeds another – his statement of self-sufficiency. Rivalry is created here as the Levite asserts his equality with any potential host in the city. This in and of itself violates the spirit and the law of hospitality and sets the stage for the rivalry of personal sacrifice found in 19:24–25. Plus there is a certain irony in the statement that granting him hospitality will cost his host nothing. As the story is played out, hosting the Levite nearly costs the Ephraimite his life and the virginity of his daughter, and it does cost the life of the Levite's concubine.[431]

Trible suggests that the Levite deliberately describes himself and his concubine as servants of the host either to flatter the old man or to use the woman "as bait" to obtain lodging for the night.[432] This sort of bribe has no place in the hospitality ritual. A stranger, whether wealthy or poor, does not have to demean himself or offer payment for hospitality – it is to be freely given, bringing honor to the host for his generosity.[433] More likely, the Levite is using sarcasm in 19:19, mixed with the polite speech expected of the stranger to his potential host. Yet there is irony here since the naming of the concubine as the "handmaid" *('āmâ)* of his host, a negative and

[429] Bichr Fares, *L'honneur chez les Arabes avant l'Islam*. Paris: Librairie d'Amerique et d'Orient, 1932: 95.

[430] D. P. Cole, *Nomad of the Nomads* (1975): 67.

[431] The whole scene is reminiscent of Gen 24:23–25, where Abraham's servant questions Rebekah about her family and asks about possible lodging. This is proper questioning since Rebekah will not be the servant's host; she simply is a source of information. Her response includes an abbreviated version of the Levite's speech: "We have both straw and provender enough, and room to lodge in." In this case, however, this places the servant in the position of one who will be the recipient of this bounty, not one who boasts of possessing it.

[432] P. Trible, *Texts of Terror* (1984): 72.

[433] J. Pitt-Rivers, "The Stranger, the Guest, and the Hostile Host," in *Contributions to Mediterranean Sociology* (1968): 23.

demeaning term,[434] may eventually explain the offer made by the Ephraimite to the crowd when they threaten his guest (see the comment on 19:24).

Following the boastful speech of the Levite, the Ephraimite humbly offers himself as host (Judg 19:20–21), promising to "care for all your wants," and, like Lot, pleading that the stranger "not spend the night in the square" (compare Gen 19:3). His concern appears to be genuine, but his invitation is a violation of custom because of his sojourner status. Since the pattern of violation began with the failure of the men of Gibeah to offer the Levite hospitality, it does not seem odd that the Levite would accept this improper invitation. As he said he would, the Ephraimite provides for the needs of the Levite and his animals. All the conventions of hospitality are followed, including the foot-washing ritual prior to the meal (see Gen 18:4).[435] The strict adherence to custom by the writer thereby heightens the irony associated with the improper invitation and with the inhospitable events to come.

There are some exact parallels between the scenes in Judg 19:22–26 and Gen 19:4–5. A meal is interrupted by a knock on the door and the demand to send out the stranger to be abused by the crowd. In Gen 19:4, however, a legal formula is used to show that the entire citizenry of Sodom was assembled outside Lot's house.[436] The legal character of that statement makes it sound like an official town council meeting in which the actions of Lot and his guests will be judged. In Judg 19:22, the situation reads more like a gang of hooligans, left unchecked by the citizens of Gibeah, who plan to prey on a weak old man and his guests.

In the scene in Judges the legal ramifications of the situation are not as well defined. If these are simply ruffians, then the direct parallels with Gen 19 are weakened, but the ironic reversal is heightened. It can thus be compared to the step taken by the Levite of thrusting his concubine out to the crowd in 19:25. The parallel between this and the actions of the angels in Gen 19:10–11 to save Lot is also weak, but it works in a literary sense as a way of heightening the impression of the lawless world in the Judges period.

The men in Judg 19 are not representing the legal rights of the town of Gibeah, as are the men in Gen 19:4. However, the failure of the town to control this irresponsible element compounds the initial failure to offer the

---

434 T. J. Schneider, *Judges* (2000): 259.
435 T. Raymond Hobbs, "Hospitality in the First Testament and the 'Teleological Fallacy'," *JSOT* 95 (2001): 13–19.
436 V. H. Matthews, "Hospitality and Hostility in Genesis 19 and Judges 19," *BTB* 22 (1992): 5.

Levite hospitality. A case could be made that the Levite was open to attack from any group in Gibeah once he accepted the improper invitation from the Ephraimite. However, the circumstances, as is so often the case in the Judges material, lend themselves to a sense of lawlessness that breeds the sort of outrage that is about to occur in this narrative.

Like Lot, the Ephraimite endangers himself in v. 23, as is required by custom, by protecting his guest. However, because a person's identity originates with birth site and can never totally be changed to another, the Ephraimite, as a resident alien, had no legal right to offer the Levite hospitality. He is now asserting that he does have the right to protect his guest, judging their actions, and calling the men assembled outside his house "my brothers."

Of interest is the repeated use of the phrase "the master of the house." While the Ephraimite is a sojourner and not a permanent resident of Gibeah, he, like all heads of households, is master of his own house. Lot asserts his right as a householder by closing his door behind him in Gen 19:6. This marks the boundary between the domain of the homeowner and the outside world. The door is not used as a symbol in Judg 19:23, and the phrase describing him as "master" may only serve to increase the irony of a master without mastery over the situation.

It is possible that the writer felt compelled to provide symmetry between this narrative and its original form in Gen 19. Since Lot offered two women to the mob in Sodom (Gen 19:8), the mechanics of the framework could demand that the Ephraimite offer two women to the mob in Gibeah.[437] The symmetry is broken, however, since the concubine is probably not a virgin like both of Lot's daughters (her earlier flight, however, may have prevented the consummation of the marriage).

The parallel continues with the invitation to "ravish them" and thus assuage their violent desires. The situation in Judg 19:24 may therefore be intended to portray a skewed world in which no man or woman is safe from harm, or one in which the "contest of courtesy" between the host and guest results in escalating offers that will eventually result in the sacrifice of the Levite's concubine as he wins this ritual conflict.[438] The Ephraimite's

---

[437] S. Lasine, "Guest and Host in Judges 19," *JSOT* 29 (1984): 39.

[438] David Penchansky, "Staying the Night: Intertextuality in Genesis and Judges." Pages 81–82 in *Reading between Texts: Intertextuality and the Hebrew Bible*. Edited by Danna N. Fewell. Louisville, Ky.: Westminster/John Knox, 1992. T. R. Hobbs, "Hospitality in the First Testament," *JSOT* 95 (2001): 23, suggests that the Ephraimite's insistence on protecting his guest may be based on the fact that both he and the Levite are from Ephraim. Thus he is not extending his sphere of protection over a foreigner, as Lot does in Gen 19:6–8.

invitation that the men do "whatever you want" is suggestive of the final phrase in this narrative (Judg 21:25b): "all the people did what was right in their own eyes." The creed for this period is summed up in that statement and seems to explain everything that happens, no matter how incongruous with normal custom or action.[439]

Trible uses this passage to claim that "the rules of hospitality in Israel protect only males."[440] However, women are legal extensions of their husbands and thus would come under the same protections guaranteed to their husbands – as long as their husbands identified them as such. In addition, any action taken against the wife would dishonor the husband.[441]

Taking a different tack in his study, Lasine points to v. 24 as the key to the reversal in the story.[442] He believes that the Ephraimite has shifted his role from hospitable to inhospitable host by "callously" offering the Levite's concubine to the crowd in order to save his honor and perhaps his own life. This could certainly be interpreted as another violation of the hospitality code since the concubine could not be legally separated from the Levite and thus was protected by the customs of hospitality to the same degree. At this point, however, the statement in v. 19 should be recalled, in which the Levite describes her as the Ephraimite's "handmaid," not his wife. The old man may now be taking the Levite at his word and offering in turn what he has been offered by the Levite to the crowd. This could simply be a further reflection of the principle that the guest is placed completely at the mercy of his host.[443]

This interchange or negotiation is less dramatic than that in Gen 19:9. The citizens of Gibeah simply ignore the Ephraimite's offer without accusing him of "playing the judge." They also make no attempt to speak to the Levite, ignoring him and treating him as an object rather than as a person with a defined social status.[444] Ironically, this is the same way that the Levite has

---

[439] Hans W. Jungling, *Richter 19-Ein Pladoyer für das Königtum: Stilistische Analyse der Tendenzerzählung Ri 19, 1–30a; 21, 25.* AB 84. Rome: Pontifical Biblical Institute, 1981: 279.

[440] P. Trible, *Texts of Terror* (1984): 75.

[441] Anton Blok, "Rams and Billy-Goats: A Key to the Mediterranean Code of Honour," *Man* 16 (1981): 434.

[442] S. Lasine, "Guest and Host in Judges 19," *JSOT* 29 (1984): 39.

[443] Michael Herzfeld, "'As in Your Own House': Hospitality, Ethnography, and the Stereotype of Mediterranean Society." Page 79 in *Honor and Shame and the Unity of the Mediterranean.* Edited by David D. Gilmore. Washington, D.C.: American Anthropological Association, 1987.

[444] K. A. Stone, "Gender and Homosexuality," *JSOT* 67 (1995): 99.

treated his concubine throughout much of the narrative, and he, in the end, does not bother to consult her prior to pushing her out the door.[445]

There is a sense of urgency in the Judges account, brought on by a lack of reasoning in the actions of the mob, which is intent on gaining dominance over the Levite. This may in turn explain the Levite's precipitous action of thrusting his concubine out the door and into the hands of the crowd. Lasine points to this passage as evidence of the attempt by the author to generate "outrage" among his readers when they compare the actions of the angels in Gen 19:10–11 with the Levite's act.[446] In both cases the life of the host is saved by his guest(s), but clearly the solution provided by Lot's guests is preferable to that of the Levite.

In both narratives the guest is forced to save his own life and that of his host. The irony of this reversal climaxes the narrative, although a sense of disgust lingers over the violence done to the Levite's concubine. She is a victim whose only attempt to assert her independence was thwarted by her father, her husband, and the citizens of Gibeah (by failing to carry out their proper role as host).[447] The Levite chooses to sacrifice her to save himself from being raped and thus "feminized" by the ruffians of Gibeah.[448] He has taken literally the Ephraimite's invitation to do what is "good in your eyes."[449] At the same time the degrees of potential social dishonor are demonstrated in these actions. Apparently, it is better in the eyes of the host to sacrifice his daughter and the Levite's concubine than the Levite to save his honor as a host.[450] And, it is better for the Levite to sacrifice his concubine than to submit himself to the sexual abuse of the mob.[451]

Although it did not come into play when the Ephraimite spoke to the mob, the door now functions as a significant symbol in the narrative. The

---

[445] S. Niditch, "The 'Sodomite' Theme," *CBQ* 44 (1982): 370; K. G. Bohmbach, "Conventions/ Contraventions," *JSOT* 83 (1999): 87.

[446] S. Lasine, "Guest and Host in Judges 19," *JSOT* 29 (1984): 52, n. 5.

[447] S. Niditch, "The 'Sodomite' Theme," *CBQ* 44 (1982): 371.

[448] K. A. Stone, "Gender and Homosexuality," *JSOT* 67 (1995): 97.

[449] This callous act might be compared to Abram's statement to Sarai about Hagar in Gen 16:6: "Do to her as you please."

[450] K. A. Stone, "Gender and Homosexuality," *JSOT* 67 (1995): 100, notes that the Ephraimite's decision may be based on the perception that his daughter is a "proper sexual object" and that the Levite is a "proper sexual subject," who is entitled to hospitality.

[451] Stanley H. Brandes, "Like Wounded Stags: Male Sexual Ideology in an Andalusian Town." Pages 232–34 in *Sexual Meanings: The Cultural Construction of Gender and Sexuality.* Edited by Sherry B. Ortner and Harriet Whitehead. Cambridge: Cambridge University Press, 1981.

"perverse lot" had beat upon the door (v. 22a), and now the dying concubine crawls back to what should have been a place of sanctuary. Note that the text is careful not to mention the doorway prior to this. It simply says the Ephraimite "went out to them" (v. 23) and the Levite "put her out to them" (v. 25), but in neither case does it say the doorway was crossed or that the door was opened or closed.

This could be a way to remove the legal ramifications associated with the entrance to the house from the episode and once again to differentiate this version of the framework story from that in Gen 19:5–10. In that episode, the crowd did not beat on the door; "they called to Lot" (v. 5). Lot "went out the door to the men, [and] shut the door after him" (v. 6). Incensed by Lot's refusal to give up his guests, the mob "drew near to break the door" (v. 9b), and the angels pulled Lot back into the house "and shut the door" (v. 10). Throughout this narrative, the door is used as a symbol of ownership and personal space. At first the men of Sodom seem reluctant to violate this custom, even by knocking, and it is only after they become infuriated by Lot's "judging" them that they attack the door.

In the Judges account, however, the confrontation begins with a blatant attack on personal privacy as the mob "started pounding on the door." Safety is often associated with justice in village custom (Exod 21:6; Deut 22:13–21), and the lack of it in this text is exemplified by the omission of any mention of the door. It then becomes the height of irony that the concubine should, with her last bit of strength, stumble back to "the door of the man's house," perhaps in a final attempt to elicit justice from her husband and the community.[452]

The manner in which her hands stretched out upon the threshold of the doorway is suggestive of another broken body. In 1 Sam 5:4, the "head of Dagon and both his hands were lying cut off upon the threshold" of his temple in Ashdod. In both cases the hands upon the threshold suggest submission to a fate they could not control, but it may also be an indictment of the Levite's action toward his concubine.[453]

The remainder of the narrative in Judg 19 deals with the aftermath of the crime committed at Gibeah. The Levite, referred to here as "her master," callously orders the ravaged woman to "get up" so they can resume their

---

[452] V. H. Matthews, "Entrance Ways," *Fides et Historia* 19 (1987): 34.
[453] S. Niditch, "The 'Sodomite' Theme," *CBQ* 44 (1982): 270–71; D. Penchansky, "Staying the Night," in *Reading between Texts* (1992): 83.

journey. Presumably, he has spent a comfortable and secure night during her ordeal, and now, without any thought for what she suffered on his behalf, he simply plans to complete what he had started. Seeing that she is unable to respond, he casually ties her body to his donkey and returns to his house.[454] He has no sympathy for her condition. What empathy there is for her suffering must be evoked from the reader.[455]

The story now provides lurid details of one last indignity perpetrated on the concubine's body as it is transformed into a "message" to serve the Levite's purposes.[456] She is carved up into twelve pieces, and the grisly evidence is dispatched as bloody invitations to a general assembly of the tribes. There are clear parallels between this action and Saul's call to arms in 1 Sam 11:7. It may function as part of an extended political polemic against Saul's family, tying Gibeah and the carving up of Saul's team of oxen to the dismemberment of the Levite's concubine.[457] Another possibility is a somewhat contrived or forced motif intended to remind the readers both of Saul's heroic act of marshaling the people to save Jabesh-gilead and of this scandalous and self-serving episode during the Judges period.[458]

Both of these versions of the story of the inappropriate host center on the obligations of the visited community (Sodom and Gibeah) to provide hospitality. It is the failure of the citizenry that is highlighted, but the narrative also contains a subplot, in which a righteous man is saved despite his own violations of custom. Instead of a citizen of the town offering hospitality, in both cases it is a resident alien who, without the right to do so, brings the visitor(s) into his house. Although the customary pattern seems to be operating here, from the moment when Lot and the Ephraimite invite the angels and the Levite, respectively, to share the comforts of their home, the reader realizes that this narrative can only end in tragedy for the town and its inhabitants.

---

[454] Koala Jones-Warsaw, "Toward a Womanist Hermeneutic: A Reading of Judges 19–21." Pages 177–78 in *A Feminist Companion to Judges*. Edited by Athalya Brenner. Sheffield, Eng.: Sheffield Academic Press, 1993.

[455] Alice A. Keefe, "Rapes of Women/Wars of Men," *Semeia* 61 (1993): 90.

[456] Mieke Bal, "A Body of Writing: Judges 19." Page 223 in *A Feminist Companion to Judges*. Edited by Athalya Brenner. Sheffield, Eng.: Sheffield Academic Press, 1993.

[457] S. Lasine, "Guest and Host in Judges 19," *JSOT* 29 (1984): 41–43; S. S. Brooks, "Was There a Concubine?" *Bulletin of the Anglo-Israel Archaeological Society* 15 (1996–97): 33.

[458] Yairah Amit, "Literature in the Service of Politics: Studies in Judges 19–21." Pages 31–35 in *Politics and Theopolitics in the Bible and Postbiblical Literature*. Edited by H. G. Reventlow, Y. Hoffman, and B. Uffenheimer. JSOTSup 171. Sheffield, Eng.: Sheffield Academic Press, 1994.

CHAPTER 20

(1) Then all the Israelites came out, from Dan to Beersheba, including the land of Gilead, and the congregation assembled in one body before the Lord at Mizpah. (2) The chiefs of all the people, of all the tribes of Israel, presented themselves in the assembly of the people of God, four hundred thousand foot-soldiers bearing arms. (3) (Now the Benjaminites heard that the people of Israel had gone up to Mizpah.) And the Israelites said, "Tell us, how did this criminal act come about?" (4) The Levite, the husband of the woman who was murdered, answered, "I came to Gibeah that belongs to Benjamin, I and my concubine, to spend the night. (5) The lords of Gibeah rose up against me, and surrounded the house at night. They intended to kill me, and they raped my concubine until she died. (6) Then I took my concubine and cut her into pieces, and sent her throughout the whole extent of Israel's territory; for they have committed a vile outrage in Israel. (7) So now, you Israelites, all of you, give your advice and counsel here." (8) All the people got up as one, saying, "We will not any of us go to our tents, nor will any of us return to our houses. (9) But now this is what we will do to Gibeah: we will go up against it by lot. (10) We will take ten men of a hundred throughout all the tribes of Israel, and a hundred of a thousand, and a thousand of ten thousand to bring provisions for the troops, who are going to repay Gibeah of Benjamin for all the disgrace that they have done in Israel." (11) So all the men of Israel gathered against the city, united as one. (12) The tribes of Israel sent men through all the tribe of Benjamin, saying, "What crime is this that has been committed among you? (13) Now then, hand over those scoundrels in Gibeah, so that we may put them to death, and purge the evil from Israel." But the Benjaminites would not listen to their kinsfolk, the Israelites. (14) The Benjaminites came together out of the towns to Gibeah, to go out to battle against the Israelites. (15) On that day the Benjaminites mustered twenty-six thousand armed men from their towns, besides the inhabitants of Gibeah. (16) Of all this force, there were seven hundred picked men who were left-handed; every one could sling a stone at a hair, and not miss. (17) And the Israelites, apart from Benjamin, mustered four hundred thousand armed men, all of them warriors. (18) The Israelites proceeded to go up to Bethel, where they inquired of God, "Which of us shall go up first to battle against the Benjaminites?" And the Lord answered, "Judah shall go up first." (19) Then the Israelites got up in the morning, and encamped against Gibeah. (20) The Israelites were out to battle against Benjamin; and the Israelites drew up the battle line against them at Gibeah. (21) The Benjaminites

there's nothing like a common enemy to unite people.

came out of Gibeah, and struck down on that day twenty-two thousand of the Israelites.[459] (23) The Israelites went up and wept before the Lord until the evening; and they inquired of the Lord, "Shall we again draw near to battle against our kinsfolk the Benjaminites?" And the Lord said, "Go up against them." (22) The Israelites took courage, and again formed the battle line in the same place where they had formed it on the first day. (24) So the Israelites advanced against the Benjaminites the second day. (25) Benjamin moved out against them from Gibeah the second day, and struck down eighteen thousand of the Israelites, all of them armed men. (26) Then all the Israelites, the whole army, went back to Bethel and wept, sitting there before the Lord; they fasted that day until evening. Then they offered burnt offerings and sacrifices of well-being before the Lord. (27) And the Israelites inquired of the Lord (for the ark of the covenant of God was there in those days, (28) and Phineas son of Eleazar, son of Aaron, ministered before it in those days), saying, "Shall we go out once more to battle against our kinsfolk the Benjaminites, or shall we desist?" The Lord answered, "Go up, for tomorrow I will give them into your hand." (29) So Israel stationed men in ambush around Gibeah. (30) Then the Israelites went up against the Benjaminites on the third day, and set themselves in array against the Gibeah, as before. (31) When the Benjaminites went out against the army, they were drawn away from the city. As before they began to inflict casualties on the troops, along the main roads, one of which goes up to Bethel and the other to Gibeah, as well as in the open country, killing about thirty men of Israel. (32) The Benjaminites thought, "They are being routed before us, as previously." But the Israelites said, "Let us retreat and draw them away from the city toward the roads." (33) The main body of the Israelites drew back its battle line to Baal-tamar, while those Israelites who were in ambush rushed out of their place west of Geba. (34) There came against Gibeah ten thousand picked men out of all Israel, and the battle was fierce. But the Benjaminites did not realize that disaster was close upon them. (35) The Lord defeated Benjamin before Israel; and the Israelites destroyed twenty-five thousand one hundred men of Benjamin that day, all of them armed. (36) Then the Benjaminites saw that they were defeated. The Israelites gave ground to Benjamin, because they trusted to the troops in ambush that they had stationed against Gibeah. (37) The troops in ambush rushed quickly upon Gibeah. Then they put the whole city to the sword. (38) Now the agreement between the main body of Israel and the men in ambush was that when they sent up a cloud of smoke out of the city

---

[459] The NRSV translators have reversed the order of vv. 22 and 23 to provide a more logical story line.

(39) the main body of Israel should turn in battle. But Benjamin had begun to inflict casualties on the Israelites, killing about thirty of them; so they thought, "Surely they are defeated before us, as in the first battle." (40) But when the cloud, a column of smoke, began to rise out of the city, the Benjaminites looked behind them – and there was the whole city going up in smoke toward the sky! (41) Then the main body of Israel turned, and the Benjaminites were dismayed, for they saw that disaster was close upon them. (42) Therefore they turned away from the Israelites in the direction of the wilderness; but the battle overtook them, and those who came out of the city were slaughtering them in between. (43) Cutting down the Benjaminites, they pursued them from Nohah and trod them down as far as a place east of Gibeah. (44) Eighteen thousand Benjaminites fell, all of them courageous fighters. (45) When they turned and fled toward the wilderness to the rock of Rimmon, five thousand of them were cut down on the main roads, and they were pursued as far as Gidom, and two thousand of them were slain. (46) So all who fell that day of Benjamin were twenty-five thousand arms-bearing men, all of them courageous fighters. (47) But six hundred turned and fled toward the wilderness to the rock of Rimmon for four months. (48) Meanwhile, the Israelites turned back against the Benjaminites, and put them to the sword – the city, the people, the animals, and all that remained. Also the remaining towns they set on fire.

Chapter 20 provides a continuation of the plea of the Levite for justice against the men of Gibeah.[460] This could explain the emphasis contained in the Levite's charge against the men of the Gibeah that they had first attempted to kill him (v. 5), a Levite, a person of elevated social caste (compare Micah's happiness at attracting a Levite to serve his shrine in Judg 17:10–13).[461] The crime is therefore the antisocial behavior of the "lords of Gibeah,"[462] and the concubine's rape is secondary, even collateral damage.

It is also clear that the version of the story that the Levite tells the assembly of the Israelites at Mizpah is shaded to disguise his own cowardly act and to paint the leaders of Gibeah as responsible for this outrage instead of a group

---

[460] It has been argued that chapters 20 and 21 are later appendages to existing stories that have been compiled in the postexilic period by the priestly editors (A. D. H. Mayes, "Deuteronomistic Royal Ideology," *BibInt* 9 [2001]: 254; U. Becker, *Richterzeit und Königtum* [1990]: 257–99). T. J. Schneider, *Judges* (2000): 272, makes a convincing statement, however, that the more important issue is their linkage to the central argument of the Book of Judges: the spiraling downward progression of social and religious decline by the judges and the people.

[461] R. H. O'Connell, *Rhetoric of the Book of Judges* (1996): 253.

[462] S. Niditch, "The 'Sodomite' Theme," *CBQ* 44 (1982): 377 .

of ruffians. He calls on them to invoke the legal principle of *lex talionis* (an eye for an eye [Exod 21:23–25]) to restore his honor as well as the honor of the Israelites themselves.[463] As a result the town rather than the actual culprits is indicted (vv. 9–10), and when the Israelites demand that "those scoundrels in Gibeah" be turned over to them (v. 13), the rest of the Benjaminites are faced with the loss of Gibeah's entire population.

There are two interesting parallels to this story in which the Israelites demand that the "scoundrels of Gibeah" be surrendered to them. First, it provides a reversal of the scene in Judg 19:22–25. Instead of the scoundrels making the demand that the "old Ephraimite" send out his guest to them, the Israelites demand that the scoundrels be turned over to them so that they can be executed. Second, just as the ruffians in Gibeah "would not listen" to the argument of the Ephraimite (19:25), the Benjaminites also reject legal demands and "would not listen to their kinsfolk" (20:13b). The explanation for this position is found in the tribes' assurance that this action will remove the disgrace and corruption that the Benjaminites represent for the whole body of Israel (a nice irony considering the disgrace that has been perpetrated on the body of the concubine). The outraged tribes' justification for violence is very close to the legal principle invoked in the execution of Achan and his family in Josh 7:16–26. In both narratives the following story elements occur:

JOSH 7:16–26 AND JUDGES 20: THE "PURGING OF EVIL" FROM ISRAEL
1. Tribes are called into assembly
2. Tribes are confronted with a criminal act and they suffer a military defeat
3. Tribes are told to separate out the lawbreaker(s) so that evil can be purged from Israel
4. A collective action takes place in which persons, their animals, and their property are destroyed (a principle of *ḥērem*)

The prelude to the civil war between the Benjaminites and the rest of the Israelite tribes thus has its roots in the besmirched honor of a Levite and the precipitous anger of the Israelites themselves. Rather than consulting God at their general assembly, they proclaim a rash vow to remain in the field until revenge has been taken against Gibeah (vv. 8–10). It becomes clear that

---

[463] R. H. O'Connell, *Rhetoric of the Book of Judges* (1996): 253.

all parties involved will ultimately be faced with the consequences of their failure to obey the law, ascertain the facts of the situation from more than a single witness, or seek divine guidance.[464] It is a true irony that the one occasion in the Book of Judges when "all the men of Israel gathered . . . united as one" (v. 11) is in a war against their own kin.

When the Israelites do finally go to Bethel to consult God on the coming battle (v. 18), the response is exactly the same as the one in Judg 1:1–2 prior to commencing the conquest of the Canaanites, "Judah shall go up first."[465] This provides a literary frame to the book, an inclusio, which ties events as well as themes together. Clearly, Benjamin has now been equated with the enemy, and, just as the fight against the Canaanites is not a complete success (1:19–21, 27–36), so too will this fight against the Benjaminites prove to be a struggle greater than one would expect between 26,000 and 400,000 warriors. After suffering a stunning defeat in their initial battle, the Israelites, like Joshua (Josh 7:6–9) mourn and ask God why this has happened. There is also a change in their rhetoric. Now the Benjaminites are referred to as their "kinsfolk" and thus are less demonized, and the fervor for war has clearly diminished.[466] While they may be reluctant to resume the conflict, God orders them into battle once more.

After a second devastating defeat, the confused Israelites depart in a body for Bethel, where they make sacrifices and once again consult God on the advisability of this conflict. In vv. 27–28 there is a gloss embedded into the text, which adds the information that the Ark of the Covenant was housed in Bethel and that Phineas, the grandson of Aaron, is serving as its officiant. This stands in contrast to the illegitimate shrine of Micah, with its idols and Gershom, the grandson of Moses, as its priest in residence.[467] Quite likely, this is an intentional insertion by the editor pointing to the legitimacy of the Jerusalem cult versus that in the northern kingdom at Dan. It also provides a cultic history for Bethel, which was corrupted by Jeroboam's Sin (golden calf and non-Levitical priests; 1 Kings 12:28–31), and then purified by the "righteous king" Josiah in the seventh century BCE (2 Kings 23:4–16).

[464] R. G. Boling, *Judges* (1975): 288; Philip Satterthwaite, "Narrative Artistry in the Composition of Judges XX 29FF," *VT* 42 (1992): 81.

[465] B. G. Webb, *Book of Judges* (1987): 193, notes the appropriateness of this choice since the Levite's concubine was from the territory of Judah, and thus the act against her could be construed as an act against the entire tribe.

[466] P. Satterthwaite, "Narrative Artistry," *VT* 42 (1992): 82.

[467] T. J. Schneider, *Judges* (2000): 275.

As in many Israelite narratives, the third time an action is taken will prove to be the decisive one (compare 2 Kings 1:9–16). Having secured for the first time in this narrative a divine promise of military success (compare Josh 8:7; 10:19; Judg 3:28), the Israelites developed a more skillful battle plan (prior attempts had been frontal assaults based on superior numbers). It includes a feigned attack and retreat that draws the Benjaminites out into open country, where they will be more vulnerable (v. 32). There is also an ambush set to take the city of Gibeah and to fall upon the Benjaminites from behind (compare the attack on Ai in Josh 8:1–23).

The account of the third day of civil conflict is the most detailed of any battle saga in the Book of Judges. It also presents some confusing narrative problems, which may be the result of a misunderstanding of the editor's intent or a failure to understand military terminology by the translators.[468] For example, vv. 29–36a appear to complete the initial chronicle of this battle, with the Benjaminites recognizing their vulnerable position and imminent defeat. This first section also includes the statement that Yahweh inflicted the defeat on the Benjaminites (v. 35), thereby drawing this story away from its previously lawless character to one more typical of conquest accounts, in which the divine warrior intervenes to provide a victory (compare Josh 10:8–13).

Starting at v. 36b, there is a second telling of the story from the perspective of the Benjaminites. It contains some details not found in the first account and extends to v. 44. In particular, this section includes the mention of the smoke signal that is to be used to spring the trap on the Benjaminites (compare Josh 8:20). Once they see Gibeah in flames and the swift about-face of the previously retreating Israelites (v. 41), the Benjaminites are scissored between two contingents of the enemy, and they flee toward the wilderness as a general slaughter begins.

The aftermath of the battle begins at v. 45, with the scene shifting first to a group of Benjaminites who flee to the rugged area around the rock of Rimmon[469] and then to the Israelites (v. 48), who abandon their chase of the fleeing soldiers and return to finish the campaign by destroying Benjaminite

---

[468] E. John Revell, "The Battle with Benjamin (Judges XX 29–48) and Hebrew Narrative Techniques," *VT* 35 (1985): 431.

[469] Patrick M. Arnold, "Rimmon (Place)." Page 774 of vol. 5 in *The Anchor Bible Dictionary.* Edited by David N. Freedman. New York: Doubleday, 1992, notes the parallel incident in 1 Sam 13:15, in which Saul and 600 men rally in preparation to battle the Philistines at the "Pomegranate Rock" near Gibeah (1 Sam 14:2). The repetition of 600 men associated with a Benjaminite leader serves as yet another tie between the story in Judg 20–21 and Saul's career.

towns.[470] This quick shift sets up the conditions in chapter 21, in which 600 Benjaminite warriors are found to have survived the slaughter but whose families have been killed in the general destruction of Gibeah and the other Benjaminite settlements.

The confusion over the structure of this battle account has been attributed to a "composite composition" by a number of commentators.[471] However, the editor is in fact employing a literary technique known as resumptive repetition to explain the apparent duplication of phrases. In this way, the varied perspectives of the three different groups of Benjaminites and Israelites that are scattered about the battlefield can be described effectively.[472] As the narrator shifts from one contemporary scene to another, there must be some repetition included in the text so that the reader is made aware of the temporal and spatial context of a newly described scene. In this way the suspense attached to the Israelite strategy, the movement of forces about the battlefield, and the unforgiving nature of the pursuit as the Benjaminites flee for their lives are depicted. Ultimately, all the waste associated with this civil war is epitomized by the systematic destruction of persons and property.[473]

CHAPTER 21

(1) Now the Israelites had sworn at Mizpah, "No one of us shall give his daughter in marriage to Benjamin." (2) And the people came to Bethel, and sat there until evening before God, and they lifted up their voices and wept bitterly. (3) They said, "O Lord, the God of Israel, why has it come to pass that today there should be one tribe lacking in Israel?" (4) On the next day, the people got up early, and built an altar there, and offered burnt offerings and sacrifices of well-being. (5) Then the Israelites said, "Which of all the tribes of Israel did not come up in the assembly to the Lord?" For a solemn oath had been taken concerning whoever did not come up to the Lord to Mizpah, saying, "That one shall be put to death." (6) But the Israelites had compassion for Benjamin their kin, and said, "One tribe is cut off from Israel this day. (7) What shall we do for wives for those who are left, since we have sworn by the Lord that we

---

[470] E. J. Revell, "Battle with Benjamin," *VT* 35 (1985): 432.

[471] C. F. Burney, *The Book of Judges*, 2nd ed. London: Rivingtons, 1920: 447; J. A. Soggin, *Judges* (1987): 293–94.

[472] E. J. Revell, "Battle with Benjamin," *VT* 35 (1985): 426–30.

[473] P. Satterthwaite, "Narrative Artistry," *VT* 42 (1992): 88–89.

will not give them any of our daughters as wives?" (8) Then they said, "Is there anyone from the tribes of Israel who did not come up to the Lord to Mizpah?" It turned out that no one from Jabesh-gilead had come to the camp, to the assembly. (9) For when the roll was called among the people, not one of the inhabitants of Jabesh-gilead was there. (10) So the congregation sent twelve thousand soldiers there and commanded them, "Go, put the inhabitants of Jabesh-gilead to the sword, including the women and the little ones. (11) This is what you shall do; every male and every woman that has lain with a male you shall devote to destruction." (12) And they found among the inhabitants of Jabesh-gilead four hundred young virgins who had never slept with a man and brought them to the camp at Shiloh, which is in the land of Canaan. (13) Then the whole congregation sent word to the Benjaminites who were at the rock of Rimmon and proclaimed peace to them. (14) Benjamin returned at that time; and they gave them the women whom they had saved alive of the women of Jabesh-gilead; but they did not suffice for them. (15) The people had compassion on Benjamin because the Lord had made a breach in the tribes of Israel. (16) So the elders of the congregation said, "What shall we do for wives for those who are left, since there are no women left in Benjamin?" (17) And they said, "There must be heirs for the survivors of Benjamin, in order that a tribe may not be blotted out from Israel. (18) Yet we cannot give any of our daughters to them as wives." (19) So they said, "Look, the yearly festival of the Lord is taking place at Shiloh, which is north of Bethel, on the east of the highway that goes up from Bethel to Shechem, and south of Lebonah." (20) And they instructed the Benjaminites, saying, "Go and lie in wait in the vineyards, (21) and watch; when the young women of Shiloh come out to dance in the dances, then come out of the vineyards and each of you carry off a wife for himself from the young women of Shiloh, and go to the land of Benjamin. (22) Then if their fathers or their brothers come to complain to us, we will say to them, "'Be generous and allow us to have them; because we did not capture in battle a wife for each man. But neither did you incur guilt by giving your daughters to them.'" (23) The Benjaminites did so; they took wives for each of them from the dancers whom they abducted. Then they went and returned to their territory, and rebuilt the towns, and lived in them. (24) So the Israelites departed from there at that time by tribes and families, and they went out from there to their own territories. (25) In those days there was no king in Israel; all the people did what was right in their own eyes.

The narrative in Judg 21 is dominated by the dilemma of finding suitable wives for the 600 surviving Benjaminite warriors. The situation is complicated because the Israelites have taken an oath not to give their daughters to the tribe of Benjamin, and this will drastically restrict the choices left to supply the Benjaminites with wives. A partial solution is found as a result of a separate oath taken by the Israelites at their assembly at Mizpah. They had sworn to kill any member of the Israelite tribes who failed to appear at their assembly (compare Saul's oath in 1 Sam 11:7). Obviously, the men of Benjamin had not attended, and they had been duly, if not completely, punished. Now, in a shocked reaction to what they have done, and even blaming it on God's creating a "breach in the tribes of Israel" (v. 15), the elders decide to spare the 600 Benjaminites so that one of the twelve tribes would not become extinct.

After reviewing the records of the assembly, the elders discover that the men of Jabesh-gilead had not attended and were therefore to be considered oath-breakers, subject to the full wrath of the assembled tribes. The Israelites need merely to destroy the city and put the people to the sword, sparing 400 virgins, who can be given as spoil (compare Judg 5:30) to the Benjaminites as a sign that peace is truly proclaimed between them and the rest of Israel.[474]

The raid against Jabesh-gilead is yet another link between Saul's career and the Judges account. Jabesh-gilead serves as an inclusio in the Saul narrative. He opens his career as a war chief by relieving the siege of Jabesh-gilead by the Ammonites in 1 Sam 11:5–11.[475] Then after his death in battle at Mt. Gilboa, Saul's body is impaled before the walls of Beth-shemesh by the victorious Philistines (1 Sam 31:8–10). To repay his previous military service to their town and to provide the king/chief with an honorable burial, the men of Jabesh-gilead secretly removed his body, cremated it, and had the remains interred under a sacred tamarisk tree within their territory (1 Sam 31:12–13). Now, in this account in Judg 21, the only Israelites, other than the men of Benjamin, who had failed to answer the call to arms in the civil war were the men of Jabesh-gilead. This cannot be a coincidence and must be a contrived element designed once again to demonize Saul's tribe and family.[476] The marriage between the surviving Benjaminites and the 400 virgins of the oath-breaking city of Jabesh-gilead are thus the ancestors of Saul's rejuvenated tribe.

For the remaining 200 Benjaminites a novel legal loophole is devised. The Israelites may not give, that is contract, a marriage for their daughters with the Benjaminites, but this does not mean that the warriors cannot obtain

[474] S. Niditch, *War in the Hebrew Bible* (1993): 135.
[475] See V. H. Matthews and D. C. Benjamin, *Social World of Ancient Israel* (1993): 101–9.
[476] Y. Amit, "Literature in the Service of Politics," in *Politics and Theopolitics* (1994): 32.

brides by capture.[477] This practice is also legislated in Exod 22:16–17 and
Deut 22:28–29. In the former, a man who has sexual intercourse with an
unbethrothed virgin is required by law to pay the normal bride-price, but
her father has the option of refusing to allow him to marry his daughter.
The example in Deuteronomy instead requires the rapist to pay 50 shekels of
silver to her father and marry the young woman, and he is forbidden ever to
divorce her. It is this latter statute, which dates to the end of the monarchic
period, that applies to the case of "rape-capture" in Judg 21:19–21.[478] Based
on this law there are no circumstances in which the father could deny giving
his daughter to her "captor," and the stipulation against divorce provides
her with legal protections that could balance the father's ire at the loss of his
child.[479]

The callous nature of this solution rivals that of the Levite when he thrust
his concubine out to the mob in Gibeah (19:25) and is yet one more attempt
by the narrator to chronicle the lawlessness of this period in which women
are so cavalierly and brutally treated.[480] In fact, the young women dancing
so joyously in the vineyard festival at Shiloh are physically raped and their
families are financially victimized.[481] These households lose the economic
value attached to arranged marriages and are forced to be content with an
apparent tribal altruism: that they have helped to save a fellow tribe and
in the process have been spared any guilt that would have been incurred
if they had contracted marriage arrangements with the Benjaminites. Such
a bitter pill would not have been easy to swallow, but they have no real
choice given the political decision of the elders of the other tribes. With the
"problem" solved and battle lust deflated by these forced nuptials, all that
remains is for the tribes to return to their home territories.[482] The similar
language of Judg 2:6 and 21:24 thus provides another framing device, tying

---

[477]   Note the capture of a bride by the Ugaritic hero Keret in *KTU* 1.14–16 (see Johannes C. de
Moor, *An Anthology of Religious Texts from Ugarit.* Leiden, Neth.: Brill, 1987: 191–223).

[478]   Tikva Frymer-Kensky, "Virginity in the Bible." Pages 92–93 in *Gender and Law in the
Hebrew Bible and the Ancient Near East.* Edited by Victor H. Matthews et al. JSOTSup 262.
Sheffield, Eng.: Sheffield Academic Press, 1998.

[479]   Carolyn Pressler, *The View of Women Found in the Deuteronomic Family Laws.* BZAW 216.
Berlin: Walter de Gruyter, 1993: 39.

[480]   Daniel I. Block, "Unspeakable Crimes: The Abuse of Women in the Book of Judges," *SBJT*
2 (3, 1998): 52–54.

[481]   Alice Bach, "Rereading the Body Politic: Women and Violence in Judges 21," *BibInt* 6
(1998): 3.

[482]   Susan Ackerman, *Warrior, Dancer, Seductress, Queen: Women in Judges and Biblical Israel.*
New York: Doubleday, 1998: 257–59, makes an excellent case for this final chapter in Judges
being paired with the much more hopeful story in 1 Sam 1:1–2:10, which also takes place
during the vineyard festival at Shiloh and involves the annunciation of Hannah and birth
of Samuel.

the book together and leaving the readers to shake their heads at the summary statement in v. 25 that nothing more could be expected of a people without a king.[483]

BRIDGING THE HORIZONS

It is possible that chapters 17–21 in Judges are the most difficult for modern readers to reconcile with their normal or idealized expectations of the biblical account. There are no redeeming characters here, and the blatant acts of antisocial behavior, idolatry, brutality, disloyalty, and even madness are beyond belief. What, then, can be concluded about why they are included in the book and about what value they have to our understanding of the covenantal relationship with God? Here are a few thoughts to consider.

(1) The almost comic exchange between Micah and his mother over the theft of her silver is an amplified version of the breakdown of the family in every time and place. Children do not always measure up to the standards that parents expect, and it is often a parent who is the last to realize that their son or daughter is responsible for an act of theft or other violation of the standard code of conduct. To be sure, Micah's mother's willingness to forgive her son is commendable and so is her intent to dedicate a portion of the silver to God, possibly as a sin-offering for her son's act. However, that pledge of devotion is neutralized by her using it to mold an idol. If we use our funds to purchase items for a church that glorify ourselves, pointing with great pride as "our donation" rather than seeing it as an advancement of God's mission on earth, then we are also guilty of her sin of idolatry.

(2) Too often we are tempted to place a minister or priest on a pedestal, assuming that they can serve as a spotless example to the faithful of proper action and personal devotion. This makes any infraction that they may commit even greater in the eyes of the people, which in turn can lead people to leaving the faith community or to becoming cynical with regard to the clergy. Certainly, the Levites in these narratives are not exemplary characters. The one in the Micah account seems more interested in finding employment than in remaining true to the God he serves and the covenant expressed in the Ten Commandments. The other, in chapter 19, cares only for his own safety and callously uses the body of his murdered concubine to call for revenge. Negative examples, however, can be useful. Ministers must strive not to

---

[483] M. Z. Brettler, *Book of Judges* (2002): 98.

lose sight of the calling that brought them to their position of authority and responsibility within the faith community. They must continually reexamine what they are doing and what they are advocating in their preaching and instruction to ensure that the message and liturgy are consistent with the beliefs of the church. Furthermore, they must strive to be courageous in the face of all types of adversity, both physical and emotional. Sharing their concerns with other clergy and with the members of their congregation helps make this manageable and prevents the isolation that so often can plague a minister's life and career.

(3) Life is filled with choices and their consequences. The decision of the concubine in Judg 19 to leave her husband, the delay that sent them away from her father's house too late in the afternoon to reach their destination before dark, and the decision to go to Gibeah rather than a Canaanite village all determined the fate of the people involved. Of course, it is easy to look at a story in hindsight and point out where mistakes were made. Maybe the concubine and her husband could have worked out their differences and prevented this whole tragedy. Perhaps the couple could have stayed one more night with the father-in-law and set out early the next day so that they would not have had to stop for the night and face the uncertain hospitality of a strange village. But it is not what could have been done that matters. What unfolds is how life works, and we all make decisions constantly that may be for the best or that may turn out disastrously. Perhaps the key is to think carefully whenever possible before acting. Examine the possible consequences and meet what comes with as much grace and wit as we can, realizing that there will always be unexpected events and reactions.

(4) "In those days there was no king in Israel; all the people did what was right in their own eyes" (Judg 21:25). This final phrase in the Book of Judges sums up the continual slide of the people into social and political anarchy. Without leadership, without attention to the covenant or to God's direction, they had the option of "flying blind" through life (compare Saul's desperate acts at the end of his reign in 1 Sam 28:3–10). Their lack of any clear code of conduct allowed for rampant violence, intrigue, and haphazard religious practice. What good can come of total reliance on a personal sense of right and wrong? There are no social standards, no precedents in law, and no authoritative leaders calling for proper conduct. Demagogues too often take advantage of

such a situation, promising to lead the people out of the wilderness, which often leads to destruction for their followers. The warning of the Book of Judges is to keep sight of the heritage you have been given. The Israelites had been delivered from Egypt by a triumphant and caring God and had received the Ten Commandments to provide them with a code of conduct as members of the covenantal community. But, as when Moses was too long on Mt. Sinai (Exod 32:1), they lost their courage and fell into idolatry and unfaithfulness. Judges is a warning, but it is also a piece of wisdom literature reminding the reader that there are standards that can be obeyed and a divine promise of aid if they do not rely solely on their own judgment.

PART TWO

The Book of Ruth

4. Introduction

A personal sense of identity in the village culture of ancient Israel is defined for each individual in terms of his or her membership in a family, a clan, or a tribe and by gender. This understanding of membership within a specific group is further qualified by the location of their home village or town, their geographical region within Israelite territory, and their geopolitical relations with both their neighbors and other nations. In the normal course of events, it would have been inconceivable for people in this ancient society even to consider making a conscious decision on what their identity should be. However, the Book of Ruth contains such a story. Ruth, who has become a liminal or socially undefined figure by her decisions and actions, must establish a new identity within a strange community. In essence, she must "find her place," both physically and socially, in Bethlehem.[1] In addition, the two widows in the story must find a means both to save the memory of Naomi's husband's household and to preserve their lives.[2]

Ruth's social drama involves a processional pattern, much like that described by the anthropologist Victor Turner. He notes a four-stage sequence:

1. Breach between social elements
2. Crisis
3. Adjustment or redress

---

[1]   The humanistic geographer Edward C. Relph, *Place and Placelessness*. London: Pion, 1976: 1, states that "to be human is to live in a world that is filled with significant places; to be human is to have and to know *your* place."

[2]   Peter W. Coxon, "Was Naomi a Scold? A Response to Fewell and Gunn," *JSOT* 45 (1989): 27, emphasizes the awkwardness of Naomi's situation, returned to her hometown after a period of ten years and yet unrecognizable to the townswomen (Ruth 1:19). This may actually be a reflection of her diminished social and economic condition, but it also is an indicator of just how desperate a situation Ruth and Naomi face.

4. Either reintegration of the group, person, or "element" into the social
structure or recognition of an irreparable breach.[3]

Ruth's separation from Moabite territory and community functions as her
breach. A crisis then occurs when she must face her liminality in the new
social setting of Bethlehem. For there to be adjustment or redress, Ruth and
Naomi have to operate within the legal guarantees and social customs of this
village culture. However, Ruth's liminal character,[4] as both a resident alien
and a widow, allows her to transgress some physical and social barriers, and
she and Naomi take steps to ensure their reintegration into the community.

Given this processional model Ruth's dilemma is not just her own problem. The community in Bethlehem, Naomi's kinsman Boaz, and the kinsman
redeemer will all have to come to terms with her legal and social claims on
them. In addition, the firmly established, comfortably understood identity of
places associated with the tribal territory of Judah, the village of Bethlehem,
Boaz's field, and the village threshing floor will also be affected by Ruth's
activities and physical presence.

RECONSTRUCTING AN ANCIENT STORY

The story of Ruth and Boaz contains reflections of how the original audience identified with and reacted to the narrative based on culturally defined norms, values, and language. Of course, ancient Israelite culture no
longer exists, and its members cannot be observed or interviewed to obtain firsthand information. As a result, reconstruction of the emic (insider)
viewpoint becomes a matter of interpretation (in fact an etic – outsider or

---

3   Victor Turner, "Social Dramas and Stories About Them." Page 145 in *On Narrative*.
    Edited by W. J. Thomas Mitchell. Chicago: University of Chicago Press, 1981. His
    model is derived from Arnold Van Gennep's study of rites of passage (*The Rites
    of Passage*. London: Routledge and Kegan Paul, 1909), and he describes it as com-
    prising three phases: separation, margin or limen, and reaggregation. See also
    Victor Turner and Edith Turner, *Image and Pilgrimage in Christian Culture: Anthro-
    pological Perspectives*. New York: Columbia University Press, 1978: 249, and Victor Turner,
    The Ritual Process: Structure and Anti-Structure. Ithaca, N.Y.: Cornell University Press,
    1969: 94.
4   V. Turner, *Ritual Process* (1969): 95, describes the attributes of liminality as "necessarily
    ambiguous," being "neither here nor there; they are betwixt and between the positions
    assigned and arrayed by law, custom, convention, and ceremonial." Because of this Ruth
    may be able to slip between the social cracks and engage in activity that would not be
    acceptable or normally assigned to a woman in that society.

observer – process) and is subject to the degree of objectivity applied to the text and to archaeological data from the settlement period.[5]

Even with these limitations, there is still a possibility of deriving insights into what the insiders can tell us about their world. However, it is imperative that modern readers/scholars be careful not to fall into the trap of becoming "passive documenters of indigenous claims."[6] The biblical writers seldom explain everyday acts or behaviors. These social cues are so much a part of their own existence that to explain them would be redundant to their audience.[7]

The Book of Ruth is a tightly written, composite tale dating to the beginning of the postexilic period.[8] It contains a relatively authentic look at the social world of a small village in ancient Israel. At the same time, it contains a political and social agenda that dates to either the late preexilic or early postexilic period. The emphasis on David's genealogy and the mixed marriage between Boaz and the Moabite Ruth may indicate a minority voice, raising a religious argument against the enforcement of endogmatic marriage practices by Ezra and Nehemiah in the fifth century BCE.[9] Other attempts at

[5] Kenneth L. Pike, *Language in Relation to a Unified Theory of the Structure of Human Behavior*, 2nd ed. The Hague, Neth.: Mouton, 1967, first formulated the use of emic/etic. See the reexamination of emic (insider) and etic (outsider) analysis in Marvin Harris, *Cultural Materialism: The Struggle for a Science of Culture*. New York: Random House, 1979: 32–41, and his contention that etic structures cannot, as Pike asserts, provide "stepping-stones" to emic structures. Instead the researcher should "describe both [emics and etics] and if possible explain one in terms of the other" (p. 36).

[6] Russell T. McCutcheon, "Introduction." Pages 17–18 in *The Insider/Outsider Problem in the Study of Religion*. Edited by Russell T. McCutcheon. London: Cassell, 1999. See also M. Harris, *Cultural Materialism* 1979: 37, for a warning about collecting emic data.

[7] Anne Buttimer, "Home, Reach, and the Sense of Place." Page 171 in *The Human Experience of Place and Space*. Edited by Anne Buttimer and David Seamon. London: Croom Helm, 1980, argues that "the meanings of place to those who live in them has more to do with everyday living and doing than with thinking." Thus to provide explanations in a story of everyday realities would be superfluous.

[8] Note the very careful linguistic analysis in Frederic W. Bush, *Ruth, Esther*. Dallas: Word, 1996: 18–30, demonstrating the number of instances of Late Biblical Hebrew in the text of Ruth. His conclusion is that the author, while being very familiar with the grammatical usage of Standard Biblical Hebrew, still injects several forms from his own era and thus provides the key to dating this story. Marjo C. A. Korpel, *The Structure of the Book of Ruth*. Assen, Neth.: Koninklijke van Gorcum, 2001: 224–27, uses the unique phrase "in the days when the Judges judged" (1:1) to argue for a date "long after the rise of the Davidic dynasty."

[9] M. C. A. Korpel, *Structure of Book of Ruth* (2001): 230–33; Yair Zakovitch, *Das Buch Ruth: Ein jüdischer Kommentar*. Stuttgart, Ger.: Verlag Kotholisches Bibelwerk, 1999: 38–41, 62–64.

interpreting the purposes behind the Book of Ruth include the positions that the story is part of the dynastic "apology" supporting the reign of David's family,[10] or that it is perhaps a political prop shoring up Josiah's attempt to reunite the country following the demise of the Assyrian empire.[11]

A CLOSER LOOK AT ENDOGAMY

Endogamy is the custom of marrying within a specific group (kinship, religious community, or ethnic designation). It first appears as a means in the ancestral narratives to preserve the cultural identity of Abraham's clan as they first settle in Canaan (Gen 24:1–9; 26:34–35; 28:1–5). Thus Abraham is most insistent that his son Isaac remain in Canaan while a servant is sent back to Harran to arrange a marriage for him with a girl from their own clan. The seriousness of the matter is punctuated by an oath that requires the servant to put his hand under Abraham's thigh and touch the genitals (Gen 24:2–4).[12] By obtaining the "proper bride" the patriarch can ensure continuity of cultural values. In addition, by bringing a bride from the "Old Country," focus is retained on living in the new land. It also prevents Isaac from being disinherited by departing the Promised Land.[13] The custom of endogamy provides a more acceptable reason for Jacob to journey to Mesopotamia: he is seeking a bride rather than fleeing his brother Esau's wrath over the stolen blessing.[14]

The emphasis on "marrying in" is seldom mentioned after these early stories, although Samson's parents do plead with their son to seek out a bride from "among your kin, or among all our people" rather than to pursue "a wife from the uncircumcised Philistines" (Judg 14:3). In the exilic and postexilic period, the effort to maintain a distinct cultural identity by the diasporic community in Mesopotamia leads them to emphasize endogamy

[10] Athalya Brenner, "Naomi and Ruth." Pages 80–81 in *A Feminist Companion to Ruth*. Edited by Athalya Brenner. Sheffield, Eng.: Sheffield Academic Press, 1993, links this story to that of Lot's daughters (Gen 19:30–38) and to Tamar and Judah (Gen 38) as anticipations of "David's foreign connections and his weakness for women."

[11] See the summary of these arguments in Kirsten Nielsen, *Ruth*. OTL. Louisville, Ky.: Westminster/John Knox, 1997: 28–29, and in Jack M. Sasson, *Ruth: A New Translation with a Philological Commentary and a Formalist-Folklorist Interpretation*, 2nd ed. Sheffield, Eng.: Sheffield Academic Press, 1989: 240–52.

[12] Gordon Wenham, *Genesis 16–50*. Dallas: Word, 1994: 141.

[13] Victor P. Hamilton, *The Book of Genesis, Chapters 18–50*. Grand Rapids, Mich.: Eerdmans, 1995: 140.

[14] Michael Fishbane, *Text and Texture: Close Reading of Selected Biblical Texts*. New York: Schocken Books, 1979: 49.

as a strict marriage custom.[15] However, it is apparent that many of the exiles who returned to Jerusalem and formed the restored community chose to intermarry with local families, perhaps to gain economic advantage or title to land. When Ezra and Nehemiah arrived as representatives of the Persian government, they strictly enforced endogamy, ordering that those Israelites who had contracted mixed marriages must divorce their wives and disown their children (Ezra 9–10:17; Neh 13:23–27). Their insistence on endogamy may be attributed to their membership in the diasporic community as well as to pressure from the Persian government to maintain clear cultural identifiers among its subject peoples.[16]

While this short story is set in the period of the Judges, its theme and its use of legal structures from the Deuteronomic Code also suggest a date of composition in the postexilic period. Its placement in the canon immediately after Judges is based on similarity of story type as well as an attempt to connect the Judges period with the story of the rise of David in the Books of Samuel.[17] The once-upon-a-time quality of the opening phrase, "In the days when the Judges ruled," adds to the sense of antiquity and allows the narrator to focus on matters of the social order without tying them more specifically to actual historical events.[18]

On a basic level the Book of Ruth is structured in such a way that the events of chapters 1 and 4 form a pair and those of chapter 2 and 3 combine to provide a central narrative.[19] The first chapter concerns itself with the systematic loss of husband and sons by Naomi, leaving her empty. This is coupled with Ruth's assimilation ritual (1:16–17) and the potential that this daughter-in-law has to care for Naomi and restore the fortunes of Elimelech's family. Ruth 4 then takes up the situation by ensuring that Ruth and Naomi have a redeemer, who provides for their physical needs and gives them a son and who will carry on the name of Elimelech and become the ancestor of David.

Chapters 2 and 3 contain the scenes in which Ruth and Boaz meet and form an alliance. These episodes contain aspects of the law of levirate

---

[15]   Victor H. Matthews, "The Social Context of Law in the Second Temple Period," *BTB* 28 (1998): 10–11.
[16]   Victor H. Matthews, *A Brief History of Ancient Israel.* Louisville, Ky.: Westminster/John Knox, 2002: 123–24.
[17]   Tod Linafelt and Timothy K. Beal. *Ruth and Esther.* Collegeville, Minn.: Liturgical Press, 1999: xviii–xx.
[18]   G. R. H. Wright, "The Mother-Maid at Bethlehem," *ZAW* 98 (1986): 57.
[19]   M. C. A. Korpel, *Structure of Book of Ruth* (2001): 27.

obligation (see Gen 38 and Deut 25:5–10), display the importance of significant space in the village culture, and demonstrate the manner in which Ruth is able to convince Boaz to serve as her legal advocate in the gate court. An additional factor woven into the story by the writer is resistance against the increasing emphasis on endogamy, which was being forced on the Jerusalem community during the time of Ezra and Nehemiah (Ezra 9–10; Neh 13:23–27). In portraying this, the book forms the basis for a more universal understanding of the covenant. It also stands as a broad argument against the policy of "ethnic purity" found in Deut 12–26 and especially the prohibition against the Moabites in Deut 23:4.[20]

The story of Ruth can also be seen as a miniversion of the Exodus account and of the return from exile as envisioned in Isa 40, Jer 32, and Ezek 37. It contains these common elements:

1. Forced departure from the land due to famine (see Gen 12:10; 41:57–46:7)
2. Eventual return after the death of the old way of life and old leadership (Mahlon and sons); compare wilderness experience and Moses' death (Num 27:12–23; Deut 31:1–8; 34:1–9)
3. Restoration of legal rights to the land through struggle (aspects of the conquest narrative [Josh 1] as well as the struggle with the "adversaries of Judah and Benjamin" described in Ezra 4)
4. Renewal of the covenant with messianic hope; tie to David (see Ezek 34:11–31; Isa 9:6–7; 11:1–5.

Note the transformation aspects of the story. Ruth, a non-Israelite, is transformed through a conversion ritual into a law-abiding member of the covenant with Yahweh. This could be compared to the transformation of the "mixed multitude" who leave Egypt and who are then transformed into the Israelite people during the wilderness and conquest period. It could also relate to the universalism of the third Isaiah (Isa 56–66) who recognized Sabbath worship and belief as the only criteria for membership in the covenant community.

---

[20]   John B. Curtis, "Second Thoughts on the Purpose of the Book of Ruth," *Proceedings, Eastern Great Lakes and Midwest Biblical Society* 16 (1996): 142–43.

5. Suggested Reading

Since Ruth is a compact piece of literature, there are relatively few commentaries that deal only with this book. I have found Frederic W. Bush, *Ruth, Esther* (Dallas: Word, 1996) the most useful for the discussion of linguistic issues and the overall coverage of the material. The commentary by Edward F. Campbell Jr., *Ruth*, AB 7 (Garden City, N.Y.: Doubleday, 1975) remains the standard work for literary analysis. He also provides excellent, if now quite dated, comments on the social world and archaeological aspects of Ruth. The most recently published commentary, Tod Linafelt and Timothy K. Beal, *Ruth and Esther* (Collegeville, Minn.: Liturgical Press, 1999), highlights the ambiguities in the text and refuses to accept the stereotypical labels that so many others have assigned to the scenes and the characters. In particular Linafelt notes the conflicting desires and interests of the various characters, and he goes beyond the apparent romantic aspects of the story to discuss motivations and apparent double entendres in the narrative. Yet another unconventional volume in this genre is Jack M. Sasson, *Ruth: A New Translation with a Philological Commentary and a Formalist-Folklorist Interpretation*, 2nd ed. (Sheffield, Eng.: Sheffield Academic Press, 1989), which provides a philological commentary and makes use of the techniques for the study of Russian fairy tales developed by Vladimir Propp.[1]

Other commentaries that have contributed to the study of Ruth include:

Hubbard, Robert L., Jr. *The Book of Ruth*. NICOT. Grand Rapids, Mich.: Eerdmans, 1988.
Nielsen, Kirsten. *Ruth*. OTL. Louisville, Ky.: Westminster/John Knox, 1997.
Rudolph, Wilhelm. *Das Buch Ruth, Das Hohelied, Die Klagelieder*, 2nd ed. Gütersloh, Ger.: Gerd Mohn, 1962.

---

[1]   Vladimir Propp, *Morphology of the Folktale*, 2nd ed. Austin: University of Texas, 1962.

Van Wolde, Ellen. *Ruth and Naomi.* London: SCM 1997.

Zakovitch, Yair. *Das Buch Ruth: Ein jüdischer Kommentar.* Stuttgart, Ger.: Verlag Kotholisches Bibelwerk, 1999.

Zenger, Erich. *Das Buch Ruth.* Zurich, Switz.: Theologischer Verlag, 1986.

LITERARY STUDIES

Ruth is a tightly written short story with structural elements that are fairly easy to analyze. Among the most helpful monographs detailing the literary character of Ruth is that of Marjo C. A. Korpel, *The Structure of the Book of Ruth* (Assen, Neth.: Koninklijke van Gorcum, 2001). In his technical treatment, he provides charts as well as linguistic analyses for each verse. Another resource that provides strong arguments about the literary units within Ruth and the central themes is Danna N. Fewell and David Gunn, *Compromising Redemption: Relating Characters in the Book of Ruth* (Louisville, Ky.: Westminster/John Knox, 1990b). The articles contained in *The Feminist Companion to Ruth*, edited by Athalya Brenner are close readings of the text, with a feminist perspective. Among the other literary studies I would suggest are:

Bauckham, Richard. "The Book of Ruth and the Possibility of a Feminist Canonical Hermeneutic." *BibInt* 5 (1997): 29–45.

Brenner, Athalya. "Naomi and Ruth." Pages 70–84 in *A Feminist Companion to Ruth.* Edited by Athalya Brenner. Sheffield, Eng.: Sheffield Academic Press, 1993.

"The Food of Love: Gendered Food and Food Imagery in the Song of Songs." *Semeia* 86 (1999a): 101–12.

"Ruth as a Foreign Worker and the Politics of Exogamy." Pages 158–62 in *Ruth and Esther: A Feminist Companion to the Bible,* 2nd series. Edited by Athalya Brenner. Sheffield, Eng.: Sheffield Academic Press, 1999b.

Coxon, Peter W. "Was Naomi a Scold? A Response to Fewell and Gunn." *JSOT* 45 (1989): 25–37.

Curtis, John B. "Second Thoughts on the Purpose of the Book of Ruth." *Proceedings, Eastern Great Lakes and Midwest Biblical Society* 16 (1996): 141–49.

Fewell, Danna N., and David Gunn. " 'A Son Is Born to Naomi!': Literary Allusions and Interpretation in the Book of Ruth." *JSOT* 40 (1988): 99–108.

LEGAL AND SOCIAL WORLD STUDIES

A large proportion of the scholarship on Ruth has centered on legal issues, especially the terms of levirate marriage or obligation. Timothy M. Willis, *The Elders of the City: A Study of the Elders-Laws in Deuteronomy* (Atlanta: SBL, 2001) provides an in-depth analysis of the institution of village elders, their responsibilities, and the narrative and legally based units that include them as principal characters. For a thorough review of marriage customs in ancient Israel, with comparisons to other ancient Near Eastern cultures, see Raymond Westbrook, *Old Babylonian Marriage* (Horn, Austria: Verlag Ferdinand Berger & Sohne Gesellschaft, 1988) and *Property and the Family in Biblical Laws*, JSOTSup 113 (Sheffield, Eng.: Sheffield Academic Press, 1991).

Additional sources providing coverage of these issues include:

Beattie, D. R. G. "The Book of Ruth as Evidence for Israelite Legal Practices." *VT* 24 (1974): 251–67.

Campbell, Edward F., Jr. "Naomi, Boaz, and Ruth: Ḥesed and Change." *Austin Seminary Bulletin* 105 (1990): 64–74.

Carasik, Michael. "Ruth 2, 7: Why the Overseer Was Embarrassed." *ZAW* 107 (1995): 493–94.

Carmichael, Calum M. "A Ceremonial Crux: Removing a Man's Sandal as a Female Gesture of Contempt." *JBL* 96 (1977): 321–36.

Hamlin, E. John. "Terms for Gender and Status in the Book of Ruth." *Proceedings, Eastern Great Lakes and Midwest Biblical Society* 15 (1995): 133–43.

Kruger, P. A. "The Hem of the Garment of Marriage: The Meaning of the Symbolic Gesture in Ruth 3:9 and Ezek 16:8." *JNSL* 12 (1984): 79–86.

Leggett, Donald A. *The Levirate and Goel Institutions in the Old Testament, with Special Attention to the Book of Ruth.* Cherry Hill, N.J.: Mack, 1974.

Manor, Dale. "A Brief History of Levirate Marriage as It Relates to the Bible." *ResQ* 27 (1984): 129–42.

Meyers, Carol. "Procreation, Production, and Protection." *JAAR* 51 (1983): 569–93.

——. " 'To Her Mother's House': Considering a Counterpart to the Israelite *Bêt'āb*." Pages 39–51 in *The Bible and the Politics of Exegesis*. Edited by David Jobling et al. Cleveland, Ohio: Pilgrim Press, 1991.

——. "Returning Home: Ruth 1.8 and the Gendering of the Book of Ruth." Pages 85–114 in *A Feminist Companion to Ruth*. Edited by Athalya Brenner. Sheffield, Eng.: Sheffield Academic Press, 1993.

Sakenfeld, Katharine D. "The Story of Ruth: Economic Survival." Pages 215–27 in *Realia Dei: Essays in Archaeology and Biblical Interpretation*. Edited by Prescott H. Williams and Theodore Hiebert. Atlanta: Scholars Press, 1999.

Saxegaard, Kristen M. " 'More Than Seven Sons': Ruth as Example of the Good Son." *SJOT* 15 (2001): 257–75.

Shepherd, David. "Violence in the Fields? Translating, Reading, and Revising in Ruth 2." *CBQ* 63 (2001): 444–63.

Smith-Christopher, David L. "The Mixed Marriage Crisis in Ezra 9–10 and Nehemiah 13: A Study of the Sociology of the Post-Exilic Judean Community." Pages 243–65 in *Second Temple Studies, 2*. Edited by Tamara C. Eshkenazi and Kent Richards. Atlanta: Scholars Press, 1994.

Thompson, Thomas L., and Dorothy Thompson. "Some Legal Problems in the Book of Ruth." *VT* 18 (1968): 79–99.

Wright, G. R. H. "The Mother-Maid at Bethlehem." *ZAW* 98 (1986): 56–72.

Zakovitch, Yair. "The Woman's Rights in the Biblical Law of Divorce." *Jewish Law Annual* 4 (1981): 28–46.

For smaller issues or information on individual characters or social customs described in Ruth, I suggest that readers consult either a one-volume Bible dictionary or the multivolume *Anchor Bible Dictionary* (New York: Doubleday, 1992), edited by David N. Freedman.

6. Commentary

CHAPTER 1

(1) In the days when the Judges ruled, there was a famine in the land, and a certain man of Bethlehem in Judah went to live in the country of Moab, he and his wife and two sons. (2) The name of the man was Elimelech and the name of his wife Naomi, and the names of his two sons were Mahlon and Chilion; they were Ephrathites from Bethlehem in Judah. They went into the country of Moab and remained there. (3) But Elimelech, the husband of Naomi, died, and she was left with her two sons. (4) These took Moabite wives; the name of the one was Orpah and the name of the other Ruth. When they had lived there about ten years, (5) both Mahlon and Chilion also died, so that the woman was left without her two sons and her husband. (6) Then she started to return with her daughters-in-law from the country of Moab, for she had heard in the country of Moab that the Lord had considered his people and given them food. (7) So she set out from the place where she had been living, she and her two daughters-in-law, and they went on their way to go back to the land of Judah. (8) But Naomi said to her two daughters-in-law, "Go back each of you to your mother's house. May the Lord deal kindly with you, as you have dealt with the dead and with me. (9) The Lord grant that you may find security, each of you in the house of your husband." Then she kissed them, and they wept aloud. (10) They said to her, "No, we will return with you to your people." (11) But Naomi said, "Turn back, my daughters, why will you go with me? Do I still have sons in my womb that they may become your husbands? (12) Turn back, my daughters, go your way, for I am too old to have a husband. Even if I thought there was hope for me, even if I should have a husband tonight and bear sons, (13) would you then wait until they were grown? Would you then refrain from marrying? No, my daughters, it has been far more bitter for me than for you,

because the hand of the Lord has turned against me." (14) Then they wept aloud again. Orpah kissed her mother-in-law, but Ruth clung to her. (15) So she said, "See, your sister-in-law has gone back to her people and to her gods; return after your sister-in-law." (16) But Ruth said, "Do not press me to leave you or to turn back from following you! Where you go, I will go; where you lodge, I will lodge; your people shall be my people, and your God my God. (17) Where you die, I will die – there will I be buried. May the Lord do thus and so to me, and more as well, if even death parts me from you!" (18) When Naomi saw that she was determined to go with her, she said no more to her. (19) So the two of them went on until they came to Bethlehem. When they came to Bethlehem, the whole town was stirred because of them; and the women said, "Is this Naomi?" (20) She said to them, "Call me no longer Naomi, call me Mara, for the Almighty has dealt bitterly with me. (21) I went away full, but the Lord has brought me back empty; why call me Naomi when the Lord has dealt harshly with me, and the Almighty has brought calamity upon me?" (22) So Naomi returned together with Ruth the Moabite, her daughter-in-law, who came back with her from the country of Moab. They came to Bethlehem at the beginning of the barley harvest.

*A*s in the case of Abram's and Sarai's forced movement from Canaan to Egypt in Gen 12:10 because of a famine, the story of Ruth begins with a famine that drives Elimelech and his family to resettle in Moab.[1] The "highly variable rainfall" in the highlands of ancient Canaan were always a factor that the village farmers and herdsmen had to contend with year after year.[2] In Elimelech's case, he chose to seek "greener pastures" to the east. This type of "migration in search of economic survival" is simply a fact of life in marginal environments.[3]

There is a distinctive pattern that runs through the entire story that begins with the death of the three men in Elimelech's family, leaving Naomi without support. It then begins to turn from loss to gain as Ruth pledges herself to

[1]   Danna N. Fewell and David M. Gunn, "'A Son Is Born to Naomi!': Literary Allusions and Interpretation in the Book of Ruth," *JSOT* 40 (1988): 103, see this destination as an unpropitious beginning, given the negative attitude toward Moab in Gen 19:30–38 and Num 25. However, Moab is also the refuge for David's family in 1 Sam 22:3–4. Coupled as it is with the Davidic genealogical note in Ruth 4:18–22, this text indicates that Moab is not always considered an enemy people.

[2]   David C. Hopkins, *The Highlands of Canaan*. Sheffield, Eng.: Almond Press, 1985: 107–8.

[3]   Katharine D. Sakenfeld, "The Story of Ruth: Economic Survival." Page 217 in *Realia Dei: Essays in Archaeology and Biblical Interpretation*. Edited by Prescott H. Williams and Theodore Hiebert. Atlanta: Scholars Press, 1999.

her mother-in-law. At that point Boaz emerges as the legal advocate for the two widows. The story resolves with the birth of Ruth's son and the public acknowledgment by the women of the village of Bethlehem (who first appear in a dismal scene in 1:19–21) that Naomi's household has been restored. This transforming process emphasizes Yahweh's gracious provision for her family (see the acknowledgment by the village women in 4:14–15). The focus and structural links in this tale are between Naomi's needs and how they are eventually fulfilled and the strategies that she employs to achieve survival and the specific aid she receives from God and others.[4]

PROGRESSION OF LOSS

1. Death of Elimelech: Naomi left with her two sons (1:3).
2. Mahlon and Chilion die: Naomi left without her sons and husband (1:5).
3. Orpah is convinced to return to her "mother's house," only Ruth remains (1:14–15).
4. With the village women as witnesses, Naomi renames herself Mara (meaning "bitter") for her losses (1:19–21).

PROGRESSION OF GAIN

1. Ruth pledges to remain with Naomi: the two women go to Bethlehem (1:16–19).
2. Boaz pledges to serve as redeemer/advocate: Naomi and Ruth gain legal support at the gate court (3:10–13; 4:1–12).
3. Ruth gives birth to a son: Naomi receives the child in place of her lost sons (4:13–16).
4. The village women bless and certify Naomi's household as restored (4:14–17).

No specific cause is given for the death of Naomi's husband and sons (compare the pointed explanation for the deaths of Er and Onan in Gen 38:7–10). As a result it is not possible to make the case that they were being punished for their move to Moab. Plus, despite a ten-year stay in Moab and marriages of indeterminate length, it is not possible to ascribe the lack of children to divine punishment or displeasure. The general dearth of details simply provides the prologue to Naomi's legal status as a widow with neither a husband nor a surviving son to care for her. This in turn leads to

---

4 Edward F. Campbell Jr., "Naomi, Boaz, and Ruth: Ḥesed and Change," *Austin Seminary Bulletin* 105 (1990): 72.

her decision to return to Bethlehem, where, she has heard, the famine had ended (compare Gen 42:1) and where she has relatives who owe her legal obligations. Appended to this narrative is the dialogue between Naomi and her daughters-in-law over their future.

The drama begins as the three women actually leave the environs of their Moabite village. This is the moment of crisis when decisions must be made, and it is in this familiar "lived space" that the significance of space is made clear in this story.[5] Faced with the need to depart, the three women engage in a face-saving dialogue, built around and playing upon the use of the Hebrew word "turn" or "return" (*šûb*) and tied to the basic characteristics of familiar and unfamiliar space.[6] In the following list, the use of *šûb* is traced throughout the dialogue scene to show how it provides structure.

DIALOGUE BETWEEN NAOMI AND HER DAUGHTERS-IN-LAW

1. Naomi started "**to return**" along with the daughters-in-law to "**go back** to the land of Judah," but before they had gone far Naomi tells them to "**go back** . . . to your mother's house. . . . May you each find **security** in the house of your husband." She **kisses** them and they **weep** (1:6–9).
2. Orpah and Ruth say, "**we will return** with you to your people" (1:10).
3. Naomi replies, "**Turn back**. . . . Do I still have sons in my womb" (1:11).
4. Naomi adds, "**Turn back** . . . I am too old to have a husband. . . . If I . . . bear sons, would you then wait until they were grown?" (1:12–13).
5. They weep. Orpah kisses Naomi and "**goes back** to her people" (1:14–15).
6. Ruth refuses "**to turn back** from following" Naomi (1:16).
7. After Ruth pledges not to "**turn back**," Naomi says "no more to her" (1:16–18).

The dialogue begins in v. 8 when Naomi tells her daughters-in-law to "go back . . . to your mother's house," a place that they would associate with

---

5   Timothy Cresswell, *In Place, Out of Place: Geography, Ideology, and Transgression*. Minneapolis: University of Minnesota Press, 1996: 17, notes that "by acting in space in a particular way the actor is inserted into a particular relation with [his/her society's] ideology."

6   Compare a similar use of dialogue in Gen 23, in which Abraham bargains with Ephron for the purchase of the cave of Machpelah as his wife's burial site. Each man will take turns making magnanimous statements that eventually lead to a resolution and a completion of the transaction. What is at stake here and in the Ruth story is the honor of the participants, and it is a contest to see who can offer the most before the other gives in and accepts the final price offered.

comfort and all things familiar. This opening statement thereby initiates a rhetorical fencing match between the women, designed to show how each party is attempting to care for the needs of the other.[7] The next step occurs in v. 10 when the daughters-in-law insist that they will return with Naomi "to her people," a group unknown to them and a place where they will be termed "strangers."[8] In response to this magnanimous gesture, Naomi repeats for a second time that they should "turn back," and she focuses on her barrenness and the inability of an extinct household to supply them with their levirate rights (v. 11).

The second round of dialogue begins with Naomi, who for a third time tells the two young women to "turn back," but this time her speech is expanded to include not only her barren womb but the physical inability to bear any more children at her age. At the heart of this statement lies her inability to provide security for the other women, and this is a source of shame that she alleviates by giving them their freedom. The blessing that she uses, referring to "the dead," may also be all-encompassing (v. 9), including herself as no longer among the living since she has no means of support. Baring her soul, Naomi proclaims that God has made her life "bitter" (v. 13), a claim she will repeat in v. 20 to the women of Bethlehem.

As is so often the case in Hebrew narrative, once something has been said or has transpired three times, the drama can move on (see 1 Sam 3:4–8). Thus Orpah makes the symbolic gesture of accepting Naomi's offer by kissing her mother-in-law (v. 14), and then the women weep aloud. The kisses and the weeping in vv. 9 and 14 form an inclusio framing the entire dialogue.[9]

Turning now to Ruth, Naomi addresses her remaining daughter-in-law, encouraging her to follow Orpah back to her people and "her gods" (v. 15).

---

[7] The suggestion that the daughters-in-law return to their "mother's house" may seem unusual given that in most cases reference would be to their "father's house," as in Gen 38:11 or Lev 22:13 (see Edward F. Campbell Jr., *Ruth*. AB 7. Garden City, N.Y.: Doubleday, 1975: 64; Jack M. Sasson, *Ruth: A New Translation with a Philological Commentary and a Formalist-Folklorist Interpretation*, 2nd ed. Sheffield, Eng.: Sheffield Academic Press, 1989: 23. However, given the influence that women had on affairs within the household and that Naomi, a female authority figure in this episode, is speaking to another female, it is not out of place or incongruous for her to refer to a "mother's house" (see Carol L. Meyers, "'To Her Mother's House': Considering a Counterpart to the Israelite *Bêt'āb*." Page 50 in *The Bible and the Politics of Exegesis*. Edited by David Jobling et al. Cleveland, Ohio: Pilgrim Press, 1991).

[8] T. Cresswell, *In Place, Out of Place* (1996): 3, notes that every society has an understanding that some things or persons belong or do not belong within a specific place.

[9] See Gen 29:11; 33:4; 45:15 for other examples in which a kiss and weeping are combined as part of an emotional scene.

This highlights the social and religious differences between the Moabites and the Israelites and sets the stage for Ruth's assimilation ritual. Having been given the easier choice to return to the familiar, Ruth instead chooses the more difficult course of pledging herself to serve Naomi and Naomi's God. In so doing, Ruth is about to discover that the ability to fill or use particular social space is based on the communal expectations attached to that place.[10] Bethlehem will be her new social space, and she will have to conform to the social customs and practices of that place.

The arrangement between Naomi and Ruth could be seen as a contractual one. The assimilation ritual that transforms Ruth from a Moabite to a member in good standing of Naomi's household is more than an emotional display by a daughter-in-law who cannot bear to send her mother-in-law off to face her loss and poverty alone. Brenner makes the case for Ruth as a "female foreign worker," who obligates herself contractually to work and care for Naomi in exchange for the benefits attached to adopting a new social identity in Bethlehem.[11] This argument, which posits a situation comparable to a slave's pledge to "love" his master in Exod 21:2–5,[12] is based in part on Sasson[13] and his emphasis on both the sense of lifelong obligation proposed by Ruth and her addition of an oath in the name of Yahweh to demonstrate her determination – a determination that Naomi cannot deny.

Ruth's statement of commitment to Naomi is counterbalanced by the scene in which Naomi publicly renames herself Mara (bitter) before the women of Bethlehem (1:19–21). Her entrance into the village causes a stir since there were probably few events to break up the regularity of daily life (compare 1 Sam 18:7, where the welcome is more joyous). There is a parallel in the question raised by the village women, "Is this Naomi?" and the questions spoken by Boaz in 2:5 and 3:9. In each case a formal attempt is made to define a person socially as well as to recognize their presence.

Naomi, in this case, refuses to be inserted once again into the social category that she once filled. She is bereft of her husband and sons, and the Lord has brought her back (again using the term *šûb*) to them "empty."

---

10 See the discussion in T. Cresswell, *In Place, Out of Place* (1996): 21–27, on the transgression of place as a form of social resistance.

11 Athalya Brenner, "Ruth as a Foreign Worker and the Politics of Exogamy." Pages 158–62 in *Ruth and Esther: A Feminist Companion to the Bible*, 2nd series. Edited by Athalya Brenner. Sheffield, Eng.: Sheffield Academic Press, 1999b.

12 See V. H. Matthews, "Female Voices: Upholding the Honor of the Household," *BTB* 24 (1994b): 129–32.

13 J. M. Sasson, *Ruth* (1989): 30.

Thus she rejects being called "pleasant" (Naomi) and cries out that God, not fate or chance, has done this to her. This could be seen as a lawsuit initiated by Naomi against God, calling for justice or relief from her situation.[14] It also can be identified as a "theology of complaint" found in Job's cry, "Do not human beings have a hard service on earth" (Job 7:1) and in Jeremiah's assertion that he has become a "laughingstock" after God "enticed" him to speak (Jer 20:7). Naomi feels free to point to God's actions (a form of theodicy or explanation of divine activity) and to cry out for retribution on the basis of her claims. She has not lost her faith but instead makes a case to a God, whom she believes has sovereignty over creation and can render aid.[15] Ultimately, she will be heard and her present state of emptiness will be filled.

The rather dry summary statement supplied by the narrator in v. 22 provides a sober response to Naomi's charges, pointing out that the two women had made a safe journey to Bethlehem at harvest time, a period when the village will be "full" of God's bounty.[16] In addition, vv. 19–21 serve to foreshadow the legal setting in chapter 4, where Boaz opens his conversation with Naomi's next-of-kin by saying she "is selling the parcel of land that belonged to our kinsman Elimelech" (4:3). It could be that by publicly declaring that she is without resources Naomi has put up the "for sale" sign on her property and thereby set things in motion that will eventually lead to the financial redemption of the two widows.[17]

CHAPTER 2

(1) Now Naomi had a kinsman on her husband's side, a prominent rich man, of the family of Elimelech, whose name was Boaz. (2) And Ruth the Moabite said to Naomi, "Let me go to the field and glean among the ears of grain, behind someone in whose sight I may find favor." She said to her, "Go, my daughter." (3) So she went. She came and gleaned in the field behind the reapers. As it happened, she came to the part of the field belonging to Boaz, who was of the family of Elimelech. (4) Just then Boaz came from Bethlehem. He said to

14   E. F. Campbell Jr., *Ruth* (1975): 83.
15   F. W. Bush, *Ruth, Esther* (1996): 95.
16   M. C. A. Korpel, *Structure of Book of Ruth* (2001): 82.
17   See Raymond Westbrook, *Property and the Family in Biblical Laws.* JSOTSup 113. Sheffield, Eng.: Sheffield Academic Press, 1991: 65–67; D. R. G. Beattie, "The Book of Ruth as Evidence for Israelite Legal Practices," *VT* 24 (1974): 257–58.

the reapers, "The Lord be with you." They answered, "The Lord bless you."
(5) Then Boaz said to his servant who was in charge of the reapers, "To
whom does this young woman belong?" (6) The servant who was in charge of
the reapers answered, "She is the Moabite who came back with Naomi from
the country of Moab. (7) She said, 'Please, let me glean and gather among the
sheaves behind the reapers.' So she came, and she has been on her feet from
early this morning until now, without resting even for a moment." (8) Then
Boaz said to Ruth, "Now listen, my daughter, do not go to glean in another
field or leave this one, but keep close to my young women. (9) Keep your eyes
on the field that is being reaped, and follow behind them. I have ordered the
young men not to bother you. If you get thirsty, go to the vessels and drink
from what the young men have drawn." (10) Then she fell prostrate, with her
face to the ground, and said to him, "Why have I found favor in your sight, that
you should take notice of me, when I am a foreigner?" (11) But Boaz answered
her, "All that you have done for your mother-in-law since the death of your
husband has been fully told me, and how you left your father and mother and
your native land and came to a people that you did not know before. (12) May
the Lord reward you for your deeds, and may you have a full reward from
the Lord, the God of Israel, under whose wings you have come for refuge!"
(13) Then she said, "May I continue to find favor in your sight, my lord, for
you have comforted me and spoken kindly to your servant, even though I am
not one of your servants." (14) At mealtime Boaz said to her, "Come here, and
eat some of this bread, and dip your morsel in the sour wine." So she sat beside
the reapers, and he heaped up for her some parched grain. She ate until she
was satisfied, and she had some left over. (15) When she got up to glean, Boaz
instructed his young men, "Let her glean even among the standing sheaves,
and do not reproach her. (16) You must also pull out some handfuls for her
from the bundles, and leave them for her to glean, and do not rebuke her."
(17) So she gleaned in the field until evening. Then she beat out what she had
gleaned, and it was about an ephah of barley. (18) She picked it up and came
into town, and her mother-in-law saw how much she had gleaned. Then she
took out and gave her what was left over after she herself had been satisfied.
(19) Her mother-in-law said to her, "Where did you glean today? And where
have you worked? Blessed be the man who took notice of you." So she told her
mother-in-law with whom she had worked, and said, "The name of the man
with whom I worked today is Boaz." (20) Then Naomi said to her daughter-
in-law, "Blessed be he by the Lord, whose kindness has not forsaken the living
or the dead!" Naomi also said to her, "The man is a relative of ours, one of our
nearest kin." (21) Then Ruth the Moabite said, "He even said to me, 'Stay close

by my servants, until they have finished all my harvest.'" (22) Naomi said to
Ruth, her daughter-in-law, "It is better, my daughter, that you go out with his
young women, otherwise you might be bothered in another field." (23) So she
stayed close to the young women of Boaz, gleaning until the end of the barley
and wheat harvests; and she lived with her mother-in-law.

RUTH GLEANING IN BOAZ'S FIELD

When Ruth and Naomi return to Bethlehem, they are destitute widows
whose only property seems to be a field that belonged to Naomi's husband
Elimelech (4:3). The text then provides two significant cultural notes that
indicate to the reader why the story line works – in other words, gives it
that touch of physical and social reality that satisfies the reader. First, the
narrative states (1:22b) that this is the time of the barley harvest (mid- to
late April, as the rainy season came to an end), and this "time cue" drives
the rest of the action in the story.[18] If it had been another season, the two
women might well have been unable to interact so directly with Boaz or
achieve long-term security. Second, since there is no mention of the land
owned by Elimelech being in production during the ten years that they had
been absent,[19] Ruth and Naomi must rely on the law that allows "widows,
orphans, and strangers" to glean in the harvested fields of other property
owners (Lev 19:9; 23:22; Deut 24:19–21). Ruth is completely within her rights
to suggest that she "glean among the ears of grain, behind someone *in whose
sight I may find favor*" [my emphasis] (2:2). Given this economic and social
reality, Ruth enters the field with the full knowledge that she is seeking a
sponsor or patron for herself and Naomi.

The question arises why both women do not go to glean that day. It is
possible that Naomi stays behind because of her intention to remain in
seclusion, in mourning for her husband and sons, playing on her renaming
of herself as Mara (1:20–22).[20] Of course she may also be too old to work, just
as she notes that she is "too old to have a husband" (1:12). Perhaps by sending

---

18 Similar examples of time cues can be found in the editorial note in Exod 9:31 indicating
    the damage to the barley and flax that were nearly ready to harvest, and in 2 Sam 21:9–10,
    which describes the length of time Rizpah protected the bodies of her slain sons.

19 Timothy M. Willis, *The Elders of the City: A Study of the Elders-Laws in Deuteronomy*.
    Atlanta: SBL, 2001: 269, notes that the lack of men in Naomi's family means that Elimelech's
    land was probably lying fallow when the women returned to Bethlehem.

20 Kristen M. Saxegaard, "'More Than Seven Sons': Ruth as Example of the Good Son,"
    SJOT 15 (2001): 264, notes that despite Naomi's losses she is not another Job character. In
    fact, "Ruth is Naomi's new son" and hope for the future. Such a gender reversal does fit

Ruth alone, the storyteller wishes to elicit a greater sense of the plight of two women,[21] or possibly Naomi hopes to use the younger woman to attract a potential patron (i.e., Boaz) to assist them, although there are no specific instructions given to Ruth about which field to enter.[22]

Even if Naomi did not set this up, the story is clearly following agricultural protocol, starting with the harvest and eventually shifting to the processing and distribution of the grain on the threshing floor. It also draws on the likelihood that the community would be more sensitive to the needs of the poor during this period of bounty.[23] Not only will nothing go to waste or be left in the fields (Jer 6:9; Mic 7:1), but the people can feel that they are truly serving the community by ensuring the survival of even the weakest among them. In the light of this traditional obligation (Jer 49:9), this episode, as well as the future of Naomi's household, hinges on Ruth meeting Boaz in a legally significant setting and receiving a favorable response to her plea on their behalf.

Apparently the fields near Bethlehem were divided among several landowners, with the arable strips of land marked off by boundary stones (Deut 19:14; Ps 16:6). The story appears to suggest that it is only by chance, not intention, that Ruth enters Boaz's portion (2:3b: "As it happens"), but this seems unlikely and may be a sort of tongue-in-cheek remark. The relationship between Boaz and Naomi had prefaced Ruth's declaration that she would go out and glean in the fields (2:1). It therefore couples the community's obligation to support the destitute widows with a familial obligation

---

some of the aggressive actions taken by Ruth, but the story also depends on her role as a widow, who is subject to the laws and the decisions of the male elders.

21 Carol L. Meyers, "Returning Home: Ruth 1.8 and the Gendering of the Book of Ruth." Pages 93–94 in *A Feminist Companion to Ruth*. Edited by Athalya Brenner. Sheffield, Eng.: Sheffield Academic Press, 1993, notes that Boaz and Naomi never have direct contact in the story. Using Claudia Camp, *Wisdom and the Feminine in the Book of Proverbs*. Sheffield, Eng.: JSOT Press, 1985: 124–47, who suggests that women achieve their goals through "indirect action," Meyers posits this distancing of Naomi is designed to raise Ruth to prominence and prevents a social confrontation that might have resulted if Naomi had directly petitioned Boaz for help.

22 As Gillian Rose, *Feminism and Geography: The Limits of Geographical Knowledge*. Minneapolis: University of Minnesota Press, 1993: 146, puts it, women are generally "positioned in a space" that is not their own to control. Placed in situations such as Boaz's field, the newly arrived Ruth is vulnerable both as a stranger and as someone who has not yet obtained an identity that will make her and her neighbors comfortable.

23 Oded Borowski, *Agriculture in Iron Age Israel*. Winona Lake, Ind.: Eisenbrauns, 1987:59, points to the joy of harvest in Isa 9:3 and Ps 126:5 as further evidence of a time when the needs of the community were being met, and as a result the people could afford to be more generous with their harvested grain.

owed to Naomi by her husband's clan ties.[24] Whatever the rhetorical intent of the author here,[25] the opening statement is certainly a narrative aside intended to warn the reader that Ruth, whether instructed to or not, will find herself in the company of Boaz that day.

By setting foot within the confines of Boaz's fields, she becomes his legal responsibility and is subject to his control while occupying his private space. Subsequently, it will be Boaz's entrance into the field, long after the reapers have begun their work, and his question, "To whom does this young woman belong?" (2:5), that set things in motion. His question is also a means of social recognition, taking note of her presence and providing an opportunity for her legal identity to be made known publicly. Boaz already is aware of this information, since he later acknowledges who she is and what she has been doing to assist Naomi (2:11).[26] However, in his role as landowner, village elder, and Naomi's kinsman, it is necessary that he begin making a legal case for this care by asking for Ruth's social credentials.

The situation could easily be compared to the hospitality protocol, which also is triggered by the entrance of a stranger into the sphere of responsibility of a household or a citizen of a town.[27] Boaz's public statement, extending his hospitality and protection to Ruth while she is working in the fields, is an indication of his acceptance of her as his responsibility, and this will be reiterated in the promise he later makes to her on the threshing floor: that he will protect her and serve as her advocate before the village assembly (3:11). His blessing in the name of "the Lord, the God of Israel" (v. 12) can be seen as a response to Ruth's commitment to worship Naomi's God rather than the gods of her own people. Plus, Boaz's benediction, noting that Ruth has come for shelter under the "wings" of God, serves as a precursor to Ruth's request that Boaz (God's representative in this economically stressed situation) "spread your cloak over your servant" (3:9).

---

[24] K. Nielsen, *Ruth* (1997): 53, notes that this statement is a signal that Naomi and Ruth can expect to receive help from the family.

[25] T. Linafelt and T. K. Beal, *Ruth and Esther*. Collegeville, Minn.: Liturgical Press, 1999: 24–25, emphasize that Boaz's name is not "revealed" until the end of the sentence and matches this to Ruth's later revelation to Naomi of their benefactor (2:19). This may be a rhetorical device to add greater significance to Boaz's appearance and thus punctuate his importance to the reader.

[26] Peter W. Coxon, "Was Naomi a Scold? A Response to Fewell and Gunn," *JSOT* 45 (1989): 28.

[27] See V. H. Matthews, "Hospitality and Hostility in Judges 4," *BTB* 21 (1991): 13–21, for a discussion of the hospitality protocol.

HOSPITALITY PROTOCOL AND GLEANING

1. Sphere or zone of responsibility: Once a stranger enters this private space, the property owner is compelled by tradition and law to offer hospitality. For travelers, this includes a meal, foot washing, rest, and conversation. When a gleaner enters a field, the owner is required by law (Lev 19:9; 23:22) to allow them to take what they can from the discarded harvested ears (*šibbōllet*) or from the unharvested "corners" of the field (*pē'â*). It is up to the owner to expand on this minimal requirement of public almsgiving.

2. Transformation of stranger: The invitation of hospitality, which may or may not be accepted without prejudice, transforms the potential threat into a temporary ally and also provides the stranger with an identity. Any stranger is a potential enemy and is dealt with most efficiently by changing him/her into a noncombatant while in guest status. Boaz announces his intent to offer hospitality by asking who Ruth is, and she demonstrates her willingness to accept his generosity by bowing to the ground.

3. Obligation to protect the stranger: Once the guest/gleaner accepts hospitality, the host/owner is expected to protect this person as long as the latter remain within the former's territory.

Interestingly, both Ruth and Boaz function in this episode as role models for the village community. Ruth, who is still a liminal character, not yet identified as a member of the Bethlehem community except through her link to Naomi, plays the role of the hard-working, responsible resident alien, who identifies herself to the steward as Naomi's daughter-in-law. She asks permission to glean among the sheaves and then works, without a break, from early morning until Boaz comes to inspect his workers (2:6–7). Subsequently, Boaz, the courteous and engaged field owner (2:4), takes note of a new person in the community (presumably something fairly unusual in the small village) and demonstrates great generosity toward Ruth. This indicates that he is a venerated village elder and is considered to be a legal role model.

Ruth in turn shows her pleasure and surprise at his acceptance of a "foreigner" and his apparent willingness to give her the "status of being a member of his family group."[28] This social definition will be reiterated in

---

[28] E. John Hamlin, "Terms for Gender and Status in the Book of Ruth," *Proceedings, Eastern Great Lakes and Midwest Biblical Society* 15 (1995): 135.

4:5–10, where Boaz makes the statement before witnesses that he is willing to acquire "Ruth the Moabite, the wife of Mahlon" to be his wife.

In addition, and perhaps anticipating the sexual connotations of the second scene on the threshing floor, Boaz councils Ruth to (1) stay and glean only in his field (his zone of responsibility), (2) stay close to his young women so that she will not be bothered by his young men,[29] and (3) share water rights, drinking from their storage jars of water as she needed (2:8–9).[30] All of this suggests the establishment of a patron/client relationship and also protects and emphasizes her sexuality – a key to the legal scene in chapter 4. Ruth, perhaps surprised that someone from Israel would extend such generosity to "a foreigner" (2:10), prostrates herself before him and blesses him for his kindness, even though she is not one of his servants (2:13).[31] Ruth's action serves as a precursor to her going to the threshing floor and lying at Boaz's feet (3:7). In fact, the writer appears to be employing a concentric (or chiastic) ABB′A′ structure tying these two episodes together:

A   Boaz offers his protection and grants her privilege and food (2:8–9).

B   Ruth prostrates herself in acceptance of a client role (2:10–13).

B′   Ruth lies at Boaz's feet claiming client status (3:7–9).

A′   Boaz promises his protection and provides her with food (3:11–15).

His concern for her matches his interest in maintaining his image of propriety at the threshing floor when he tells Ruth to remain with him until morning rather than getting up in the middle of the night and possibly starting a scandal (3:13).[32] Furthermore, he instructs his workers to see to it that Ruth is given special privileges in gleaning, even from the "standing

---

[29]   Compare Dinah's fate when she left the protective care of her encampment in Gen 34:1–2. Ellen Van Wolde, *Ruth and Naomi*. London: SCM, 1997: 45, goes so far as to say that "women were often molested, assaulted, or abducted when in the fields." This is perhaps overstated given what the text provides here, but it is quite possible that Ruth did face some real harassment from the field workers, as Michael Carasik, "Ruth 2,7: Why the Overseer Was Embarrassed," *ZAW* 107 (1995): 493–94, suggests.

[30]   Many stories contain the extension of water rights, either as an expression of hospitality or acceptance: Abraham's servant (Gen 24:14–19); Egyptian straggler (1 Sam 30:11); enemies (Prov 25:21).

[31]   Compare Abigail's subservience, bowing to the ground before David in 1 Sam 25:23, begging for the life of her household. E. J. Hamlin, "Terms for Gender and Status," *Proceedings, Eastern Great Lakes and Midwest Biblical Society* 15 (1995): 136–37, notes that Ruth's speech is a subtle attempt to suggest that she would like to come under his protection, like his other female servants.

[32]   Compare the concern expressed by Lot when he attempts to convince the visitors at Sodom's gate in Gen 19:2–3.

[unharvested] sheaves" (*ŏmārîm*; 2:15). What she garners from this day's work is an ephah of barley (about two-thirds of a bushel), a quantity matched by what he later gives her on the threshing floor (3:15), yet another tie between the two episodes.

To complete this portion of the story line, Ruth then returns home. As she has been told by the field owner, Naomi also encourages Ruth to stay "close to the young women of Boaz" as she continues to work during the harvest (2:22).[33] In this way the person legally responsible for Ruth steps aside in favor of a stronger and wealthier male patron, anticipating the formal bond that will eventually be established between them. In the process, the degree to which Ruth is considered a liminal character is reduced, and she has thus taken a step toward full membership in the Bethlehem community. Thereafter Ruth, the one-time "foreigner," is identified by her membership among these "young women" (Ruth 2:22–23; 3:2). The implicit strategy is one of survival, not only for these two women but for the household of Naomi's husband. However, for them to survive and uphold the honor of their household, they must transcend the label of widow and become, once again, productive members of their society.

CHAPTER 3

(1) Naomi her mother-in-law said to her, "My daughter, I need to seek some security for you, so that it may be well with you. (2) Now here is our kinsman Boaz, with whose young women you have been working. See, he is winnowing barley tonight at the threshing floor. (3) Now wash and anoint yourself, and put on your best clothes and go down to the threshing floor; but do not make yourself known to the man until he has finished eating and drinking. (4) When he lies down; then, go and uncover his feet and lie down; and he will tell you what to do." (5) She said to her, "All that you tell me I will do." (6) So she went down to the threshing floor and did just as her mother-in-law had instructed her. (7) When Boaz had eaten and drunk, and he was in a contented mood, he went to lie down at the end of the heap of grain. Then she came stealthily and uncovered his feet, and lay down. (8) At midnight the man was startled, and turned over, and there, lying at his feet, was a woman! (9) He said, "Who

---

[33] David Shepherd, "Violence in the Fields? Translating, Reading, and Revising in Ruth 2,"
     CBQ 63 (2001): 459, concludes from this and from Boaz's warning in 2:9 that there is a
     euphemism being employed that implies a real threat of harassment or even assault.

are you?" And she answered, "I am Ruth, your servant; spread your cloak over your servant, for you are next-of-kin." (10) He said, "May you be blessed by the Lord, my daughter; this instance of your loyalty is better than the first; you have not gone after young men, whether poor or rich. (11) And now, my daughter, do not be afraid, I will do for you all that you ask, for all the assembly of my people know that you are a worthy woman. (12) But now, though it is true that I am a near kinsman, there is another kinsman more closely related than I. (13) Remain this night, and in the morning, if he will act as next-of-kin for you, good; let him do it. If he is not willing to act as next-of-kin for you, then, as the Lord lives, I will act as next-of-kin for you. Lie down until the morning." (14) So she lay at his feet until morning, but got up before one person could recognize another; for he said, "It must not be known that the woman came to the threshing floor." (15) Then he said, "Bring the cloak you are wearing and hold it out." So she held it, and he measured out six measures of barley, and put it on her back; then he went into the city. (16) She came to her mother-in-law, who said, "How did things go with you, my daughter?" Then she told her all that the man had done for her, (17) saying, "He gave me these six measures of barley, for he said, 'Do not go back to your mother-in-law empty-handed.'" (18) She replied, "Wait, my daughter, until you learn how the matter turns out, for the man will not rest, but will settle the matter today."

RUTH AND BOAZ ON THE THRESHING FLOOR

Initially, what can be drawn from the scene involving Boaz on the threshing floor is an established landowner, who in the proper season (Job 5:24) has brought his harvested grain to a common agricultural facility where it can be processed (threshed, winnowed, and sieved) and distributed. The threshing floor is defined by the community based on (1) its practical function, (2) its social attributes (i.e., what is done there beyond its primary function), and (3) its metaphorical meaning, based on (1) and (2). Thus initially a threshing floor has an agricultural function that is defined by its basic utilitarian characteristics (location and physical layout).[34]

In the village culture, which serves as the setting for this episode, the threshing floor was centrally located between adjoining fields or even

---

[34] Note the many examples in which the threshing floor and the winepress are coupled as economic indicators of prosperity or the abundance of the land. In both places food is distributed to the people, as well as to the Levites and, as in this case, to freed debt slaves (see Num 18:27; Deut 16:13; 2 Kings 6:27).

between villages and thus functioned as public space.[35] All of the farm-ers would transport their stalks of grain to this flat and open space where the prevailing west winds would help in separating the wheat from the chaffs of grain (Hos 13:3).[36] Once the grain was ready to be distributed, a recog-nizable system was used to determine the amount that went to each field owner and the portion that would be set aside for others. The owner of the grain, of course, expects to receive the bulk of the produce, but there are other claimants. Levites take their portion (Num 18:30). The protected classes (widows, orphans, and strangers) may claim their portion of the har-vest under a societal/covenantal obligation to protect the destitute and the weak (see Deut 14:29; 26:12–13).[37] Plus, when the central government was established, the state demanded its portion in taxes (Neh 5:4).

Because of this repeated communal activity, the threshing floor, like the gate in urban settings, eventually acquired a degree of social authority that allowed it to function as a place for both judicial and business practices.[38] Through their continuous reliance on the threshing floor as the place of processing and distribution, it became the logical place to transact business related to the harvest, perhaps even including land sales or redemption of property. And, in addition to trade, the threshing floor functioned as a logical worship area, for giving thanks and making sacrifices to the God or gods considered responsible for the harvest (Hos 9:1).[39] In this way practical

---

[35] D. C. Hopkins, *Highlands of Canaan* (1985): 226, notes the efficiency and labor-saving aspects of a centrally located threshing floor.

[36] O. Borowski, *Agriculture in Iron Age Israel* (1987): 62–63, suggests that some threshing floors, specifically the one mentioned in Ruth 3, were privately owned while others were public property for use by the whole community. Unless the farmer had very large hold-ings, as in the latifundialization of tracts of land during the monarchy period, it seems unlikely that the threshing floor could be anything but a communal facility. On land enclosure, see D. N. Premnath, "Latifundialization and Isaiah 5.8–10," *JSOT* 40 (1988): 49–60. For a study of premodern Judean farming practices and the collective use of local threshing floors, see Lucian Turkowski, "Peasant Agriculture in the Judean Hills," *PEQ* 101 (1969): 102–5.

[37] The Deuteronomic law concerns itself with the paying of the tithe, plus these extra portions for the protected classes. This is apparently in addition to the portion of the harvest of both grain and fruits that is to be left in the field for widows, orphans, and strangers to glean (Deut 24:19–21). See similar legislation in the Holiness Code in Lev 19:9–10.

[38] For example, in 1 Kings 22:10, the authority of the threshing floor and that of the city gate are combined to magnify the importance of a judicial procedure and a prophetic pronouncement. See Maurice M. Aranov, "The Biblical Threshing-Floor in the Light of the Ancient Near Eastern Evidence: Evolution of an Institution," PhD diss., New York University, 1977: 45, for the threshing floor's use as a place of cultic activity, and pp. 132–33 for its use as a place for dispensing charity and justice.

[39] Hans W. Wolff, *Hosea.* Philadelphia: Fortress Press, 1974: 154.

necessity, regular usage, and the evolution of social convention coalesced to create public space, with all the legal implications separate from private property.

The relative extent of Boaz's wealth or influence in the community is mitigated in this story by his use of a common facility rather than one of his own.[40] It is possible that this threshing floor is Boaz's property, loaned for use by all others in the village during the harvest, but the text does not say so specifically. In any case a small village like Bethlehem would not ordinarily have more than one threshing floor, and all would make use of it during this time of ingathering.

Harvest time was a period of intense labor requiring all of the able-bodied men and women to participate (Ruth 2:23).[41] However, the narrative in Ruth suggests that women did not remain with the men on the threshing floor overnight. Boaz's counsel that Ruth remain with him until morning suggests that her presence there is unusual, and it could even be defined as a cultural and spatial transgression (3:14). Thus, as in the first episode, caution is reflected by the separation of the sexes. When Naomi counsels Ruth to prepare herself like a potential bride (bathed, anointed, and nicely clothed)[42] and to go late at night, after the winnowing had been done in the cooler atmosphere of early evening, it is a break with social convention (Ruth 3:2).[43] However, given their situation, they have little choice but to violate the social and physical boundaries set by their society.[44]

---

[40]   Note other threshing floors that are tied by name to specific individuals: Nacon (2 Sam 6:6); Araunah (2 Sam 24:16); Ornan the Jebusite (2 Chron 3:1).

[41]   Carol L. Meyers, "Procreation, Production, and Protection," *JAAR* 51 (1983): 577–79, argues quite persuasively that the intensity of labor requirements for survival in the difficult farming areas of ancient Palestine, plus exogenous factors such as petty warfare that drew a portion of the male population away from farm tasks, necessitated the use of female laborers.

[42]   Compare the brides in Isa 61:10 and Jer 2:32. The parallel between the stories in Ruth 3 and Gen 38 also include a garment motif. Both women prepare themselves for their meeting with the future father of their child by removing their widows' garments, changing their clothing and thus their social status.

[43]   D. C. Hopkins, *Highlands of Canaan* (1985): 225, and Shalom Paul and William G. Dever, *Biblical Archaeology*. Jerusalem: Keter, 1973: 158, point to the fact that the summer heat would have limited harvest and processing time to the cooler hours of the morning. It seems likely, however, that activity on the threshing floor could have continued in the late afternoon and early evening when the cooling breeze aided both the winnowing as well as the workers.

[44]   Robert D. Sack, *Human Territoriality: Its Theory and History*. Cambridge: Cambridge University Press, 1986, discusses how space is used to control human behavior. The limits attached to the use of space within a community would have been conveyed to the

It is midnight before he becomes aware of her presence (Ruth 3:8). He awakens in the dead of night, possibly because an older man sleeps less soundly and must "turn over" at points during the night.[45] When Boaz finds Ruth lying at his feet, he is startled by this break in tradition and may, in his confusion, not have recognized her in the dark. Therefore he exclaims, "Who are you?" (3:9). Boaz's query parallels his question in 2:5 and initiates the dialogue between them. Having been addressed and thereby been given permission to speak, Ruth petitions him to "spread his cloak" over her, "his servant," and to serve as her husband's legal next of kin (3:9). The gesture of covering the bride with the groom's cloak, also found in Ezek 16:8, is a symbolic act that signifies "the establishment of a new relationship and the symbolic declaration of the husband to provide for the sustenance of the future wife."[46]

Ruth's request is not just for the levirate rights owed to her deceased husband. Furthermore, she is not simply attempting, as Tamar does in Gen 38:13–19, to obtain a child. Naomi wants her to "seek some security," and Ruth intends to initiate a long-term relationship, with the object being both a husband and children.[47] Her use of the term servant parallels her speech in 2:13, where she also refers to herself as Boaz's servant. In both cases she takes on the role of client, and in both cases she is requesting the patronage that he can dispense.[48]

While Boaz has previously been willing to give Ruth special favors during the harvest and to take on more responsibility for her and Naomi's welfare than might ordinarily be the case with widows, he demurs at this point. Although he blesses her and takes note of her family loyalty (working in the field to support Naomi and now coming to him rather than a younger man for patronage), Boaz tells her that he is not the legal next of kin. He does pledge to act on Ruth's behalf to protect the legal rights of her household.

members of that community from the time they were children and presumably to strangers as well. Naomi and Ruth are therefore in conscious violation of a spatial taboo.

45 T. Linafelt and T. K. Beal, *Ruth and Esther* (1999): 53–54, discuss the ambivalence of the Hebrew verbs used in this verse, which suggest the lack of control felt during the night or even the "involuntary physical reactions" to sexual contact with Ruth. The need to "turn over" in the sense of getting up to empty his bladder may also be the source of his restiveness.

46 P. A. Kruger, "The Hem of the Garment of Marriage: The Meaning of the Symbolic Gesture in Ruth 3:9 and Ezek 16:8," *JNSL* 12 (1984): 86.

47 T. M. Willis, *Elders of the City* (2001): 264, n. 69.

48 Adele Berlin, *Poetics and Interpretation of Biblical Narrative.* Sheffield, Eng.: Almond Press, 1983: 89; Joanna W. H. Bos, "Out of the Shadows: Genesis 38; Judges 4:17–22; Ruth 3," *Semeia* 42 (1988): 60.

Finally, Boaz measures out a portion of his own grain into her cloak. It is quite possible that his use of Ruth's cloak as a practical means of carrying the grain and as a symbol of his legal responsibility for her is a parallel with her request that he "spread his cloak" (i.e., legal protection) over her. In this way he officially becomes Ruth's patron, as she requested. In addition, since he does offer to serve as levir if the nearest kin refuses to take up his obligation, the grain could also be construed as a preliminary payment of a bride-price.[49] Then Boaz will be able, in public, to become her redeemer.[50] In this way he exemplifies the legal injunction not to abuse the widow or the resident alien (Exod 22:21–24).

Quite noteworthy is that he then sends her home while he shoulders the legal task of returning to the village to call together a group of elders and to hear the testimony of the levir at the gate (Ruth 4:15). Clearly, Boaz could have taken advantage of Ruth in her vulnerable condition, but he proves himself to be a man of outstanding character. Naomi in turn reiterates to Ruth that she can trust that Boaz will not let this task wait even for a day. His resolve is clear and the final disposition of the widows is at hand.

A CLOSER LOOK AT LEVIRATE OBLIGATION

There are three examples of levirate obligation detailed in the biblical text, two in narrative passages (Gen 38; Ruth 3–4) and one in the pronouncement of a legal case study (Deut 25:5–10). By definition a levirate marriage represented a legally sanctioned union (apparently an allowed variant to the incest laws in Lev 18:16) between a widow whose husband had died without having fathered any offspring and the brother of the deceased. Comparative forms of this type of marriage are attested in Ugaritic, Hittite, and Middle Assyrian sources (see MAL A.30, 31, 33), although it is difficult to find an exact match due to individual legal situations, economic concerns, and incest customs.[51] For example, Hittite Law 193 reads: "If a man has a wife, and the

---

49 For the exchange of goods as part of the marriage negotiation, see Raymond Westbrook, *Old Babylonian Marriage*. Horn, Austria: Verlag Ferdinand Berger & Sohne Gesellschaft, 1988: 10–16. For a discussion of the social aspects of betrothal, see Nancy Tapper, "Direct Exchange and Brideprice: Alternative Forms in a Complex Marriage System," *Man* 16 (1981): 387–407.

50 Danna N. Fewell and David M. Gunn, *Compromising Redemption: Relating Characters in the Book of Ruth*. Louisville, Ky.: Westminster/John Knox, 1990b: 46–48, 54–56, also make this comparison with the Judah and Tamar story, and they take note of Boaz's demure and calculations on the best strategy to benefit both him and Ruth.

51 R. Westbrook, *Property and Family in Biblical Laws* (1991): 87–89.

man dies, his brother shall take his widow as wife. [If the brother dies,] his father shall take her."[52]

The episode in Gen 38:8–11 centers only on the necessity of preserving the deceased brother's rights as the oldest son of Judah. Neither Onan nor Shelah, the two younger brothers, is expected to actually marry Tamar. They are simply expected to "go in to" (*bō' 'el*) Tamar and impregnate her so that Er will have a son to inherit his portion. Tamar has no entitlement to marriage and is even sent back to her father's house while she waits for Shelah to grow to maturity.[53] It is interesting to note, however, that Tamar's recourse of seducing Judah parallels the particular in the Hittite law of the father taking up the levirate obligation.

A more detailed statute on the levirate custom is described in Deut 25:5–10. These verses contain the social situation of a childless widow, the exact obligations due her from her husband's family, and a form of legal recourse if that obligation is not met. According to this law, an Israelite male, "living with his brother" (presumably in the same village or clan area) is required to perform "the duties of a husband's brother" (the *yābām*) by marrying his brother's widow. This custom is designed to prevent the name and family of the deceased from dying out and at the same time to restore the childless woman to a definable category (i.e., widow with children). There are economic advantages for her and legal guarantees for both parties in this custom.[54] The child born to this union would assume the name of the deceased and thereby maintain the continuity of inheritance patterns.[55] Apparently, there was a distinct possibility that the *go'ēl* redeemer would decline to fulfill his responsibility because he would be giving up his chance to inherit his dead brother's portion.[56] A social control mechanism is included in this statute. If the levir declines to do his duty, then in the presence of the elders the widow has the right to publicly humiliate him by removing his sandal and spitting in his face.[57] Her symbolic act, the only one in which a female

---

52   Martha T. Roth, *Law Collections from Mesopotamia and Asia Minor.* Atlanta: Scholars Press, 1995: 236.

53   Victor P. Hamilton, *The Book of Genesis, Chapters 18–50.* Grand Rapids, Mich: Eerdmans, 1995: 435.

54   Carolyn Pressler, *The View of Women Found in the Deuteronomic Family Laws.* BZAW 216. Berlin: Walter de Gruyter, 1993: 73–74.

55   R. Westbrook, *Property and Family in Biblical Laws* (1991): 76–77.

56   David Daube, "The Culture of Deuteronomy," *Orita* 3 (1969): 35.

57   See Lyn M. Bechtel, "Shame as a Sanction of Social Control in Biblical Israel: Judicial, Political, and Social Shaming," *JSOT* 49 (1991): 57–60.

seems to have prominent judiciary rights, literally reverses their roles, with her spittle symbolizing the sperm he has refused to give her and the shoe representing her vagina and his rights to have intercourse with her. [58]

The example in Ruth contains some variations on the Deuteronomy procedure. It does hinge on confronting the kinsman-redeemer in public, but Ruth is not involved in the scene. Instead Boaz assembles the elders at the gate and questions the levir on his intentions. According to Nielsen, there is no mystery in this proceeding since everyone there knows what the responsibility is of a near kinsman to redeem the land and thus keep it in the control of the extended family (see Lev 25:24–34; Jer 32:7–15).[59] The question is whether Ruth is entitled to the right of levirate obligation. All the redeemer has to do is to purchase a field and, Naomi will become a ward of his household. But when Boaz raises the issue of maintaining the dead man's name, then Ruth must be considered, and the redeemer realizes he will not be able to acquire permanent title to the land.[60] He refuses to accept Ruth as part of the bargain but is not forced to undergo the humiliation of a woman removing his sandal, and Boaz is then free to make the magnanimous gesture of taking up the "right of redemption" and proclaiming his intention before witnesses to acquire Elimelech's property and to marry Ruth (4:6–9).

CHAPTER 4

(1) No sooner had Boaz gone up to the gate and sat down there than the next-of-kin, of whom Boaz had spoken, came passing by. So Boaz said, "Come over, friend; sit down here." And he went over and sat down. (2) Then Boaz took ten men of the elders of the city, and said, "Sit down here"; so they sat down. (3) He then said to the next-of-kin, "Naomi, who has come back from the country of Moab, is selling the parcel of land that belonged to our kinsman Elimelech. (4) So I thought I would tell you of it, and say: Buy it in the presence of those sitting here, and in the presence of the elders of my people. If you will redeem it, redeem it; but if you will not, tell me, so that I may know; for there

---

58 Calum M. Carmichael, "A Ceremonial Crux: Removing a Man's Sandal as a Female Gesture of Contempt," *JBL* 96 (1977): 321–26.

59 K. Nielsen, *Ruth* (1997): 83–85.

60 T. Linafelt and T. K. Beal, *Ruth and Esther* (1998): 71.

is no one prior to you to redeem it, and I come after you." So he said, "I will redeem it." (5) Then Boaz said, "The day you acquire the field from the hand of Naomi, you are also acquiring Ruth the Moabite, the widow of the dead man, to maintain the dead man's name on his inheritance." (6) At this, the next-of-kin said, "I cannot redeem it for myself without damaging my own inheritance. Take my right of redemption yourself, for I cannot redeem it." (7) Now this was the custom in former times in Israel concerning redeeming and exchanging: to confirm a transaction, the one took off his sandal and gave it to the other; this was the manner of attesting in Israel. (8) So when the next-of-kin said to Boaz, "Acquire it for yourself," he took off his sandal. (9) Then Boaz said to the elders and all the people, "Today you are witnesses that I have acquired from the hand of Naomi all that belonged to Elimelech and all that belonged to Chilion and Mahlon. (10) I have also acquired Ruth the Moabite, the wife of Mahlon, to be my wife, to maintain the dead man's name on his inheritance, in order that the name of the dead may not be cut off from his kindred and from the gate of his native place; today you are witnesses." (11) Then all the people who were at the gate, along with the elders, said, "We are witnesses. May the Lord make the woman who is coming into your house like Rachel and Leah, who together built up the house of Israel. May you produce children in Ephrathah and bestow a name in Bethlehem; (12) and through the children that the Lord will give you by this young woman, may your house be like the house of Perez, whom Tamar bore to Judah." (13) So Boaz took Ruth and she became his wife. When they came together, the Lord made her conceive, and she bore a son. (14) Then the women said to Naomi, "Blessed be the Lord, who has not left you this day without next-of-kin; and may his name be renowned in Israel! (15) He shall be to you a restorer of life and a nourisher of your old age; for your daughter-in-law who loves you, who is more to you than seven sons, has borne him." (16) Then Naomi took the child and laid him in her bosom, and became his nurse. (17) The women of the neighborhood gave him a name, saying, "A son has been born to Naomi." They named him Obed; he became the father of Jesse, the father of David. (18) Now these are the descendants of Perez: Perez became the father of Hezron, (19) Hezron of Ram, Ram of Amminadab, (20) Amminadab of Nahshon, Nahshon of Salmon, (21) Salmon of Boaz, Boaz of Obed, (22) Obed of Jesse, and Jesse of David.

*B*oaz's choice of the gate as the place to determine Ruth's and Naomi's legal future is based on unstated local tradition. There was no law that said the elders must spend their time sitting in the gate waiting to see if a legal case would be brought before them. Instead it is clear that they often chose to sit in the gate because it was a place to transact business, share gossip, and demonstrate their status as men of property and influence (see Lot in Gen 19:1 and the "well-served" husband who is "known in the city gates" in Prov 31:23). In this situation Boaz arrives early in the morning, when it can be expected that the men of the village will be passing through the gate on their way to work in the fields or to engage in business. Thus he can easily waylay both the next of kin and a requisite number of elders from his lineage group as witnesses to this lawsuit.[61]

Boaz lays out the legal situation for the elders. He notes that Naomi is either in the process of selling or has sold the property of Elimelech. This, plus the obligations owed to her by her husband's kinsmen, will provide for her needs but not those of Ruth, who is a foreigner and a widow without property.[62] Under the law of redemption (Lev 25:47–49), a kinsman has the right to redeem that property, and since the harvest has just been gathered this would be an appropriate moment for the next of kin to make his intentions plain (compare Jeremiah's right to redeem a kinsman's field in Jer 32:6–15). Willis[63] is correct in saying that Ruth's future becomes a consideration in these dealings only if the person who redeems Elimelech's land is a kinsman. All others would be concerned only with the land itself. Curiously, the next of kin, who is quick to claim the right to redeem the land, seems surprised when Boaz brings up the fact that he will also "acquire" responsibility for Ruth. Although it is possible that he had overlooked this since Ruth is a foreigner, Boaz is shrewd enough to add this detail after waving the carrot of the land. The greed of his kinsman is revealed (compare Onan's actions in Gen 38:8–10), and Boaz cannot be accused of being opportunistic.

Thus the issue that Boaz frames is whether the kinsman is willing, in the interests of his obligation to the extended family, to redeem the field and take responsibility for Ruth, a widowed Moabite.[64] Having given the kinsman an out by declaring he is willing to assume responsibility for Elimelech's

---

61 T. M. Willis, *Elders of the City* (2001): 279.
62 Donald A. Leggett, *The Levirate and Goel Institutions in the Old Testament, with Special Attention to the Book of Ruth*. Cherry Hill, N.J.: Mack, 1974: 205–8.
63 T. M. Willis, *Elders of the City* (2001): 270–72.
64 D. A. Leggett, *Levirate and Goel Institutions* (1974): 240–49. D. N. Fewell and D. M. Gunn, "'A Son Is Born to Naomi!'" *JSOT* 40 (1998): 103–7, continually point to the prejudice against Ruth as a Moabite. It is possible that the next of kin did not consider her as part of the legal transaction because no one in his village would have considered Ruth as part of the social system. That makes Boaz's action more of a match for Ruth's assimilation statement in 1:16–17. Unlike his kinsman, he is willing to put aside cultural prejudice, and this then becomes the argument against endogamic marriage practices.

household as the next in line, it is not surprising that the kinsman declines.[65] Like Onan in Gen 38:9, the kinsman knows the children born to Ruth will become his obligation, and their very existence jeopardizes the inheritance of his own heir.

When the kinsman's answer to Boaz's statement of a broader obligation is an emphatic "no," then Boaz magnanimously can step in, using this same motive of support for property rights of his kin, to redeem the property and to take on the responsibility for a childless widow without a dowry. The question might arise why Boaz is not concerned about the legal and economic obligation associated with taking Ruth into his household. However, the text does not speak to this, and it can only be speculated that either he lacks heirs of his own or his generosity to his kin is as noteworthy as is his integrity in dealing with those who are powerless in his society.

The legal reference to removing the sandal refers to a customary practice, but in this instance it is not identical to that described in Deut 25:5–10.[66] This may be due to variations in the law over time. There is also the possibility that the incident in Ruth is closer to the common practice in cases involving redemption of land rather than in cases of levirate obligation.[67] There is no sense in this passage that the next of kin is humiliated by this exchange. Having been presented with the economic factors involved in redeeming the field and acquiring responsibility for Ruth, he makes a business decision not to accept this responsibility. Although this is a public declaration, it does not appear to damage his social standing. It merely gives Boaz the legal right to step in as redeemer.[68] He makes a detailed statement describing the full parameters of this transaction, setting out exactly what he is acquiring and the purpose behind it, namely to preserve the "name" of the deceased within his kinship group and his place.[69]

The response of the elders and "all the people" who are present in the gate area is to echo Boaz's claim and bless the marriage.[70] The blessing, like

---

[65]   Thomas L. Thompson and Dorothy Thompson, "Some Legal Problems in the Book of Ruth," *VT* 18 (1968): 81.

[66]   See T. M. Willis, *Elders of the City* (2001): 275; C. M. Carmichael, "Ceremonial Crux," *JBL* 96 (1977): 323–24; Dale Manor, "A Brief History of Levirate Marriage as It Relates to the Bible," *ResQ* 27 (1984): 133.

[67]   See T. M. Willis, *Elders of the City* (2001): 275–76, for discussion of various possibilities as well as reference to the literature on this legal point.

[68]   Don C. Benjamin, *Deuteronomy and City Life*. Lanham, N.Y.: University Press of America, 1983: 249–53.

[69]   Compare the legal statements of transaction found in Gen 23:17–18 and in Jer 32:6–15.

[70]   Compare the use of this phrase "all the people" as witnesses to a legal event in the trial of Jeremiah (Jer 26:7–16).

the subsequent genealogy of Boaz's family, is political. The witnesses refer to Perez in Ruth 4:12, and this is followed by the genealogy of Perez in Ruth 4:18–22. Boaz is listed in this genealogical note as a descendant of Perez and as the ancestor, with Ruth, of King David. In this way, these two stories of levirate obligation (Gen 38 and Ruth) are tied together, and the line of David is allied with the concepts of concern for the law and the freedom to marry outside the Israelite tribes. This latter issue would be a particularly effective argument against endogamy in the postexilic period.

Finally, the song of blessing sung by the women to Naomi (Ruth 4:14–15) provides a celebration of Yahweh's role as the covenantal provider of land and children, and a fitting counterbalance to the dismal scene in 1:19–21.[71] With the fulfillment of Ruth's pledge of service to her mother-in-law, Naomi can shed her "empty" status and now rejoice in children.[72] When she places the child on her breast and the women give him a name,[73] Naomi claims Obed as her son, born in a surrogate fashion to Ruth, but now the legal heir to her husband, Elimelech (4:16–17).

The legal basis for the story is thus satisfied along with the social commentary legitimizing mixed marriages and the rights of converts to Judaism (see Isa 56:3–8).[74] After marrying Boaz, Ruth's name is not mentioned again. It might be said, therefore, that her place in the story is set aside in favor of Naomi's rights and the insertion of the male-dominated genealogy of David in vv. 18–20.[75] This submersion of her character may be simply a refocusing on the aftermath of the story, but it may also signal, once again, that Ruth is a foreigner. Despite her speech of fidelity in 1:16–17 and her actions to ensure the security of Elimelech's household, ultimately her son is defined by membership in that household rather than by the biological link to Ruth.[76]

However, Ruth has played a very significant part and cannot be set aside that easily. Perhaps, as Saxegaard notes, Ruth has become the "eighth son" in the story.[77] The women refer to her as "more to you than seven sons"

[71] T. Linafelt and T. K. Beal, *Ruth and Esther* (1999): 78–79.

[72] Frederic W. Bush, *Ruth, Esther*. Dallas: Word, 1996: 255.

[73] See Victor H. Matthews and Don C. Benjamin, *The Social World of Ancient Israel*. Peabody, Mass.: Hendrickson, 1993: 79–80, on the role of the midwife in negotiating a name for the newborn. Although the women in this passage in Ruth are not described as midwives, they function in much the same manner.

[74] Susan L. Shearman and John B. Curtis, "Divine-Human Conflicts in the Old Testament," *JNES* 28 (1969): 236.

[75] Richard Bauckham, "The Book of Ruth and the Possibility of a Feminist Canonical Hermeneutic," *BibInt* 5 (1997): 30.

[76] A. Brenner, "Ruth as a Foreign Worker," in *Ruth and Esther* (1999b): 161–62.

[77] K. M. Saxegaard, " 'More Than Seven Sons,' " *SJOT* 15 (2001): 272–73.

(v. 15), a number that exceeds the ideal of giving birth to seven sons found in Hannah's blessing (1 Sam 2:5). In this way Ruth's story is tied yet again to David, who was himself an "eighth son" (1 Sam 16:10–12). Both Ruth and David will have a connection with Moab (see 1 Sam 22:3–4), they will each overcome social obstacles, and they will be instruments in redeeming the land for generations to come.

It therefore seems likely that the canonical placement of Ruth at the transition point between the political chaos of the Judges period and the emerging monarchy in 1–2 Samuel makes eminent sense. Naomi's restoration, Ruth's marriage and family, and the genealogy of David (4:18–22) all function as responses to individual and collective needs. And, behind the scenes of this domestic drama stand the covenant promise to Israel and a God who fills the needs of those who trust in that divine power and treat each other in a similarly caring manner.

BRIDGING THE HORIZONS

The Book of Ruth contains a number of issues that have a contemporary ring to them and that can evoke helpful discussion.

(1) Immigrants find the task of blending into a newly adopted culture a challenge and an opportunity. Like Naomi in Moab and Ruth in Bethlehem, they experience new customs, language, and expectations. It is difficult to be totally accepted by the locals, and rights under the law may be confused or ignored. Ruth and Naomi face their struggle by taking advantage of a charitable system that allows them to survive through gleaning and of a legal system that requires them to depend on a male advocate to ensure their household is not extinguished.

(2) Every society must find a way to cope with widows and orphans, the elderly, and other groups that require assistance. The ancient Israelites made provision for these "protected classes" in the statutes in Exod 22:22 and Deut 24:19–21; 27:19. They felt it was important that no one be left without access to the harvest and that no one be deprived of their basic legal rights even if they were poor or had no one to stand up for them. A society that abandons the poor and the weak is a society that disregards the basic tenets of the covenant with God (see Amos 2:6–8; 8:4–6).

(3) The places where business was transacted and justice determined in the villages of ancient Israel were the threshing floor and the gate. The

significance attached to the use of particular space is the result of repeated usage and custom. In contemporary society we have courtrooms, business centers, and international deliberative bodies like the United Nations where issues of justice are raised and commercial policy is determined. Although more complex than the village setting, the principle remains the same, and it is worth reflecting on the development of customary practice and on the symbols of power and authority that we associate with these places.

(4) The future is written in the birth of every child. Naomi's future happiness and Ruth's social acceptance were based on the birth of an heir for their household. Naomi's joy when the child is placed in her lap is a reflection of her understanding that the future was now secure. The genealogy of David appended to this story (4:18–22) expands this hope to include the nation and once again demonstrates the devotion of God to fulfill the covenant promise of land and children to this people (see Gen 12:1–3; 15:5).

Author Index

Scripture and Extra-Biblical Texts Index

Subject Index